Quite Con...

With best wishes.
Mary McMahon.

Quite Contrary

AN
AUTOBIOGRAPHY
BY

MARY WHITEHOUSE

PAN BOOKS
LONDON, SYDNEY AND AUCKLAND

First published 1993 by Sidgwick & Jackson Ltd

This edition published 1994 by Pan Books Ltd
a division of Pan Macmillan Publishers Limited
Cavaye Place, London SW10 9PG
and Basingstoke

Associated companies throughout the world

ISBN 0 330 33839 0

1 3 5 7 9 8 6 4 2

A CIP catalogue record for this book is available from
the British Library

Phototypeset by Intype, London
Printed and bound in Great Britain by
Cox & Wyman Ltd, Reading, Berkshire

Dedicated to my everlastingly patient husband, Ernest

to my five delightful grandchildren, Nicola, Fiona, Katherine, Elizabeth and Daniel,

to my invaluable secretaries, Margaret Palmer and Margaret Weir, and to John Beyer, General Secretary of the National Viewers' and Listeners' Association, whose support and understanding made it all possible.

CONTENTS

PREFACE

'It *still* gives me the oddest feeling,' I said to Ernest as Radio 4 news announced on 17 July 1992 that two complaints against *The Mary Whitehouse Experience* had been upheld by the Broadcasting Standards Council.

The fact of the matter is that, in spite of all my experiences over the last thirty years, I still feel, as I am, a very ordinary person and to see my name draped in coloured, flashing lights across our television screens and to be associated with a programme which was found, for example, to be 'offensive to people suffering from a mental disability' (30 March 1992) or which included a sequence of jokes about masturbation and oral sex (16 March 1992) was quite the last thing I could have expected – or desired!

'Why did you give your name to a programme like that?' or 'Why did you let them use your name?' were questions I was constantly asked as one series after another went its sordid way. But it was all as much a surprise to me as it was to everyone else!

'There is nothing special at all about me,' I tell myself and anyone else who's listening, 'except perhaps my forebears – on both sides.' As I told in *A Most Dangerous Woman* (Lion Publishing) my mother was a Searancke. No one we knew had ever heard of her maiden name and no one could spell it, either. As children we heard vastly intriguing stories of the origins of this family, no doubt much embroidered in the telling. However, many years later my cousin, Esme Searancke, traced our lineage back to a yeoman family living in the town of Hatfield in the early 1500s.

In the nineteenth century the family broke away from Hatfield and many of them emigrated. One of them, William

1

Nicholas Searancke, eighth child of a naval captain who lost an arm fighting with Nelson at Copenhagen, trained as a surveyor, went out to California in search of gold (though there's no record that he ever found any) finished up in New Zealand and married a daughter of the Maori King Tawhiao. Princess Te Puea Harange, CBE, born in 1882, was the child of their eldest son. Like her father and grandfather before her she fought to protect Maori lands, culture and institutions, while at the same time accommodating the best of European influences. Only with the publishing of her biography in 1977 was it possible, so the blurb tells us, for the people of New Zealand fully to understand what she did, not only for the Maoris but for New Zealand. When she died in 1952 'the funeral ceremonies were the largest seen in New Zealand outside those for Prime Ministers who had died in office'.

But the Searanckes over here, including my mother's immediate family, didn't have it so good. Grandfather Searancke was a master builder in a small way, but he died as a comparatively young man just before the birth of his twelfth child, leaving his wife destitute and without any of those supportive social services which would ease the lot of any such mother today. Grandmother sought help from the other branch of the Searancke family, but they, so the story goes, were 'not interested in poor relations'.

The eldest boys of the family had to earn coppers where they could. One of them stood as a little lad of ten selling shoe-laces and tins of blacking in all weathers. The tale of his 'runny nose' as he 'shivered in the bitter winter weather' outside the local shoe-shop, which he was later to manage until he retired, is another nostalgic memory. Two of the others started as brickboys and made their way until they became well known in the East Midlands as master builders and sand merchants and I remember vividly the fun we children had in those sandpits when we went to spend holidays with our indulgent uncles.

I like to think that it was perhaps not only the lineage from which she sprang but my mother's own character which made her such a remarkable woman. It is not easy, in these days of social care and financial support that needy families can call upon almost as a matter of course, to envisage the constant anxiety and strain which surrounded not only our family but many others in the days which followed the First World War. One of my most vivid memories is of the discharged, destitute soldiers in their ragged, dirty uniforms who used to sing in the streets of Chester, where we lived, and no doubt in just about every other town, too. I remember how my mother would bring them in and warm them up with a bowl of her home-made soup and the gratitude which would light up their faces. Not that she had anything to spare, either resources or strength.

Never a physically strong woman she was possessed of a will and determination to ensure that her family was well cared for and brought up as good Christian children – a determination, it should be said, which was typical of family life at that time. But she had more than the usual anxieties attached to rearing a family. My elder sister contracted polio at the age of two and a half in the epidemic which swept Britain in 1910. I was born the same year and within the next couple of years the family was completed with the birth of two sons. So, four children under six with the eldest severely paralysed and a husband, who, dear as he was in many ways, was not the most careful in the way he spent money, laid an exceptional burden upon her.

Being something of a tomboy and spending every minute I could away from the house and the odd jobs I was expected to do there, my happiest memories of my childhood are those I spent out of doors – as a Guide, round the camp-fires we would build at every opportunity, and of course, on my bike. That vehicle was my most treasured possession. I'd been promised one if I passed a scholarship to the Chester City Grammar School, my parents being unable to afford to send me there. 'Slapdash as usual!', however, I failed but managed to win a bursarship the following year committing me to becoming a teacher. What a joy that bike was. I remember still the thrill I felt when, having sweated up to the top of a hill, I would let go the handlebars and come sailing down the other side with my arms outstretched – different traffic conditions then! But I've got another memory too. Being crippled as she was my sister could not have a bike but she made – and made is the operative word – me get her up on to the saddle, give her a push and off she'd go, swinging her bad leg back and forwards while her good leg turned the pedal. She instructed me to stand in the road from where I'd pushed her, until she returned for me to catch the bike and get her down. To this day I vividly remember my father's anger against me when he was driving his little Austin Seven through the streets of Chester to see her pedalling away among the traffic, quite unable to stop if the need arose. But somehow it never did.

As the years went on my sister, a pretty girl, became self-conscious about her handicap and refused to go out. She was, however, very clever with her hands and my mother arranged for her to go and work, without pay, at an arts and crafts studio in Chester. The strain on Mother was immense: she would push my sister in her bathchair to work – a journey of more than two miles – after she had got the rest of us off to school and then fetch her back in the afternoon in time to get us home, too. Not, of course, to mention the frequent hospital visits in the hope – quite false as it turned out – that something could be done for my sister.

So good was my sister's work at the studio that the owner pressurized my parents to sign a statement to the effect that she would never open a business in Chester, or anywhere else, within the next three years. My father's Scottish blood boiled at that and he refused. So another page in the story of the family was turned. Everyone got behind the effort to start up an arts and crafts business from home and one of my most vivid memories is of how we all worked together to market our wares. One of the most successful was our special line in suede belts, which were composed of different coloured leaves, machined together and veins marked with poker work. We would all sit round the table working like mad to fulfil the huge orders (hundreds of belts at a time) from the London stores.

Then the day came when the not-very-kind lady who rented the original arts and crafts studio from the Duke of Westminster decided to retire and my mother and sister took it over, launching a business which still flourishes today. One memory of my mother remains vividly in my mind: when the opportunity to rent the shop arrived she went personally to see the Duke's business agent, told him exactly how much money she owed, assured him that she would not take a penny piece in wages until it was all paid off – it took her twelve years – and launched into a daily behind-the-counter life from which she never sought to retire until she died at the age of eighty-three.

Yet I was, perhaps, more proud of the Hutchesons. My Dad was a Scot, one of the Hutcheson family whose forebears, George and Thomas, founded in 1641 the Hospital for Poor Boys in the Gorbals area of Glasgow which became the famous 'Hutchies' Grammar School. One of the great disappointments of my 'speaking' life was that through illness I was unable to fulfil an engagement at the school. The occasion, I feel sure, would have been full of atmosphere.

My grandfather, Walter, was a well-known Scottish artist, but it was a by no means lucrative occupation and he and his wife Jeannie had to struggle hard to bring up their seven children on his salary as illustrator for the *Glasgow Herald* and *Chatterbox*. As children we used to hear fascinating stories of how Grandfather would be called from his bed in the middle of the night to rush to a fire in the streets or the docks and then hurry back to do his engraving ready for reproduction in the morning paper. The artistic talent still so characteristic of the Hutchesons springs from his modest genius. A telling example of how gifts are passed down from one generation to the next came during a visit to us by an aunt from Glasgow. She was asking after our children and when I told her that one of our sons was studying silversmithing at Birmingham College of Art she burst out, 'Well, Mary, isn't that interesting? Your grandfather was a silversmith as a young man before he became a painter.' Something none of us had known.

In common with so many of their compatriots my father's brother and sister successfully emigrated to the USA and we still keep in touch with their children. It didn't work out well for all of them, though, especially not for my father. He, a gifted man, desperately wanted to become an artist but his father, conscious of the financial difficulties he and his wife had experienced in bringing up a family on an artist's earnings (even though he was also art master at Hutchies as well as a freelance painter and illustrator), packed him off to Nuneaton where he set him up as a gentlemen's outfitters. Poor Dad! What an unhappy and frustrated man he turned out to be. With no business acumen he was bankrupt within a couple of years.

It was in Nuneaton that he met my mother, who became a wonderful wife. But how hard things were. Following his failure in business my dad became a representative covering the whole county of Cheshire for a firm of cattle food and medicines. His job was quite a good one, bringing in anything from ten to twenty pounds a week, a lot of money in those days. But the demands of my sister's medical treatment, my mother's frequent illness and a number of unfortunate business transactions, which drained his resources for years, meant that our financial situation was always precarious. So I learnt very early to 'make do and mend' and accept with grace the clothes which were handed on to me.

Looking back I think quite the worst time of my childhood was during the dreadful foot-and-mouth disease epidemic (which affected cattle and sheep) of the 1920s which went on for many weeks. My father would go out day after day, riding his push-bike – no car then – for mile after mile in all weathers down the Cheshire lanes, tramping the muddy fields, only to be met over and over again by large No Admittance notices. I can still feel his total despondency as he returned home hopelessly day after day, and see him collapsing in a chair by the fire, as he held out his legs, one at a time, without a word, for me to take off his muddied leggings and pull off his boots. This was the time when my mother sat up through the night making little dresses for the neighbours' children. One night she stitched on and on until the needle of her hand-turned sewing-machine went through her finger.

I cannot help but believe – even more strongly as the years go on – that it was my mother's very real Christian faith and her total devotion to her children which gave her the strength to keep going in the face of quite phenomenal physical and mental pressure. Strangely enough, while I remember that we were expected to attend Sunday School every week there was little piety in the home. The one thing I do remember clearly is my mother singing to each of us, as she tucked us up in bed, this verse:

> Jesus, tender shepherd, hear us
> Bless thy little lambs tonight
> Through the darkness be thou near them
> Keep them safe till morning light.

And I seem to remember turning over and going straight off to sleep. Whether I stayed there till morning light is an entirely different matter with the temptations of the pantry only a quiet creep away down the stairs.

In no way would I wish to belittle the part that my mother's upbringing, our Sunday School teaching and the general acceptance of the Christian faith which characterized the world in which I grew up, played in profoundly affecting all my future decisions for better or worse.

Like everyone else, I have had experiences, lots of them, and not least during the last nearly thirty years I've been involved in the work for which I have become famous, or infamous, according to your viewpoint. So, I thought, why not put the record straight?

I imagine that unless one can see a pattern to one's life by the time one reaches, as I have, the advanced age of eighty-three, then one probably never will. It is fascinating to look back and see how not only were the good things good, but also how events which were, to say the least, unfortunate at the time, demanded a change of direction that, in the long run, turned out to be wholly beneficial.

This particular story has its roots in the decisions Ernest and I made that I should go back into teaching after fifteen years of marriage. But why should I do that when I had a very happy, busy life as wife and mother, lots of sporting activities – especially tennis – plus a large garden which gave me enormous pleasure? The answer lay with the tubercular infection which settled in my kidneys and laid me low for many months in the late fifties.

When I was well enough to travel my mother took me for a prolonged holiday to the Canary Islands and when I returned the doctor gave me the all clear. That was fine, but the physical strength that had enabled me to run a three-storey Victorian house, keep pace with three strapping sons, dig and plant to my heart's content had largely deserted me. Obviously I'd got to have domestic help, but we couldn't afford it. I went back into part-time teaching, which led, step by step, into the work which has occupied us all so much during the last thirty years.

I began with a temporary job in Wolverhampton and two years later took up a most interesting and challenging appointment in Madeley in Shropshire, now part of Telford New Town, as senior mistress and head of the art department at the then Madeley Secondary Modern School. On my first day there the headmaster called me to his office to say that he wished me, as senior mistress, 'responsible for the moral welfare of the girls', to become involved immediately in a new venture: sex education. I was taken aback and most reluctant to undertake it. The headmaster gave me till the next day to decide but left me in no doubt about what he intended my reply to be. There was only one thing to do: go home, discuss it with Ernest and trust that by next morning I would know what my answer would be.

I did. Provided that the headmaster would accept that I had no experience of such work – which was, after all, rather a long way from teaching pictorial composition, design, colour and texture – and that he would take responsibility for the results of that inexperience then my answer would be yes. So there I was, professionally committed to providing sex education for teenagers based on the newly published (1962) Newsom Report on Secondary Education which said that sex education should be based on 'chastity before marriage and fidelity within it', which was, in any case, how I, personally, would have wished to approach the matter. I had experienced how profound an effect such a commitment can have upon the quality of married life. There have been many times over the years since when my mind has gone back to those experiences and I have compared the standards I was then expected to maintain with those that are so current now, and the anxiety which exists about the quality and quantity of sex education in schools today.

Central to our work at school was the realization that children of the same physical age can vary enormously in their emotional and psychological development. Certain material, that was helpful to some children, was deeply emotionally upsetting to others, as with the girl who fell off her chair in a faint during one of the marriage guidance lectures with which we began the course. When I talked to her later it transpired that she had witnessed violence related to sexual demands on her mother by her father and her mind rejected the intimate information with which she was being presented in class. This brought home to me forcibly the dangers of dealing *en masse* with such fundamental issues, and consequently, a step at a time, we developed a completely new approach to the matter of sex education, independent of any involvement with the

Marriage Guidance people whose contribution did not impress us much – not least because they objected to the presence of teachers, an idea to which we gave short shrift!

We felt that, in the first place, the decision of whether or not a child should be included in the class teaching should be left with parents, so we invited them to come to the school in the evening to show them the type of material we proposed to use and to discuss all the issues involved. I remember so well the mother who said to me, 'I want to talk to her, Miss, but I don't know the words to use,' and how grateful she was for our help. We also arranged evenings when mothers came with daughters – very well attended – and others when fathers came with sons – not quite so well attended but immensely valuable all the same.

All this happened at the time of the launching of the permissive society and the 'new morality' not least, of course, through its advocacy on the television screen, notably by the BBC. Before 1963 was out I found myself having to help children whose personal lives had been directly and adversely affected by the licentiousness and immorality which increasingly characterized television programmes. And it was out of all that experience that my work developed in most unaccustomed and remarkable ways.

In an interview in *The Times* on 27 November 1991 Margaret Jay raised the matter of safe sex for teenagers and referred to the difficulties that parents find in talking to them about sex, saying, 'We find it difficult enough to talk to them about what they had for breakfast let alone whether they use a condom.' I was so struck by the inadequacy of her approach that I wrote a letter to *The Times* in which I spoke of the work we had done in that modest secondary modern school all those years ago. To my amazement and delight it was published at the top of the first column. It was even more encouraging to receive a letter in response to mine from Dr C. Everett Koop in which he said that when he was Surgeon General of the United States

we contemplated a program like you mentioned – educating parents to teach children about human development. The time may be right for another effort in this direction, and I would appreciate any additional information you have. I am especially interested if any kind of report was ever written indicating how you went about your task and what measurable results or anecdotal responses there were. I apologize for the effort this might take.

He needn't have apologized! and we gave him what help we could.

Then it was announced, as the first major story in the *Sunday Telegraph* on 25 April 1993, that 'The government is to declare war on teenage pregnancies in an effort to counter the consequences of the permissive society.' The thought of the government taking on the ramifications of the permissive society made me wonder – momentarily! – if the time had come for me to retire! It didn't last long and the first thing I did was to offer, for her consideration, the ideas we had pioneered at Madeley to Mrs Virginia Bottomley. Certainly I hoped that her plans did not stop, as the paper rather disappointingly suggested, at 'preventing unsafe sex', but at least it was a start. How things do go in circles.

I could hardly believe my eyes when they fell on a press headline which reads 'Patten crusades for sex education with moral touch'. The article is, I think, worth including here in some detail. It is from *The Times* of 23 April 1993.

A crusade to ensure that schoolchildren are taught about sex within a clear moral framework that promotes family values was launched by John Patten, the education secretary in the early summer of 1993.

His department issued guidelines stating that pupils must be told that the law forbids sexual intercourse with girls under 16 and homosexual acts between males if either party is under 21.

Furthermore, he said that teachers who give advice to under-age girls about the provision of contraception without parental knowledge or consent could face criminal charges.

The guidance offers advice to school governors, who are responsible for drawing up sex education lessons that go beyond the rudiments of reproduction, which are already included under the national curriculum.

Mr Patten said that 'all sex education should encourage children to consider the moral dimension of their actions'.

He added, 'It should recognize the value of family life and understand the importance of loving relationships and mutual respect.'

He said the advice rightly recognized that parents were the key figures in helping children to cope with the physical and emotional aspects of growing up and in preparing them for the responsibilities of sexual maturity.

The guidelines say schools cannot avoid tackling controversial matters such as contraception and abortion, as at least 8,500 under-age girls become pregnant each year. However, the government hopes to halve the rate of conception among the under–16s by the end of the decade as part of its Health of the Nation initiative.

The government guidelines stated that sex education should encourage pupils to consider 'the importance of self-restraint, dignity and respect for themselves and others'. Pupils should be helped to recognize the physical, emotional and moral risks of promiscuity.

Schools should foster a recognition that both sexes should behave responsibly in sexual matters. Pupils should be helped to appreciate the benefits of stable married and family life and the responsibilities of parenthood.

On the specific question of giving advice about contraceptive provision to girls under 16 without parental knowledge, the guidance says it would be 'an inappropriate exercise of a teacher's professional responsibilities and could, depending on the circumstances, amount to a criminal offence'. The Minister went on to declare that 'A teacher approached by a pupil for such advice should instead encourage them to go to their parents,' and to state that, 'There is no place in any school in any circumstance for teaching that advocates homosexual behaviour, presents it as the norm or encourages homosexual experimentation. In teaching older pupils about Aids and HIV, schools should warn about the health risks of promiscuity.'

CHAPTER ONE

BACK TO THE BEGINNING

It certainly gave me a strange feeling to walk out on to the platform of Birmingham Town Hall in 1992 for the first time in nearly thirty years. It wasn't quite how I'd remembered it: there were no banks of flowers round the apron of the platform, only the upstairs was full, instead of every seat in the hall, and there were no television cameras, reporters and no cheers, only very welcome clapping. To what was I comparing the Annual Conference of the Women's Gas Federation? Why, our own first public meeting to launch the 'Clean Up TV Campaign' on 4 May 1964.

I started my address by telling them the story of how just four of us, the Revd Basil Buckland, his wife Norah, my husband Ernest and myself, had issued our 'Clean Up TV Manifesto' and why and how four people, then totally inexperienced in public affairs, had come to find themselves at the centre of what *The Times* next morning called 'the most extraordinary meeting ever held in the Birmingham Town Hall'. And with memories of Lloyd George and his escape through the back door disguised as a policeman this was saying something!

What made us begin in the first place? Nineteen sixty-three was, by any standards, an extraordinary year, a climactic year, the year of the Profumo scandal, the publication of *Honest to God* by John Robinson, Bishop of Woolwich, 'kitchen sink' plays, which were dramas full of 'dirt' both in language and behaviour, late-night satire; the year in which Dr Peter Henderson, Principal Medical Officer at the Ministry of Education announced that it was not unchaste to have premarital sex. Dr Alex Comfort defined (on television) a chivalrous boy 'as one who takes contraceptives with him when he goes to meet his girl-friend' and the BBC gave the 'full treatment' to the exponents of the 'new morality' and censored, by exclusion, the protagonists of established morality.

Homosexuality, prostitution and sexual intercourse became the routine accompaniment of the evening meal and the topic of excited conversation in the cloakrooms and playgrounds as, night after night, the Profumo affair – in which Minister of War John Profumo was involved with prostitutes Christine Keeler and Mandy Rice-Davies – unfolded before our eyes. Suddenly 'they' were seen to have less than feet of clay, and a totally different way of life became accessible to all of us, including children, if only via the television screen. How 'accessible' I was soon to discover.

Not much goes on at school without it coming to the ears of the staff by one means or another, and it wasn't long before I found myself talking to a group of three girls and two boys who had, according to other children in the class, been 'doing things they shouldn't'.

'Why?' I asked them.

'Well, Miss, we watched them girls on TV and it looked as if it was easy, and see how well they done out of it, Miss, so we thought we'd try.' Shamefaced and rebellious, but little more than children.

Coming into school one Monday morning at the height of the *Honest to God* debate – and what a height! It spiralled upwards day after day for weeks on end – I was met at the gate by a group of fourth-year girls. Had I seen *Meeting Point*, the BBC's religious programme the night before? they asked excitedly. 'It was about premarital sex and ever so interesting.'

I quietened them down and promised we would discuss it during social studies later in the morning. As soon as the bell rang for change of lessons the girls came rushing in as one of them cried, 'I know what's right now, Miss.'

'Good. Well, you tell us,' I said hopefully.

The girl told me that when she heard what the programme was to be about, her father insisted that she and her two sisters should stop what they were doing and watch it. At the end of it they were all quite convinced, she told me, 'that we shouldn't have intercourse until we're engaged'.

What Kind of Loving? was a classic example of the way in which the BBC, with its penchant for 'South Bank' religion was allowing itself to be used as a launching platform for the 'new morality'. Paul Johnson writing in *New Statesman* had this to say about the programme:

> Amazing the advice young people get nowadays. I switched on BBC Television to hear a panel of experts talking about premarital sex. They consisted of a psychologist, a bishop's wife, a headmistress and a clergyman . . . Although none of them dare to say it outright, they all seemed in favour of sex before marriage if certain conditions were fulfilled.
>
> Nobody was prepared to take the orthodox line of traditional Christian morals. The clergyman was twice pressed to say whether or not fornication was a sin, but declined to give any direct answer.

This incident made a tremendous impression on me. These were average girls: if, within one short programme, their whole approach to the question of premarital sex had been moved into a sub-Christian dimension, was it not logical to assume that the programme had had the same effect upon impressionable teenagers all over the country?

My objection was not to discussion of the subject, but to the refusal of those, who might be expected to be clear and able spokesmen of the Church, to commit themselves to a firm position on right or wrong. The programme remains a landmark in the establishment of the permissive society and a classic example of the power of television to create and change patterns of thought and behaviour.

The country was in an uproar as women's organizations, magistrates, Church leaders, feature writers, and public and private figures joined in the chorus of protest, which Sir Hugh Carleton Greene, then Director-General of the BBC, was to dismiss as the voice of the 'lunatic fringe' while being forced for the first, but by no means the last, time to bow to its intensity. *That Was The Week That Was* was taken off the air at the end of 1963 with Greene still defending it. 'I enjoyed it. It was very good. It was positive and exhilarating. I have no objection to the language used,' he said.

What was he defending, and enjoying, and approving?

A show 'as smutty as a train window in a Crewe railway siding', (*Daily Sketch*) . . . which was 'adding a new quality to its irresponsible offensiveness – it is now sinister' (*Time and Tide*), which, week after week, 'raised questions of taste, fairness, propriety and even libel' and which 'enabled its scriptwriters to disseminate personal abuse, and bitter attacks upon authority of every kind' (*Daily Telegraph*).

As the year went on it became increasingly clear from the evidence reaching me as a teacher and the Bucklands in their parish work, that we should try to do something about the BBC. But easier said than done. I shall always remember the four of us sitting together looking down at the 2000 copies of the 'Clean Up TV Campaign' petition we'd had printed, but without any idea of how to get it launched.

We suddenly remembered – and we lived in the Midlands then – that the Birmingham *Evening Mail* had, along with many other newspapers, expressed concern about the goings-on at the BBC, and decided to ring them up. It seemed only minutes before a reporter was sitting on our sofa.

'Do you propose to hold a public meeting?' he asked.

Thinking quickly what a good idea that was, I said, 'Yes.'

'And where will you hold it – the Birmingham Town Hall?'

Not having any idea that the Town Hall held 2000 people, I gave another cheerful 'Yes.' So there we were, four of us, a petition with not a single name on it and a commitment to a public meeting, which, in the event, made history. I recall praying all through the day at school that the Lord would give us 250 people so that the press would not be able to say the hall was empty.

Thirty-nine coachloads arrived from all over the country, from places as far apart as Devon and Scotland, and the singing of 'Jerusalem' by that great crowd was something I shall never forget. It had its dangerous moments, too, as when long-haired students caused a disruption, rushed the platform and tried to seize the microphone from me. We had envisaged that the Town Hall meeting would mark the climax of the campaign but so great was the atmosphere created by it that I found myself saying, 'Ladies and gentlemen, far from this being the end of the campaign, it is but the beginning.' And so indeed it was. The press coverage of the event was massive. BBC Television transmitted only shots of the disruption so that when people reached home that night they found anxious relations waiting up for them, believing that the whole meeting had been a disaster when, in fact, it had turned out to be what *The Times* next morning called 'one of the most memorable meetings ever held in the Birmingham Town Hall'.

The paper described how

About 2,000 supporters of a campaign to 'clean up' BBC television attended a meeting in Birmingham Town Hall tonight. Women from Glasgow, London, Liverpool and Plymouth were among the audience, which decided to ask the Queen and the Duke of Edinburgh for their support.

It was decided to send a telegram asking the Queen and the Duke to give encouragement and support to our efforts to bring about a radical change in the policy of entertainers in general and the Governors of the British Broadcasting Corporation in particular. In view of the terrifying increase in promiscuity and its attendant horrors we are desperately anxious to banish from our homes and theatres those who seek to demoralize and corrupt our young people.'

The meeting had received messages of support from the Archbishop of Canterbury, the Archbishop of York, the Bishops of Blackburn and Shrewsbury and many other well-known people.

Why had the BBC been singled out? Mr. J. W. Pepper, a Birmingham councillor and chairman of the meeting, said that plays and films were censored and could be visited selectively. But there was no control over the programmes which came into one's home and which could change their complexion suddenly and without warning.

He added: 'As the BBC is a public corporation quite as much as the nationalized industries, it should be possible for the listening and viewing public to have something to say about what they have to watch and listen to.'

Mrs Norah Buckland, wife of the rector of Longton, Stoke-on-Trent, and one of the two founders of the movement, condemned 'dirty plays' and also the talk by Dr A. Comfort in which intercourse outside marriage was advocated.

Mrs Mary Whitehouse, the other founder of the movement, appealed to sympathizers to ask their parliamentary candidates to come right out into the open with their views on the campaign. One of her complaints against the BBC was that it was adolescent. Its main aim should be to lead the people on and up, not down and out.

What sort of people came to this meeting? Although men were present, most of the audience were middle-aged women. Perhaps never in the history of Birmingham Town Hall has such a successful meeting been sponsored by such a flimsy organization. There are no committee members, no officers and no hard plans for the future except for the hope that the people at this meeting will go out and spread the word in other parts of the country.

Among the diverse ideas brought out by various speakers were: that there were those abroad who would like to see the new morality destroy the moral fibre of the country, that only improving programmes should be shown on television, and that the devil would greatly approve of what goes on in BBC Television.

There are those who will find it easy enough to laugh at the women who were here tonight. Yet a good many of the speakers had experience as teachers or social workers who were seriously concerned with social questions in the field. And could it not be argued, perhaps, that the wife of the rector of Longton is likely to know at least as much about the realities of social problems as the authors of the plays which so often distress her.

There is another story which I shall never forget. In reply to my request, following the Town Hall meeting, for an interview with Sir Hugh Greene, I received a letter from his deputy, Mr Harman Grisewood, brother of Freddie Grisewood, the much loved Question Master, informing me that the DG was out of the country. If I cared to postpone my visit I could see him when he returned several weeks later, otherwise he himself would be very happy to meet me and hear what I had to say. Since I had to be back at school before Sir Hugh Greene returned, I accepted with alacrity the invitation to go to Broadcasting House the following week.

Mr Grisewood's courtesy and concern over what I had to tell him was marked, and it was obvious that he also was deeply troubled about some of the things which were happening at the BBC. I told him of the effect of the *Meeting Point* programme on the girls' attitude to premarital sex. But, he asked me, is it not true that the majority of young people now accept premarital sex as normal?

'No, I don't think it is, certainly not among the young people I know,' I replied. Then, tentatively, I told him how much I wished he could meet some of them. To my great surprise and delight he said that he and his wife would be pleased to have supper with me and some of my young friends.

It was, in Mr Grisewood's words, 'a most memorable evening', but nothing moved him more than Pauline's story. At fourteen she was mature beyond her years. The child of a broken home, she and her younger sister, for whom she felt greatly responsible, had been left in the care of a grandmother. She sat now talking to the Deputy Director-General of the BBC and told him how 'Daddy had come back to see Mummy four times to try and sort it out. I don't think they wanted to separate really, but they're both very proud people and I don't think they know how to talk out their troubles.' And she leaned forward to ask him earnestly, 'Don't you think it would be wonderful if the BBC could put on plays which would help families like ours to stay together, instead of ones in which, whenever there's trouble, people fly for a cigarette or a drink or out through the front door?'

They were sitting side by side on a settee in the small London flat where Mr and Mrs Grisewood had come to have supper with us. Besides Pauline there was her friend, Anne, our son Richard, then at Birmingham College of Art, a Rhodes Scholar from Oxford and several other young people all of whom left them in no doubt that the standards of 'swinging' London were not theirs.

Mr Grisewood wrote to me afterwards saying how much the whole evening had meant to them both, that he would always remember what Pauline and the others had said to him and would bear it very much in mind in the months ahead. It wasn't long before Harman Grisewood resigned. He was, to my mind, too sincere and too gentle a Christian to be at ease among the demolition men who frequented the BBC at that time.

This initiative really changed the whole of 'the work'. Up till then we were a spontaneous, grass roots movement, collecting signatures, organizing meetings, making press statements, meeting MPs and clergymen and other public figures just as it seemed appropriate. But it was an organization, albeit not of charity status but with only three paid employees where the majority of the work, including my own, was carried out voluntarily.

It was at this point that the BBC began to mount its counter-attack. It had been prepared so far to give us a certain rein in the belief that as soon as we had finished with the manifesto we would get back to normal living, and look back on the excitement of the campaign as something to tell our grandchildren about.

It was as a spontaneous reaction to that first packed-beyond-capacity meeting at the Birmingham Town Hall that we first spoke of the need for some kind of an 'independent broadcasting council' to represent the viewer whose comments on and reactions to programmes were so summarily dismissed or ignored by the BBC in particular at that time and for many years after. It seemed impossible to get through to the authorities – and that was the experience not only of individuals but also of our organizations, public bodies, Churches and even of Parliament itself. In spite of the constant barrage of criticism, particularly from the BBC, we pressed on with our demand for such a body, in and out of season.

So great was the public support for our campaign that our parliamentary advisers felt we should form ourselves into a properly constituted body and the National Viewers' and Listeners' Association (National VALA) was launched on 29 November 1965 at a press conference in Fleet Street. At this first meeting the Association announced its intention of pressing for the setting up of a Viewers' and Listeners' Council. National VALA's Chairman at that time was the late James Dance, MP for Bromsgrove. One day in December 1966 Jimmy rang to ask whether Ernest and I would go to see him at his home that afternoon. 'I've something very important to tell you. I can't talk about it on the telephone.'

We went, and heard how Mr Gibson-Watt, MP, then Conservative spokesman on broadcasting, had been approached by Lord Normanbrook, Chairman of the BBC, who had told him that he wished to meet Mr Dance privately in his capacity as Chairman of National VALA.

Gibson-Watt passed this message on to Jimmy, who told us

that he and Lord Normanbrook had had lunch together at Broadcasting House that week and had talked alone together for over two hours. The 'alone together' is vitally important, for when we eventually published this story the BBC denied that the Chairman had ever spoken in the terms he did to Jimmy.

Jimmy Dance told us – and I never doubted his integrity either in this regard or any other – that Lord Normanbrook had spoken to him of the 'total rift' between himself and Sir Hugh Greene, then Director-General of the BBC, of his deep concern about the country in general and the BBC in particular. He confessed also to the deep hurt he had felt when we had described as 'arrogant' his refusal to meet a deputation from the mass meeting at Birmingham Town Hall.

Jimmy told the Chairman how sorry he was that he had taken it as a personal slight, but hoped he would agree that we'd had 'a fair amount of aggravation!' 'We both laughed at that, and the atmosphere became much more relaxed and friendly,' Jimmy said, and after some general discussion Lord Normanbrook came to what he described as his 'main purpose in proposing the meeting'. He was, he said, most anxious to do everything possible to bring about an improvement in standards and re-establish public confidence in the BBC. He shared our belief in the need for much closer liaison between the Corporation and the public, and was interested in our suggestion of a Viewers' and Listeners' Council. Did Mr Dance think that Mrs Whitehouse would be prepared to set up such a Council? (How strange all this sounds now that the Broadcasting Standards Council has been in existence for several years!)

When Jimmy left, Lord Normanbrook asked him to put the proposal to me with the request that, should I decide to accept his invitation, I would ensure that such a council would be composed of a representative cross-section of society, rather than exclusively of members or supporters of National VALA. In return he gave an assurance that there was every likelihood that such a council would be able to meet regularly with the governors of the BBC (an idea which has not yet been put in practice) and, once it had been established, no doubt with the governors of the ITA. Lord Normanbrook was anxious that all these arrangements should be carried out in complete secrecy so that no word of what was happening should leak until we were ready to present it as a *fait accompli.*

'Will you do it?' asked Jimmy. I was completely dumb-founded by the proposition but said that I would certainly try. It took me several weeks to adjust to the idea that the Chairman of the BBC should have approached me in this way, and I would sometimes shake Ernest awake in the middle of the night to ask if it was really true. 'Yes, of course it is. Go to sleep!' he'd reply with some exasperation.

The more I thought about it the more difficult the exercise appeared, especially as it had to be so secretive, until I remembered again one of the great lessons I'd learnt from the experience of the recent past. Always go through 'open doors' to particular people. I was determined, after the intrigue which followed the launching of National VALA, not to get involved with representatives of official bodies of any kind.

Shortly afterwards, however, Lord Normanbrook became seriously ill and by the following June, before the Council had time to get itself established, he was dead. Before long Lord Hill had been brought from the ITA to take his place. Where did we go from there? We felt the best thing was to discuss the situation with the new Chairman and several of us met him early in October 1967.

By this time I had begun to see that Lord Normanbrook's proposal could never work. As he saw it the Broadcasting Council would be, to put it bluntly, appointed by me, and that would not have been acceptable on any level. What we had in mind was a council which could genuinely be the vehicle of public opinion as a whole.

We had also suggested that any conclusion arrived at by the Council should be broadcast at the same time as the offending programme was transmitted and that arrangement has been incorporated into the terms of reference of the Broadcasting Standards Council as it stands today. Furthermore, we proposed that the governors of the BBC and the Chairman of the IBA (Independent Broadcasting Authority, now ITC, the Independent Television Commission) 'come regularly to the television screen to explain the policy of their different bodies', pointing out that prime ministers and leaders of the opposition do that so why should broadcasting be any different?

That such a Council was not the mad idea many professionals always claimed it to be is evidenced by this quote from an article by Ralph Bettinson in *Television Mail* as long ago as July 1965:

There is surely a proper function for a Viewer's and Listeners' Association as distinct from the Advisory Councils with which the BBC and ITA are already furnished. It can serve a constructive purpose, having nothing to do with censorship. It can bridge the gap between the public and the authorities ... Such an Association could make a valuable contribution to the future development of television in this country.

The idea was also mooted on television by me – in the BBC's *Talkback* in October 1967. Sir Hugh Greene's deputy Stuart Hood referred to the great majority of people who complained about BBC programmes as being 'cranks' and 'pathologically obscene'! I wasn't having that! So I left a message on the BBC answer phone saying I would like to take part in the programme to refute Mr Hood's remarks. Next day I received a telegram: 'We shall indeed be pleased to give you the opportunity of meeting Stuart Hood in *Talkback* next Tuesday night.' What an experience that was! The idea of the programme was that selected viewers should meet a representative of the BBC to express their complaints. I expected to be one of a panel who would be feeling much the same as me – but not this time. One after another, the panel disassociated itself from me and supported Stuart Hood. I managed, however, to state the case for an independent broadcasting council through which the public could make its voice heard. Uproar – from what seemed not only a loaded panel but also a loaded audience.

'Decline and fall of super critic,' shouted the *Daily Mirror* next day while the *Sun* told me to 'dig a hole' for myself and jump into it. As I travelled to a meeting in Plymouth next day I felt sick and desperate and had to talk about it all to the only other occupant of the carriage. He was marvellous and kept my mind off myself with stories of his own experience. He'd been a lawyer at a war crimes tribunal in Jordan for whom he was to act as unofficial ambassador. He gave me enormous encouragement, took me to dinner, and made me promise to keep in touch, so that by the time I reached Plymouth and Westward TV I felt more relaxed. At one point in the evening, he said, 'The British public being what it is, a wholesale attack on you like that will do you nothing but good.' The BBC later admitted it had received over 800 letters, many supporting the idea of a Broadcasting Standards Council and even including money to be forwarded to us.

Alasdair Milne, Director-General from 1981 to 1986, writing in his *Memoirs of a British Broadcaster* referred to the problems National VALA had with the late Sir Hugh Greene, when he was Director-General. He acknowledged the developing controversy on taste and standards on television, and referred to the 'early clashes' Greene had had with us 'to the point where she [me!] identified the cloven hoof in him and he refused to speak to her or correspond with her', and added, 'An odd stance, I always thought, on his part, because you did not need to agree with a word Mary said, but you could still have an agreeable exchange with her.' Well, that was something.

It was clear from our meeting with Lord Hill that he, too, had his doubts about the proposed Council. I wrote in my diary on the day we went to see him (9 November 1967): 'He was not prepared to have any kind of "special relationship" with us, which is not what we wanted anyway. After we'd talked generally about programme standards he said he would "certainly be willing to hear the views of any council we like to set up and the more serious research it did the better".' But, of course, we did not set up any such council though we made sure that the idea of one did not die by constantly propagating it in public meetings around the country, in our publications and through our contacts with MPs.

The nearest we got to a successful outcome came just before the election of 1974 when we met at the Home Office with the then Conservative Home Secretary Robert Carr, who showed himself sympathetic to such a proposition. But the change of government flattened all our hopes. We received nothing but discouragement from the Labour government so long as it remained in power and it was not until the Conservatives returned under Mrs Thatcher that the idea again became a possibility and then a reality.

'Mary, do you know you are in this week's issue of the *Radio Times*?' said the voice at the other end of the telephone. The shock brought forth my never very deeply buried Cheshire colloquialism. 'Don't be daft,' I said. 'Well, your hat is there, if you're not,' said my friend faintly from the south coast. How ridiculous, I thought, and grabbed the current *Radio Times*. On an inside page there was, indeed, a bad representation of my hat. Who would be interested in me or it, I wondered.

Turning over the pages I came upon details of a new serial, *Swizzlewick* by David Turner. The lady in the hat was a Mrs Smallgood who, along with her friend, was to launch a 'Freedom from sex' campaign in mythical Swizzlewick. Well, well! One of the chief characters listed was a councillor by the name of Salt. Hadn't Councillor Pepper chaired our Birmingham Meeting? We could hardly wait for Tuesday night and the first episode. Later we met a character called Ernest, a postman. Did I not have a husband whose name was Ernest, and was not our home called Postman's Piece? Our interest grew.

Swizzlewick caused an uproar. Midlands local government and council officials saw this 'skit', which showed councillors to be stupid and corrupt, as a gross insult to public-spirited men giving freely of their time; parents were furious that family viewing time should be taken up with what the *Catholic Pictorial* described as 'obscene offerings of adolescent smut'; and television critics could find little to praise. The serial's official justification – to take the lid off council pomposity and teach people to laugh at themselves – was sound, but there was an odd note of 'We'll show them' which gave the programme a bitter tang.

On Friday 24 August 1964, the Birmingham *Evening Mail* carried a critical report, by the television correspondent Ivor Jay, of the coming Tuesday's episode. The next afternoon at a meeting in Birmingham of the Clean Up TV Campaign I was offered, completely out of the blue and by someone I did not know, a copy of the script of this episode, 'Campaigners All', to do 'what you like with'. After looking at it, I had no doubts about what I wanted to do – send it to the Postmaster-General, who was the Minister responsible for the BBC. But how to get it there quickly? As soon as I got home I rang up an MP who I was sure would help. I was given a special code number and told to take the envelope containing the script to the postmaster at the General Post Office in Wolverhampton immediately. It was in the hands of the Postmaster-General within hours.

Tuesday came. 'Will you know if there are alterations to

the script, Mrs Whitehouse?' enquired the newspapers who had carried the story of what I had done with the script. I said I thought I would have a general idea. In the event two and a half minutes was cut or, as one paper pointed out next day, 250 to 300 words. It was the scene in which one of the characters was to be shown coming out of the room of Blousie, the prostitute, with his clothes in disarray.

Many newspapermen have asked who gave me the script, but I have not said and never will. One persistent reporter called it a day when I reminded him that several members of his profession had gone to jail for refusing to disclose their sources, adding that I was sure he would not expect me to disclose mine. Nevertheless when I was approached by the Birmingham *Evening Mail* and asked whether or not I had received the script from a member of their staff, I immediately said I had not. In spite of that assurance Ivor Jay was denied admission to programme previews and could not adequately carry out his job as TV critic.

Within a day or two all the papers carried the news that David Turner had left *Swizzlewick* in protest at what he described as 'unethical cuts'. And that was that – or nearly.

There is one episode of *Swizzlewick* which I am not likely to forget. One of my sons and I saw it together, and possibly few others watching would realize the significance of what we saw.

Ernest was recovering at our home from delayed shock following an accident in which, during a foggy night, he had run over and killed a young man who had laid himself across the way. The road was dark, twisting and unlighted. It was a nightmare experience for him as he drove round the corner, suddenly saw a body lying there and realized he could do nothing to avoid hitting it. Although the young man had left a note explaining his state of mind, and the inquest jury expressed sympathy for my husband and exonerated him from all responsibility, months later he collapsed from nervous strain. He was awaiting with some interest the advent of Ernest, the postman, into the serial and this evening, having some work to attend to, had asked me to call him when he appeared.

I shall never forget the incident I saw, although it was over in a few minutes. Ernest, the postman, is not well. Something must be done about it: let us lay him down on the settee. What a strange malady. He is suffering from guilt after having hit a dog with a football. He must be given psychological treatment. What about a little hypnosis? Realizing how the story was developing, I knew I must keep my husband out of the room until the episode was over. It was many months later, when he was fully recovered, before I told him what had happened. He was astounded and asked why I had not taken up the matter at the time. But how could I have done so without distressing him?

Whether this was a coincidence or not, I felt sure that had Ernest seen that episode he would have suffered a setback just as he was recovering peace of mind, and would have needed all my attention. He has, of course, been as fully committed to our campaign as I have. Without the inspiration of his deep personal faith, his selfless willingness to accept the inevitable domestic upheavals, the humour and vigour with which he has chaired many meetings, the story of the last thirty years could never have been written.

CHAPTER TWO

DOWN UNDER

There's one thing about having the kind of life I live, I never know what's going to happen next. This time it was my seventy-ninth birthday in 1989 and I was busy arranging some of the flowers which had arrived. I glanced through the windows and saw a not very young woman, looking weary and disconsolate, in the middle of the drive. She had obviously been to the door of the cottage part of the house, received no reply and was thinking that no one was at home. I thought she must have come to visit my daughter-in-law, who was working in her studio further down the drive, and out I went to direct her.

'Mary!' she exclaimed, a smile spreading across her tired face and then, as I hadn't recognized her, her face fell. 'Don't you recognize me?' she asked. 'We met the last time you came to speak in Australia in 1984 – I came up to the platform afterwards to ask what I could do to help and you said would I like to start a branch in Perth and I did!'

Beryl van Luyn was spending a couple of weeks in London, had heard on the radio that it was my birthday and had decided on the spot to come and see us. If she'd given us a ring we could have made the trip considerably easier but, to a Western Australian, distance was no object: she had feet to walk on and a tongue in her head! She took a train to Colchester, but instead of asking one of the taxi men to take her to where we lived she asked for the bus station, and walked the couple of miles here in most unsuitable shoes. She got off the bus at the end of our lane and walked another mile, before hoping desperately that the gate she had walked through was ours! I couldn't help but think that only an Australian would have set off so determinedly with so little information. We fed her, brought her up to date and put her back

on a train to London but, of course, the experience took me
back to my adventures in Australia and the wonderful times
I'd had there – even though some of them had been pretty
fraught!

Way back in January 1973 we were enjoying the last swim of
our 'away from it all' holiday in the Gambia, West Africa, when
suddenly, and quite unexpectedly, I felt very strange indeed. I
now only vaguely remember the doctor murmuring something
about 'sunstroke', and the nice couple from the chalet next
door who came in to help us pack and to get a very sick-feeling
me on to the plane. I thought no more about this odd attack
until early May, two days after accepting an invitation to go to
Sydney to launch the Australian Festival of Light that autumn,
when I collapsed with malignant tertian malaria which kept
me out of action for the entire summer.

However, 'you can't possibly go' changed, as I regained
strength, to 'you can't possibly go alone', and the tour went
ahead on the understanding that Ernest would accompany me
to make sure that I didn't overdo it. But ten days before we
were due to leave, the doctor told him, 'No flying for you,' as
the strain of past months had pushed up his blood pressure.

So there was I, not yet up for breakfast, and about to be
launched – or so it seemed to me – into the nearest thing to
outer space I was ever likely to experience, and entirely on my
own. How would it feel to stand on a platform again? Would
I remember what I had to say? How would the Aussies react
to it even if I did? Suppose I wasn't strong enough to cope, all
those miles from home? It was too late to cancel the many
arrangements which had been made for my visit, so go I must.

Four days' holiday were planned for me in Singapore –
but what in the world, apart from sleeping, would I do with
myself? I needn't have worried. No sooner was I on the airport
concourse than the first call came, and in the next few days it
seemed that everyone at home who knew anyone in Singapore
had made up their minds that I would not be lonely.

'What would you like to do?' brought, among other
delights, a night under the sky with the Filipino Ballet, and
the first of those almost unreal experiences which characterized the whole trip when the couple who had been so kind

when I was taken ill in The Gambia, strolled by as we sat chatting after the performance. 'I don't believe it!' we all exclaimed. Which was pretty much the reaction that came from one of my old sparring partners at the BBC as he spotted me getting out of a taxi next day. 'Good God, what's she doing here?' he asked his companion. 'Having lunch with me,' was the reply.

The other side of the world's not so far away, after all, I thought as I left for Darwin – to fly smack into an airport strike, an electricity strike, a postal strike (what had we said about writing every day?) and three of the most hectic, remarkable and rewarding weeks of my life.

'We don't have public meetings much in Darwin,' they told me.

'So how many are you expecting tonight?' I asked.

'Maybe as few as six. Fifty will be good.'

But there were three hundred warm, friendly Australians, predominantly young parents, many of them civil servants who worked in the outposts of administration. It soon became clear that we spoke the same language and shared the same concerns and by the end of the evening my wobbly legs had stiffened up and I had addressed my first public meeting since early May. As I wrote to Ernest on 6 October:

> Since I left Singapore on Monday night for Darwin and Brisbane I literally have not stopped – one night no sleep at all, another up at 5.30 and a constant round of meetings, TV and radio programmes which almost makes last year's American trip look like a bun fight! No doubt you realize, via the press, that all the major airports are closed by strikes, that there is an electricity strike bringing frequent blackouts and a postal strike in South Australia.
>
> But I must tell you about my Great Adventure yesterday! There were no flights out of Brisbane for Sydney where a big press and TV conference was scheduled for noon. However, one of our friends in Brisbane heard that a young pilot had flown up several businessmen in his little six-seater plane the previous night. They contacted him and persuaded him to stay overnight to take me back with him to Sydney 600 miles away. I couldn't help but

wonder what you and the boys would have thought if you'd seen it all!

As there was no radar or any other airport controls, or safety devices of any kind available, we had to keep below the cloud which was mostly around 500 feet and fly along the beaches, occasionally cutting across a flat peninsula. Just over half-way we came down on the short strip of a backwoods 'port', where there was just one fuel pump, to get refuelled – but it didn't work because of the power blackout!

After waiting some time for the pilot to make various calls through to a private airfield 12 miles out of Sydney to see if we could land there, they agreed. So off we set again – not able again to rise above 500 feet and often only just above the water – with the feeling that if we hit a sizeable air pocket we might drop neatly onto it! However, I have to report that, greatly to my surprise, I enjoyed every minute of it and wouldn't have missed it for the world. I reckon I saw more of Australia that day than many Australians see in a lifetime!

However, I must admit that on a number of occasions I became conscious that I could not hear any sound coming from the engine and I began to wonder if there was anything wrong with it! But I told myself firmly that as I hadn't really the faintest idea of how a car engine works I wasn't likely to be able to assess the state of an aeroplane engine. Enjoy the scenery and forget it, I told myself and indeed I did. It was only when the reception committee standing at the airport asked the pilot if he would like to come for a meal and he replied, 'No thanks, I don't like the sound of that kite at all and I'd better get her into shipshape before I do anything else', that I realized my imaginings hadn't been so wide of the mark after all!

The main press conference took place half an hour after I arrived in Sydney, followed immediately by four TV interviews for different channels and a half-hour radio programme – very tough and cheeky! Then after a cup of tea and a bite, I set off again to do two more interviews for current affairs programmes, finally getting to bed at 9.45 p.m. having started the day at 5 a.m.

A couple of days later:

> You'll find it difficult to believe, but though the new Sydney
> Opera House which the Queen opens next week was only
> three minutes walk away I never got across to look at it. I
> have asked the PRO man to send me a list of the TV and
> radio commitments I fulfilled so that you will be able to
> see the amount of coverage; it really was fantastic and the
> Sydney Town Hall meeting was the climax.
>
> There was a wonderful young group – New World
> Singers – who were absolutely superb. Right at the end I
> turned to the Minister of Transport who was the Chairman
> and said, 'I'm dying to get up and join them – come with
> me?' 'Come on, then' he said and we did just that, clapping
> our hands, singing and getting everyone to join in!
> Absolutely marvellous, the singing was so joyful and
> inspired. Out of 6½ thousand inside and outside the hall,
> there were only twelve demonstrators and they were quickly
> frogmarched off the premises – no messing about!
>
> The following day I had to get to Adelaide but because
> of the airport strike it had been arranged that the private
> plane bringing the papers to Sydney would take me back
> to Adelaide with it.
>
> We waited five hours at the airport – the plane had
> been diverted because of appalling weather conditions
> and when it finally arrived at about 5 p.m. it was a terrible
> thing, very old and only two seats for the pilot and co-pilot,
> no kind of a seat at all for me, just a hard, dirty, metal
> floor! We didn't like the look of it at all. So back we went
> and I slept for three hours, just in time to turn on the TV
> and hear that the airport strike was off! So we all felt that
> our prayers had been answered and that God had overruled
> what could have been a very unpleasant experience – six
> hours in a 'kite' like that in those conditions would just
> about have been the end.

That was only my first visit to Australia, and looking back I can
see what an incredible programme I had and only a few
months after the attack of malaria which had left me so exhausted. How did I cope? Well, I'm sure the secret lay not only
with the prayers which I knew were going up constantly for

me from family and friends at home but also with my own dependence on the Lord. Before I began to speak, whether in public meetings, on television or radio, I invariably lifted up my heart and mind and then trusted I would be given the strength, which I was. My second was in 1978 just after the *Gay News* blasphemy trial, the first such trial for fifty-two years. It had caused tremendous controversy not only in Britain but around the world, and homosexuals in Australia were determined to gain as much publicity as they could while I was there.

The first two rows of the Brisbane theatre – as was made obvious by the contrast of their clothing with the rest of the audience – were filled with homosexuals and lesbians who, at some given signal part-way through my speech, rose as one to hurl huge flour and water pastry cases, filled with beaten-up shaving cream and red dye straight at me. One hit me in the chest, two landed on my stomach, the filling from a couple slithered down my legs, while dollops stuck to my sleeves. 'At least', I said, to the audience cheering me on in the crowded hall, 'it matches my blouse!' Considering my attackers were seated only two or three yards from me they could hardly miss and in the clamour that followed they dashed out of the hall into the arms of the already alerted policemen waiting in the lobby!

They were, of course, hoping to drive me off the platform, but no way – at least not until I'd finished my speech and someone else had come to the microphone. Then occurred one of those amusing episodes which with the telling of the story lifted it on to another plane. I had slipped quietly behind the backdrop of curtains to see if I could stop the wet mush soaking further through my skirt and underclothes – I was feeling cold. In front of me I saw a pile of cheese cloth which I quickly folded over and over into a pad and pushed up my skirt to be held firmly – I hoped – by the waistband. Then back I went onto the platform telling the waiting policemen that I would talk to them at the end of the meeting, which I did. Just as we were about to leave an increasingly embarrassed officer glanced down at my legs. 'Excuse me, Miss,' he said. I looked down in the direction he was indicating and grabbed what I'm sure he thought were my pants and pulled out yards and yards of the cheesecloth! The laughter that followed was a welcome relief from the tension that had characterized the meeting.

One of the most vivid memories of that visit to Australia was of me speaking – under close police protection – for only three minutes instead of the expected fifteen outside Sydney Town Hall. The crowd and the TV cameras were kept at a safe distance but a girl, so small that I thought she was a child, moved to the front of the crowd. With her back to me she danced on the pavement – just enjoying herself, I thought. Then she turned round and we saw what it was all about: she had padded her stomach to make herself look pregnant and across the bulge she had fixed a placard declaring that 'Jesus loved me!' Whenever I recall that incident I do so with the hope that, perhaps by now, she has discovered that Jesus truly does love her.

As my visit went on so did the opposition, and some of it came from – to me – the most unexpected sources. As I told Ernest in a letter home from Launceston in Tasmania written on 1 September 1978:

Since I wrote last, the row over South Australia's Attorney General's attack on me has grown and grown like Topsy. It apparently started before I even left home. I can't remember whether I told you that he called me an 'angel of darkness', said that I was totally discredited in Britain and warned the people of Australia to have nothing to do with me (National Front, etc.). I responded by saying that I found it quite incredible that a man in his position should so demean his public office by launching a smear campaign based on unfounded accusation against a private person he has never met! I challenged him to meet me face to face on TV. He refused. The story grew and grew being the first item on the national TV programmes and coming out every hour on radio news. It lasted right through the weekend; Lance Shilton, Archbishop of Sydney, issued a statement supporting me from the Cathedral etc. etc. On Monday the Attorney General agreed to appear with me on *P.M.* between 6.05 and 6.15.

In the event he didn't turn up. In the afternoon he'd attended a Cabinet meeting and it was apparently made clear to him that his colleagues took a very poor view of his activities. Yesterday morning (Tuesday) he issued another statement saying that I had every right to speak (having previously said that I must be silenced!) and that he wished to make it clear that his were personal views and that the government was not associated with them. The silly ass got his facts all wrong – I'd stopped a programme on prison conditions being shown! He's strongly linked with the 'gay' lobby here and they're feeding him!

Anyway, as far as my tour is concerned this is just about the best thing that could have happened. The media interest is fantastic. On Monday I started at 7.15 when a reporter from the Sydney *Morning Herald* came to breakfast, staying with me for the rest of the day during which I did eleven TV and radio shows, finishing at 7.00 p.m.! It was quite amusing to hear the comments of exhausted journalists as they followed me round. Three of these programmes were shown in succession last evening on different channels and we were delighted with them all. I was quite happy and relaxed, often throwing the questions back to the interviewers and this made for quite good-humoured programmes and all the interviewers came over as very friendly.

At the lunch in Hobart, the Attorney General of Tasmania sat on my right and a Senator of the Federal Parliament on my left. Just everyone who was anyone was there, including the Lord Mayor and a leading judge and as the TV commentator said on the news, if I'm an angel of darkness, 'then there's an awful lot of angels of darkness amongst the leading lights of Tasmania!'

Fred Nile is travelling everywhere with me, and we go first class so this makes for a maximum of comfort. I have a lovely room here, it's 'The Millers Room' and it is huge and quite luxuriously furnished. While I've been writing this letter I have heard that Warren Mitchell of *Till Death Us Do Part* [BBC1] fame, who's in Australia, has written a huge article attacking me in the national paper the *Australian* and the press agency have been on for my comments so it looks as though my rest day is not going to be quite the 'away from it all' day that we all hoped! Never mind, as you know, that's how it goes.

I didn't fully understand then quite why I was given such tight police protection in every state I visited in Australia until the day came for me to leave, when I was given a copy of an A4 poster which had been distributed at a meeting, which the police infiltrated, held by homosexuals at Sydney University three weeks before my arrival in the country. It carried a picture of me with a meat cleaver plunged in my back with the caption 'Let the blood flow'. I'd found some of the police attention to my safety and welfare somewhat inhibiting and puzzling – they would not allow me even to leave my hotel to buy paper hankies unless they accompanied me – but all at once became clear and I was grateful for all the protection I had been given in every state I visited. To tell the truth, my adventures there and the great kindness and warmth – 'Keep at it, gal,' shouted across the street – has given Australia and its people a special place in my heart.

I have wondered, as time has passed, whether all the hard work and enthusiasm which were put into my visits to Australia had any lasting effect. The Australian Festival of Light has continued to battle on in some states I visited, particularly in Western Australia under the guidance of Beryl van Luyn, and in Sydney under the chairmanship of Dr David Phillips, a research scientist. However, according to his most recent news-letter, Australians are face to face with an ongoing 'avalanche of evil'. But he also tells us of victories, such as the ending of Channel 9's television series *Sex* as a result 'of enormous public pressure'. He had written to the chairmen of firms whose advertisements were associated with the programme and many of them had withdrawn their patronage, which demonstrates that advertisers are sensitive to public opinion.

Both Houses of the South Australian parliament have just passed a bill to control the display of pornography, similar to the Indecent Displays Bill passed by the British Parliament in 1981 and the Federal Government Assembly has called for a full inquiry into the way Pay TV is handled. Pornographers in Australia, as elsewhere, have long wanted access to a 24-hour cable TV channel devoted to pornographic movies, advertising sex objects and even prostitutes. The battle is ongoing and worldwide: 'Eternal vigilance is the price of freedom.'

*

'I am greatly honoured that you should have come to see me,' said Pope Paul VI to Dr Sieger Ernst, my German friend, a colleague of his and myself when we were received by His Holiness at his summer palace, Castel Gandolfo, in August 1971. To capture the atmosphere of the occasion I can only turn again to my diary:

Masses of people were gathered outside his summer palace for the Pope's public appearance later in the day but we were directed to the entrance to the palace itself. We went inside and were briefed on protocol. An interpreter took us slowly from one room to another of the magnificent building – the Papal Guards really are something! At last the moment came to enter the presence of the Pope himself and what a wonderful presence he has. He was sitting on his throne and we were alone with him, except for the interpreter who translated Sieger's German, but the Pope spoke to me in English and with great feeling about our work. He said he would remember us in his prayers and blessed our work. Then I mentioned the Festival of Light and he said he would pray especially for it. Twice he said, 'The work you do is very important,' and also indicated his pleasure that we were working on an international level and said, 'It is truly remarkable that you have done what you have done as private individuals.'

There was, inevitably the media interest in our visit. *Woman's Hour* were on the phone – could they interview me on the steps of the Vatican? Didn't get very far with that! Later the same day we had an interview lasting one and a half hours with one of the archbishops who had seen the Pope after our interview yesterday – he told us that while the Vatican had been aware of the general problem, it now understood it in greater depth, intended to do everything possible to help and would start by studying the problem with their own bishops around the world.

Did a little sightseeing – the Colosseum is most impressive – I shall long remember the view from inside, atmosphere fantastic, back at midnight! And I heard later – a bit of light relief! – the front page of the next day's *Birmingham Post* carried a big cartoon showing Frank Longford and me outside St Peter's with its nude statues

on the top of the pillars and his lordship saying to me,
'What is a nice girl like you doing in a place like this?'

Looking back now the two events in 1971 that stand out for
me are the meeting with Pope Paul VI and what I can only
describe as the clandestine meeting with the late Charles
Curran, then Director-General of the BBC. It was set up by
Bishop Butler of St Edmund's College, Ware. I was warned in
advance that it was to be very private and under no circumstances was I to mention it to anyone. But as time went on,
and after Charles Curran himself was dead, I felt free to give
my own impressions of the occasion as I wrote them down
in my diary that night.

> I liked the Bishop very much and he seemed very interested
> in and impressed by our work, as we talked before Charles
> Curran's arrival. When he came he seemed to be both shy
> and defensive. How defensive he was became very
> apparent as time went on.
>   It was very good of him to spare the time and to be
> prepared to meet me and I appreciate this enormously.
> And I suppose the very fact that we met and became *people*
> to one another was of immense value. But we certainly
> made no headway in conversation – I suppose it was like a
> 'summit conference' with nobody giving anything at all!
>   What was most disturbing was Curran's indication that
> the BBC no longer has a commitment to Christianity –
> clear that 'situational ethics' are the keynote theme. It was
> very difficult to make a considered point because, as the
> Bishop said afterwards, he would wait without really
> listening to what I was saying then come in with one of
> the usual clichés. All rather disappointing really – I'd hoped
> that we might have some meeting of minds, but the
> barriers seemed total.

All this arose from my letter to Charles Curran soon after
his appointment requesting that he would receive a deputation
from National VALA. This he refused but said he would be
very happy to meet me personally. Thinking back now, in the
light of the excellent programmes coming out of the BBC's
Religious Affairs department, his remarks about the BBC no

longer having any commitment to Christianity ring hollow. One can only say, thankfully, that times change. But in the meantime, the battle rolled on.

One of the busiest days of my trip to the United States in 1972 – made no less so by the fact that we woke up in a city crippled by an ice storm, all the schools closed for the first time in 21 years, 100,000 people without electricity, and, of course, for most of them this meant no heating and no cooking with many degrees of frost! Roads impassable at first because of sheets of ice but improved as the day went on.

My diary reminds me of the interview with the evening paper at the hotel – a conservative paper, so friendly. We then set off to meet the morning paper, having been told it was likely to be hostile but the woman who did the interview 'in depth' seemed very sympathetic too. I quoted from the words of the founder of their paper and one of America's greatest newspapermen, Joseph Pulitzer: he had said that his paper would 'always oppose privileged classes and public plunderers'. He had described broadcasters as a privileged class, and libertarians as 'public plunderers' and spoke of his determination 'to preserve that public virtue without which democratic government was a sham and a mockery'. From there I went on to do an hour-long radio show with questions coming in from listeners and at 4 p.m. a half-hour TV show.

Just enough time for me to get back to my room to rest for a short time before the dinner which precedes the making of a TV programme for private use amongst bishops, lay groups etc. Cardinal Carbenney was there. I sat next to him – a most charming, friendly and obviously saintly man. After dinner he put on his robes and was briefly interviewed by Bob Dornan who, until a few weeks ago, had his own show in California. He spoke out splendidly, then the next $2\frac{1}{2}$ hours were spent in putting the film together in ten-minute episodes. The Cardinal went back into the audience and Ray Gaver, Fred Schlaffley and myself joined Bob.

This really was something – the Cardinal refused to leave before we finished at 11.45! The Monsignor who

accompanied him said he had never stayed so long
anywhere before. It all went very well indeed and I can
see it being widely used. Probably up to date the most
important thing we've done. How to put it all into words?
Each one of these experiences is unique and so much
beyond what one could ever have dreamed.

Left for airport at 8 a.m., Los Angeles by 11.30. What
a flight, across the Grand Canyon and the Arizona Desert,
what a sight! How I would love to have gone there in
actuality. The colour of the rocks was marvellous and then
down into Los Angeles where we were met by Ray's wife
Ella and secretary Mary. Weather glorious to us, anyway.
To the natives it was cold. But it's obvious from the palm
trees, the bougainvillaea, the orchids, etc. that climate is
almost tropical. They brought us over to the Holiday Inn
in Hollywood where we are to stay – sixteen flights up
and a gorgeous view over this really incredible place.

My first job was a half-hour radio show – the interviewer,
Marc Bragg, said we might not be able to take the full
time but, in the event, ran through two tapes for an hour.
This will go out on Sunday night as a complete
programme and will also be used over a period of five days
in excerpts between music.

But then we went off to Washington. My diary again:

'What a day! Shan't forget this as long as I live, not only
for the magnificent sightseeing we did, but also for the
eight hours non-stop talking of Colonel John Hinkle who
conducted our tour. His knowledge of his city is such that
he does not stop for breath, and one is almost dizzy with
it all. But the highlights? The house, opposite the theatre
where he was shot, where Abraham Lincoln died. The bed,
the pillow, the untouched room at the end of the
passage, the front room in which his wife sat with her
children, the room leading off it where the Cabinet met.
Then to the Capitol where we went into the Senate and
the Congress – what a magnificent building this is.

It would be impossible to give a detailed account of all
we saw – every embassy, every government building, every
gallery – not from the inside, of course, because we could

not stop. We went to Mount Vernon, the house of George Washington – what a delightful and restful place – saw the homes where the slaves lived – and picked up a stone from outside one of them to bring home, and we saw his grave.

From there we raced to Arlington. John Hinkle wrote its official history and he gave us an autographed copy. His knowledge and ability to find his way around is unparalleled. As always, we were told, there was a group of people at the John Kennedy grave and memorial, though fewer than usual because the gates were closing. The grave in its unique setting is simple though very impressive with the eternal flame burning upon it. We were told that the flame can be seen at night right across Washington. Then we literally ran to the car and raced to the tomb of the unknown warrior and watched the changing of the guard. Very moving. When the custodian removed the wreath from the grave he gave me two red carnations, a piece of laurel and the ribbon from it to keep.

The Lincoln Memorial, now beautifully floodlit, was the next stop. What a sight – the Lincoln Memorial on the one hand with its magnificent statues and on the other side the floodlit Washington Memorial reflected right down the waters which stretched between the two. What a truly wonderful city this is.

John Hinkle told us how he had written the first communiqué after the declaration of war following the Japanese attack on Pearl Harbour. He was also one of the fifteen people including President Roosevelt and the Vice President present at the signing of the Declaration of War. So he certainly was able to give us the benefit of his first-hand experience and it was a great privilege to be conducted round these historic sights by him.

Finished up with dinner at a famous 'beef' restaurant – just about creased but immensely thrilled to have had such a day.

And then I came home, more stimulated than exhausted!

CHAPTER THREE

THE
DEVIL'S ADVOCATE

In my book *Whatever Happened to Sex* I wrote at length about National VALA's involvement in the trial in 1971 of Richard Handyside for his publication of *The Little Red School Book* with its obscene sexual exploitation of schoolchildren. And when one looks back now at the kind of 'advice' being given to children then by the publishers of this book, one comes to realize how greatly the thinking behind it has permeated a significant element of 'progressive' thinking about sexual behaviour among the young. The sexual anarchy which characterized not only the book's philosophy but also the philosophy behind A. S. Neill's policies at Summerhill School has deeply affected our present culture and education. Neill propagated as enlightened the ideas that God is dead, immorality is wonderful, and as for violence, well, 'You're angry, you know what to do'. Looking back, one can see how deep ran the links between sexual and political anarchy.

That *The Little Red School Book* was a political and sexual revolutionary primer there can be no doubt and if one looks now, twenty years on, at the statistics for divorce, rape, violence, broken marriages, children in care, availability of pornography, sexual abuse of children, we can see how the demolition of basic human, indeed Christian, values has profoundly affected us all in the years that have followed. When I meet the young growing up today, in universities and schools, I am ashamed of the burden we have created for them. That so many of them now want a different, more·responsible, way is something to be grateful for.

Our next legal venture centred on the efforts in 1976 of the Danish film maker Jens Jörgen Thorsen to have his pornographic and obscene film *The Sex Life of Christ* published in this country. We had been alerted to the nature of the Thorsen filmscript by Danish friends who knew that, following loud and anguished protests from Muslims as well as Christians, Thorsen had been prevented by the Danish government from getting the film made in Denmark. Several months later it was reported that he had obtained financial backing from the Swedish Film Institute until, once again, international concern made itself felt and, what was more to the point, the Swedish Church, according to one of its pastors, 'came to life for the first time in decades', expressing strong and continuous opposition to the project. The Swedish government, because of its policy of 'no censorship' found itself in considerable difficulties, but so great was the pressure from all sides that new legislation was quickly passed which made it well nigh impossible for Thorsen to make his film in Sweden. It was at this point that we heard rumours that he intended to come to Britain to make it. We were determined to do what we could to stop it. Then began some of the most hectic days I remember. Not just hectic – some had an air of almost total unreality! Like the phone call I received while having lunch at the Charing Cross hotel: the London *Evening Standard* had tracked down Thorsen; he had told the journalist that he was coming to Britain and would shortly be debating with me in the Cambridge University Union on the issue of censorship. Would I like to comment? 'Simple,' I replied. 'If they've got Thorsen, they haven't got me!' And that was that.

The script was blasphemous and obscene, and the media were greatly interested in the battle which was going on around it. Press conference followed press conference. Radio and TV interviews abounded. Jesus Christ became headline news and as I wrote in my diary: 'The prospect of this film being shown in Britain has stunned the faithful and indeed the unfaithful – if I can put it that way – in an unprecedented fashion.' Parliament, too, became involved, with Sir Bernard Braine demanding that the Prime Minister, James Callaghan, ensure that Thorsen would be denied entrance to the country. The Prime Minister's reply a few days later lifted all our hearts:

> From what I have read of this matter, Mr Thorsen would be a most unwelcome and undesirable visitor to this country and I very much hope that he would not seek to come here.

There is no doubt that to make a film such as the one I have read about would cause deep offence to the great majority of people in this country, among whom I number myself. I know that the Home Secretary [Merlyn Rees] shares my view.

As Brynmor John has explained, there is a power to refuse entry to an EEC national on issues relating to public order, public security or public health. I know that the Home Secretary will give very careful consideration to this if the need arises.

When the script arrived at our home from Denmark the next step was to get the 20,000 words translated into English. We were fortunate to have the services of a Danish woman who lived nearby. She and my secretary, Jane Morgan, worked hour after hour with great intensity and commitment to complete the job. Shortly afterwards on 5 October 1976 several of us went to the Home Office to present the translated version to Merlyn Rees and to ask him to ban Thorsen from Britain. We told him how he had been prevented from making the film in Denmark, Sweden, France, Spain and Italy because of the enormous public outcry in all those countries. 'Surely,' we asked him, 'Britain will not lag behind?'

At the press conference which followed I held up the script saying, 'The monstrously obscene homosexual intercourse between Jesus and St John at the Last Supper and the pornographic nature of the explicit sex scene which is supposed to represent His resurrection amount to the ultimate in spiritual vandalism and corruption.' Interestingly enough, the Thorsen *Jesus* film describes how 'Jesus and his gang' obtained funds for their 'revolutionary needs from armed bank robberies'. But I made it very clear at the press conference that, while we hoped for massive public support for our action – which we certainly had – under no circumstances would any kind of violence be used. It was necessary to make this unequivocal statement because already some people were threatening such action if Thorsen and his film came to Britain.

The media interest was tremendous not only in Britain but abroad. The Canadian and Australian Broadcasting Corporations both sent journalists to interview us over the weekend and, of course, the story as it unfolded was widely covered by both ITV and BBC.

The *Times* man met us before we went into the press conference. He told us that the Editor, William Rees-Mogg (now Lord) was anxious to have a copy of the script as he was considering printing it in his paper. My jaw dropped in amazement. 'He never will – not when he sees what it's really like,' I said. And indeed he did not. But next morning at the end of its news story *The Times* said, 'A copy of the book has come into the possession of *The Times*. The script is as bad as Mrs Whitehouse suggested, indeed worse.'

This was one of those rare occasions when practically the whole country stood united behind the Queen, the Archbishop of Canterbury, Dr Runcie, Cardinal Hume, the Prime Minister, James Callaghan, the press, who all combined to support the 'biggest ever lobby to the Home Secretary'! In the meantime a prayer vigil, our alternative to the violent demonstrations which had erupted in a number of European countries where Thorsen threatened to make his film, was organized outside the Home Office in Whitehall by Felicity Faulkner, a school teacher from Enfield, during her half-term holiday and I've always treasured the report she gave of her experience over that week.

'You should be round by the back door. That's where the Home Secretary goes in. I know. I clean his windows,' said a window cleaner at the Home Office.

'Sex life? Jesus Christ didn't have one!' exclaimed an outraged American.

All the world certainly converges on London. That was obvious during our week in Whitehall: Americans, Canadians, Australians, New Zealanders, Germans, Austrians, French, Dutch, Danes, Hungarians, Greeks, Israelis, Egyptians, Algerians, South Africans, Pakistanis – all stopped to express their views in support of the Britain they love to visit.

'Jens Thorsen. We are sorry we have him in our country to trouble you,' a Dane apologized.

'I'm an atheist, but this goes too far.'

The quiet vigil on Monday and Tuesday became, on the last three days, a massive 'signing up' at the request of passers-by and in just three days over 2700 signatures were collected.

'Nobody wants him here, so why didn't the government say "No" straight away?'

'There shouldn't be any need for you to stand here day after day . . .'.

'Well done! Keep it up,' said an employee of the Ministry of Defence; and from one of the Home Office staff, 'Wish I could sign but I work for the man.'

'It isn't governments which change attitudes, it's always individuals; like Shaftesbury and Wilberforce . . .'

What was frightening and disturbing were the other remarks: 'If the government doesn't take action within the law, we shall be forced to act outside it'; 'Lynch him!'; 'Shoot him. No, I'm serious. And if you give me the gun, I'll be glad to do it.'

There was the little crippled lady who could hardly hold the pen but was determined to sign; the elderly man who offered 10p to help with expenses and apologized that it couldn't be more; the painter with his pot of white paint who said, 'Just let him try to come here and I'll paint him white all over'; the youngster who exclaimed, 'That dirty film? No! We don't want that. Disgusting!'

There was the parliamentary candidate who walked with us from Victoria station at 7.30 a.m. on Monday; and the Muslim who supported the vigil all that day. There was the eighty-nine-year-old who came day after day to stand silently holding a banner; the MP who ran over from the House of Commons to tell us that we have many friends there; the postman who drew up on his bicycle to sign; the bishops who spared time from their Central Synod meetings to give support and to pray; the nuns who quietly said their rosaries . . .

It must be admitted that, on Thursday, when the rain poured down and pens wouldn't write on the sodden paper, we felt like saying, with St Theresa of Avila, 'Lord, if this is how you treat your friends, no wonder you have so few.' But, then, the witness was all the greater in the rain . . .

For the first-time 'campaigner', it was an exhilarating experience. What will stay with me? The kindness and friendliness of the London policemen; the selflessness of those who joined the vigil; the frankness of the Home Secretary, Mr Merlyn Rees, when he came, unbidden, out of the Home Office to speak to us; the overwhelmingly positive and vocal response of the young folk, which in a way was a surprise. The week's experience showed, beyond all doubt, how decent, honest, sincere and solid is the average Britisher, who wants to be proud of his country, bitterly deplores its falling standards and longs for it to stand up, fearlessly, for what it knows to be right.

And so Jens Jörgen Thorsen and his film never arrived in Britain. Victory.

CHAPTER FOUR

BLASPHEMY INDEED

I first saw a copy of the poem 'The Love That Dares To Speak Its Name' by James Kirkup on 1 November 1976 just as our campaign against the Thorsen film ended. It came in the morning's post, without any indication of where it had been published, and as I read it through the initial shock was very great. Coming so quickly after the Thorsen saga it was almost overwhelming in its immediate impact. There seemed no end to the vilification of Christ.

I felt, quite simply, deeply ashamed that Christ should be treated in this way. It seemed to me like a kind of re-crucifixion, only this time with twentieth-century weapons. I experienced out of love for Him a great longing to try to make some kind of reparation. It seemed to me that if I did nothing I would be like that Levite priest in Jesus's story of the Good Samaritan, who 'passed by on the other side'. Despite all that came and went in the months and indeed years that followed – and much did – nothing changed that initial reaction or altered my motivation.

Both the late Graham Ross-Cornes, my solicitor, and John Smyth QC were committed Christians and I knew I could trust their judgement. In the event they were both quite convinced that the poem, published in *Gay News* edition 96, which spoke of the homosexual relationships Jesus was purported to have had with His disciples and about the violation of His dead body as it hung on the cross, transgressed the law of blasphemous libel, and a private prosecution was launched in my name. The fact that there had been no blasphemy action for fifty-two years seemed to them quite irrelevant. The blasphemy law had been restated throughout the intervening years, as recently as 1975, so there was no question of us, as so many of my

47

opponents have said, turning to the use of 'outdated' legislation.

At no time did the Attorney General take over the case, although it was frequently claimed that he did. As a matter of fact, at just about the same time, but unknown to us, the Earl of Lauderdale sent a copy of the poem to the then Director of Public Prosecutions Sir Norman Skelhorn. In his reply, he said that he had been about to discuss the matter with the police when he saw the report in *The Times* that I was initiating legal action. The Director stated that he would 'consider taking over the case in the public interest' were I to request him to do so. But I felt that we had a special commitment to this case and that we neither could nor should pass it over to someone else.

It was at our first legal conference that we discovered that James Kirkup was Professor of Poetry at Massachusetts University with about six column inches to his name in *Who's Who*! Not that that really made any difference except that one could see what John Mortimer, defending counsel on this as on so many other obscenity trials, would make of it. I could hear the cries of 'Philistine!' and 'Censorship!' echoing through the land.

The opposition was not slow to mobilize. The *Guardian* (13 December) announced that a 'fighting fund' was to be launched for *Gay News* because it 'cannot possibly compete with Mary Whitehouse and her backers'. It was a strange expression to use. As I wrote in my diary, 'If by my backer they mean God Almighty, well, that is true, but if they are referring to a human backer, he doesn't exist!' As far as finance was concerned I had to trust that God would provide.

The *Gay News* trial was held at the Central Criminal Court in London from 4 to 12 July 1977, presided over by Judge King-Hamilton QC. *Gay News* was defended by Geoffrey Robertson QC and Denis Lemon, the editor, by John Mortimer QC. The events of those days were extensively written about, not only in Britain but in many countries abroad. They were reproduced on television in the BBC1 *Everyman* series and the preparation for that programme began well before the trial started. One of the many letters I received about that programme said that 'The trial came over as a classic example of British justice. Counsel on both sides were brilliant and equally matched. The Judge's summing up was masterly and the jury took their time.'

One of my most vivid memories of the trial was the sight and sound of Geoffrey Robertson, who is a 'Protestant sceptic', speaking with such intimate knowledge and perception of the New Testament and its teachings. I was told that he had 'rarely been seen without a copy in his hands for the last six months'.

At the end of the first day I told my diary:

> Mortimer, usually so confident and full of joking
> assumption that, of course, the prosecution's case is a lot
> of silly nonsense and no one could really take it seriously,
> seemed much less so today. The whole of the morning
> was spent trying to persuade the jury that the case should
> not have been brought to court at all, that there was no
> justification for a blasphemy law since Britain was no longer
> Christian, that it was an insult to other religions for
> Christians alone to be protected, and that if the poem had
> to come before the court at all it should be under the
> Obscene Publications Act. All these contentions were firmly
> dismissed by Judge King-Hamilton, who also turned down
> *Gay News*' request that they should be allowed to tape-
> record the proceedings. 'Can you give me a good reason
> why the normal procedure of the Court should be waived,
> Mr Mortimer?'
>
> John Mortimer also wanted John Smyth, prosecuting
> council, to make his opening address *before* the jury had
> seen a copy of the poem because, he said, this is a normal
> practice in obscenity cases. 'But this is not an obscenity
> case, Mr Mortimer,' said the judge. He was overruled and
> it was at this point that the jury – fourteen objections to
> its composition had been made by the defence – were given
> the poem to read for the first time. What a pregnant and
> total silence descended on the court and I felt for those
> very ordinary people who cannot have read anything like
> it before. I just prayed, and I knew that friends dotted
> about amongst the crowd of Gay-Libbers in the corridors
> outside the court were praying too, that the Holy Spirit
> would move in their hearts. John Smyth's address to them
> was splendid, very simple and illuminated by his own
> Christian faith as he went through the poem, line by line.

The following day, in fact every day of the trial, was equally dramatic. The poor jury was inside the court for only about three minutes and they spent a glorious summer day cooped up in an anteroom waiting to be recalled. Much of the argument was around the defence's request that it should be allowed to call 'expert witnesses'. I wrote in my diary that night:

> Mortimer and Robertson tried hard to persuade the judge
> that experts should be called because, they said, the tenets
> of the Christian faith have changed. Christ was a man,
> capable of sin, the jury with their lack of knowledge of
> modern theology could not know this. So my hunch was
> correct – before this case is out, if they have their way,
> Christ will be a homosexual too. The rest of the day was
> like something out of a fantasy. Mortimer would not
> concede that the man in the dock *was* Denis Lemon or
> that the copy of *Gay News* which the judge held up in his
> hand *was* a copy of *Gay News* or, for that matter, that the
> paper existed.

I shall never forget the dreadful sense of despair which overwhelmed me after hearing Geoffrey Robertson sum up for the defence seven days later. It was a truly remarkable performance. His manner was gentle and persuasive. In the silence that fell upon the court Robertson talked about God's love for sinners, and for homosexuals who, like everyone else, must have the hope of salvation and redemption – how I agreed. He spoke about the imagery which characterized the Christian faith.

Then he picked up the *Book of Common Prayer* and drew the attention of the jury to the words of the communion service: 'This is my Body – *eat* this. This is my Blood – *drink* this.' But, as I wrote that night:

> In some strange unbelievable way there has been more of
> the Gospel preached in this court this week, in spite of the
> motivation of those who preached it, than surely ever
> before in its history. God *must* have spoken through
> Robertson's words, whatever his intent. All the gays,
> secularists, and others who packed that court must have
> glimpsed something of the wonder and beauty of the
> Christian faith and God must surely have spoken in many

hearts. A wonderful example of the way he can and does use all things to his purpose.

Even so, as one legal expert said to me as I left the court that day, referring to Geoffrey Robertson's address to the jury, 'After that, the phrase "The Devil's Advocate" takes on a whole new meaning.' It did indeed.

I left the court quite overwhelmed by a feeling that, after listening to Robertson, the jury would be bound to return a verdict of 'Not Guilty'. If that was so, by bringing the case to court I could well have opened the flood gates not only to the obscene but to the unbelievably blasphemous. As I travelled home I felt utterly desolate. The burden of what I had done was, I felt, insupportable. For the whole of that weekend I felt utterly exhausted, both physically and mentally. I just lay in the garden, lovingly cared for by my family.

Late on Sunday night, one of the friends who had been in court all day with me the previous Friday rang up. 'Turn to 2 Chronicles, chapter 20, verses 15 to 18,' he said and rang off. I reached for my Bible and this is what I read:

> Thus saith the Lord unto you, be not afraid
> nor dismayed by reason of this great multitude;
> for the battle is not yours, but God's.
> Tomorrow go ye down, ye shall not need to
> fight in this battle: set yourselves, stand ye
> still, and see the salvation of the Lord . . .
> Fear not, nor be dismayed . . . for the Lord will
> be with you.

'Tomorrow go ye down'. How amazing. Those words brought peace and I fell asleep to wake rested in the morning.

It was a day carved for ever on my memory. I wrote in my diary that evening:

In his summing up Judge King-Hamilton stripped all the nonsense off Geoffrey Robertson's 'symbolism'. He praised him for the eloquence of his speech, which, however, he said was totally irrelevant. He dealt firmly with John Mortimer's references to a 'private individual' who according to him had brought the case 'out of malice', and as good as told the jury that the threat of 'the dark prison cell', to which Mortimer had told the jury they would condemn Lemon if they found him guilty, was to be put out of their minds. He instructed them to cast their minds back to the moment when they had first read the poem. That was what mattered, he said. Was it possible to conceive anything more obscene and blasphemous than, particularly, the fourth verse of the poem?

The jury went out at 12.30 p.m. and the tension outside the court as press and public waited for the members to return was intense. The prayer that we knew was going up all over the country was a great support. It was just before 5.30 p.m. when Mary Dacey, the young American girl who came every day to the trial and whom I had never met before that week, stopped as we walked together along the corridor. She said, 'I have such a strong feeling that we should stand still and pray *now* that God's will – not ours or anyone else's – shall be done in that jury room.' That is exactly what we did. Less than ten minutes later the jury returned.

As the BBC producer responsible for the *Everyman* programme said to me later: 'The emotional feeling in that court was overwhelming.' And, indeed, as the judge rose to leave after accepting the 'Guilty' verdict, there was a hush more reminiscent of a church than a court. Not a sound broke the silence.

By this time the gays who had stood outside throughout the case had, for some reason, rolled up their banners and gone home, and after the press had asked me for a comment, we walked quietly out unnoticed. There was no jubilation, only gratitude, not least for the courage and integrity of the jury who had been exposed to the most brilliant and experienced advocacy to persuade them to bring in a 'Not Guilty' verdict.

In passing sentence the following morning Judge King-Hamilton said that the publication of the poem revealed 'an astonishing and lamentable bad taste and error of judgement . . . a reckless disregard for the feelings of Christians, whether practising or non-practising, and for millions of non-Christians who sympathize with the doctrine of Christianity'. Referring to the jury's verdict, he told Lemon: 'Despite the fact that the company and yourself exercised your undoubted right to challenge the maximum possible number of jurors, which meant that a total of fourteen potential jurors were challenged off the jury to try this case, it availed you nothing because ten of the remaining had the moral courage to reach the verdict they did in accordance with their conscience and, what I venture to think, is good common sense. It is perhaps being a little too optimistic in this era of obscenity, but it is possible to hope that by this verdict the pendulum of public opinion is beginning to swing back to a more healthy climate.

'Although I sometimes read poetry and as a rule like what I read, I do not profess to be a judge of it and therefore would not presume to express an opinion as to whether this particular poem is a good one, a bad one or an indifferent one. But I have no doubt whatever, and apparently ten of the jury agree with me, that this poem is quite appalling and it contains the most scurrilous profanity and I hope never to see the like of it again.' He then sentenced Denis Lemon to nine months' imprisonment, suspended for eighteen months, and fined him £500. *Gay News* was fined £1000.

But life's funny. Not long after this I was walking in the lane outside our house when a car passed, drew up and reversed. A cheery hand was waving: it belonged to Geoffrey Robertson. We chatted for a minute or two and then he and his girlfriend came in for a cup of tea. We all got on very well!

The end of the *Gay News* trial was by no means the end of the matter, but sometimes wonderful things happen to lighten the pressure. One of these, coming just a few days after the *Gay News* verdict, and in the full flow of the public debate which followed, lifted my spirit immensely.

I was invited as a guest of the Honourable Society of the Middle Temple to dinner in Middle Temple Hall on its Grand Day. I treasure the unique memory of that night as a great privilege and a real tonic. The then Lord Chancellor, the Rt Hon. Elwyn Jones, and the Lord Chief Justice, Lord Widgery, were there and I was escorted into dinner by John Sparrow, then Warden of All Souls College, Oxford. The passing of the great silver loving-cup, the rose petals on the water in the huge silver bowls in which the gentlemen dipped their napkins and wiped their brows were something from another world.

The Lord Chancellor was very friendly, coming over to introduce himself to me and, with a twinkle in his eye, raising his glass to me from time to time during dinner. As we at the top table left to retire to the Parliament House, there was hissing from some of the lower tables, immediately followed by a burst of clapping. John Sparrow turned to me and said, 'You know who that's for? You. That's the answer to the hissing.'

I found myself seated as the guest of honour as everyone enjoyed the dessert, ginger, snuff, port and cigars and, of course, the talk. It was a glorious evening. Later we went out into the beautiful Temple Gardens. The borders of red geraniums, white petunias and blue lobelia and the new herb garden to commemorate the Queen's Jubilee were immaculately kept. They lay quiet under an intense blue sky across which rolled silver clouds illuminated by the lights of London. The Union Jack high on a nearby building curled in shining solitude against the sky. Memorable indeed.

I was glad that Denis Lemon did not go to prison. As I said in reply to a question in the *Everyman* programme on the trial (18 September 1978): 'If you are asking me if I have any bitterness, or hatred, or resentment against Denis Lemon for publishing his poem, I don't have those feelings towards him. This is something he must settle with his own conscience.'

But as Michael Tracey and David Morrison were to write later in their *Whitehouse* (Macmillan, 1979):

> With the conviction, however, came the storm, and one of such proportions that it even surprised and hurt Whitehouse, who was no newcomer to controversy and vilification. Neither was it just the crank threats which hurt her, though there were threats on her life and those of her family. Rather what hurt her was the sense of isolation. Not isolation in total terms, since she received an enormous number of letters, mainly from ordinary Church people, attesting their support and praising her efforts. What hurt her, though, was the sense of public isolation. 'The three weeks that followed the verdict – well, I hardly know how to describe them. I lost a stone in those three weeks'; and again she referred back to the difference between the response to the Thorsen situation and the response to the *Gay News* poem and once more, 'the silence of the Church'. And there is no doubt that it was a very loud and self-conscious silence. She felt, as

she put it, 'dreadfully isolated' despite the volume of support from the public.

'You see, the thing is I cared very much about the Church. I knew that what people were saying was, "Where's the Church?" and that was what was so dreadful. Here, in the first place, we'd had Jesus Christ treated like that and in the second place His Church wasn't even prepared to come out . . . It was the amazement at what was happening that shook me so profoundly. I couldn't believe it that all of a sudden what I had done was being so widely misinterpreted and that the Church allowed itself to be so overwhelmed with what you might call the general gay lobby.'

There *was* a tremendous outcry over the trial and there can be no doubt that it was to a great degree orchestrated by the Gay/Humanist lobby. As an appeal was pending, the extent of it was surprising – or perhaps I should say it *would* have been surprising in circumstances related to any issue other than homosexuality. I put some of my feelings in a letter to *The Times* (29 July 1977):

I have been reminded, many times, on reading your correspondence on the recent blasphemy case, of a game we used to play as children. Called 'Pass It On', it began with one person whispering a message to the next, and so on, the last one shouting out loud what he had heard. That this bore no relation to the original, that it was often, as it passed round the circle, deliberately embellished and distorted was all part of the fun. Only it hasn't been so funny this time.

The sight of the homosexual/intellectual/humanist lobby at bay has been at times an intimidating spectacle, but may I, before some of the wilder flights of its imagination become the established mythology of the case, put the record straight as far as I am free to do so? May I also say, in passing, that I have been amazed at the degree of licence offered by your columns in a matter which is still, with an appeal evidently pending, *sub judice*?

I do not 'pore over', or for that matter ever buy *Gay News*. I rarely see it and carry out no vendetta against it, though I have expressed concern, and will continue to do so, at the proselytizing of the immature adolescent by the so-called Gay Liberation movement.

Now I find myself falling into the same trap as so many of your correspondents. The blasphemy trial was not about homosexuality. It was about the right of Christians and sympathizers with the Christian faith not to be offended in the matter of their religious feelings. But this right has been almost submerged in an argument about the right of homosexuals not to have *their* feelings offended!

I accept no responsibility whatever for the distribution of this poem during and since the trial. If certain people decide to challenge the law that is their business, not mine. Neither do I regret the fact that millions now know something of the nature of the poem. If the publicity given to this case has profoundly shocked a public and a Church, not to mention a government, which has been unwilling by and large to face the degree of corruption within our culture, then that is a good thing, not a bad one. The shame of the publication of that poem lies on us all, not simply on those who maybe felt they had good reason for believing they could get away with it in these days of pseudo-freedom.

On 11 February 1978 a demonstration organized by the *Gay News* Defence Committee, of about 5000 gays, met in Trafalgar Square. Contingents from all over Britain carried banners decorated – if that's the word – with what could only be described as grotesque cartoons of me and chanted 'Whitehouse – kill, kill, kill.' Photographs of me were displayed side by side with ones of Hitler. Time and time again, I was accused of being motivated by a hatred of homosexuals. So perhaps I may quote here what I said in my book *Whatever Happened to Sex?*.

When I say what is true – that I am not against homosexuals as people but believe homosexual practices to be wrong, I am very conscious of the inadequacy of what probably sounds a very negative declaration. Homosexuals have as much right to be fully understood, to be treated with compassionate love as the rest of us. And as people they should be 'judged' no more no less than are those of us whose problems are perhaps less obvious but equally undesirable. Compassion without patronage, but without compromise – how to achieve it?

The natural repugnance which most people feel when homosexuality and lesbianism are mentioned can result in a harshness of attitude and thinking which is, at least, unhelpful and certainly as unChristian as the perverse practices which are condemned. But to go to the other extreme and elevate people suffering from such abnormalities into a norm for society not only threatens society but is dangerous to the individuals themselves, since it excludes them from the consideration of help and treatment. Society, to its shame, once hurled that word at the homosexual. In our crazy, 'value-free' society the 'shame' is now attached only to those who dare say that homosexuality is less than 'gay'. Such an attitude is as dogmatic, doctrinal and restrictive in its own way as was the fearful silence or sniggering scorn of earlier decades.

The *Gay News* appeal, which was heard early in 1978, was dismissed. The appeal judge found, contrary to the claims made by *Gay News* and Denis Lemon, that Judge King-Hamilton was correct in his direction to the jury that (1) it was sufficient if the jury took the view that the publication complained of vilified Christ in his life and crucifixion; and (2) it was not necessary for the Crown to establish any further intention on the part of the appellants beyond an intention to publish that which in the jury's view was a blasphemous libel. Later, *Gay News* made an appeal to the House of Lords and that, too, was dismissed.

It was made perfectly clear throughout by Judge King-Hamilton, the appeal judges and by the law lords, that criticisms and attacks on the Christian faith, as long as they are made in 'sober and temperate style', would not offend against the law of blasphemous libel. That there had been no blasphemous libel case for fifty-two years did not mean that people cared less, simply that nothing so blasphemous – apart from Jens Thorsen's film – had been published in the interim.

It is worth remembering that it was unanimously agreed by all nine judges concerned with the trial and appeal that the *Gay News* poem describing 'in explicit detail acts of sodomy and fellatio with the Body of Christ immediately after the moment of His death' (Judge Roskill) was 'quite appallingly shocking and outrageous' (Lord Russell of Killowen). It was during that hearing in the House of Lords that Lord Justice Scarman voiced these memorable words:

> I do not subscribe to the view that the common law offence of blasphemous libel serves no useful purpose in the modern law. On the contrary, I think there is a case for legislation extending it to protect the religious beliefs and feelings of non-Christians. The offence belongs to a group of criminal offences designed to safeguard the internal tranquillity of the kingdom. In an increasingly plural society, such as that of modern Britain, it is necessary not only to respect the differing religious beliefs, feelings and practices of all but also to protect them from scurrility, vilification, ridicule, and contempt . . .
>
> I will not lend my voice to a view of the law relating to blasphemous libel which would render it a dead letter, or diminish its efficacy to protect religious feeling from outrage and insult. My criticism of the common law offence of blasphemy is not that it exists but that it is not sufficiently comprehensive.

So the conviction stood.

In the years that have followed I have many times quoted Lord Justice Scarman's words, particularly his conclusion, as I have debated the issue of the blasphemy law. Those words are written on my heart and as time passes seem to me to express an even more profound truth. However, the gays were clearly bitterly angry with me, with an anger that persisted for a long time and surfaced not least in my visits to universities. The amount of opposition varied from the occasional heckle and loaded question to more dramatic happenings just like the sort of thing I had experienced at Birmingham University early in October 1977. Once again I refer to my diary:

> Very lively and interesting debate at Birmingham University tonight. Had to close the Union half an hour before it began and indeed it was packed far beyond capacity. I debated with Arthur Butterworth, warden of one of the colleges. The motion was 'That this House would find no

place for commercial pornography' and when I had proposed the motion I was given tremendous applause, which went on and on. Then Butterworth, as seems always to be the case, used the occasion for bitter personal attack – terribly bitter – called me 'evil and dangerous', linked me with the National Front and Nazism, with the persecution of homosexuals, with repression and oppression – what lay behind my 'charm and persuasiveness' was repulsive indeed. I go still inside when I hear these things and let them go over me – I have to.

During the contributions from the floor a young man took the microphone – but couldn't hold it as he was shaking so much and crying. 'I am a homosexual,' he cried, turning and pointing his finger at me as he tried to speak. 'I go in fear and trembling of my life because of *you*. I am anathema to you,' he shouted and then, dropping the microphone, he walked slowly out of the hall in tears shouting and gesticulating at me as he went. Terribly pathetic. Everyone clapped, including me – I felt I wanted to do something to make him feel less isolated. When I came to sum up I said how sorry I was that he had left the hall because I would like him to know that he was not anathema to me, that I did not hate him.

We lost the motion by 30 votes although over 100 abstained but, as the President said to me afterwards, 'Many of those really wanted to vote for you but lacked the courage', and that I can believe. When the President thanked me for coming I got a tremendous standing ovation, which was quite moving – unknown in the Union, I was told – and the crowd 'the biggest in living memory'! Well, I hope perhaps I gave them something worthwhile to think about – that is the real value of such an occasion.

Afterwards as I left the hall and walked down the steps into the main lobby I saw the young man standing there with a number of his friends, and I went to him with my hand stretched out. 'I'm sorry you did not hear what I said after you left,' I said to him.

'But I did, Mrs Whitehouse,' he replied. 'I was standing outside the hall listening – and I'm sorry I said the things I did about you.' Then he hastily added, 'But I'm so afraid!'

I put my hand on his shoulder. 'I'm sorry – but does it surprise you to know that I suffer from misunderstanding, too?' and I asked him to try to understand and accept that because people like me 'believe homosexual practices to be wrong that does not at all mean that we hate and despise homosexuals as people'.

I suppose of all my debating experiences the worst ever had been at Leicester University in the late sixties, though I don't remember the wording of the motion because we never got round to debating it. I was, after all, still rather new to the game. I'd been invited to debate with John Trevelyan, then Secretary of the British Board of Film Censors, but when I arrived there was no sign of him. In his place was Edward Bond, the playwright, author of the notorious play *Saved* which had been shown at the Royal Court Theatre several years previously. It was of this play that Penelope Gilliatt wrote in the *Spectator*: 'I spent a lot of the first act shaking with claustrophobia and thinking I was going to be sick. The scene where a baby is pelted to death is nauseating. The swagger of sex jokes is almost worse . . .'

In a packed-beyond-capacity house Bond opened the proceedings by referring not to the motion but to the obscene descriptions of me that he said he'd read on the walls of the lavatory he had just visited. Bond whipped up the audience into what could only be described as a frenzy. He accused me, among other things, of being 'responsible for the Moors murders'.

When I stood up to speak the obscenities flowed thick and fast, both from the mouths of individuals and as endless chants from students standing up and gesticulating in the gallery, while on the floor others crawled round and round my feet. A madhouse? Indeed, it seemed very much like it as I battled on for about forty minutes, unable to make my voice heard, let alone present any argument. The President of the Union found it impossible to control the meeting, though one of Bond's visiting supporters took the microphone and disassociated himself from what was happening.

Whenever I tell this story people say to me, 'Why on earth did you stand there all that time?' I wasn't capable of thinking very coherently about it, I just had a gut feeling that as long as I stood in front of them I was a challenge. I was, after all, more than old enough to be their mother. Would they allow what was happening to me to happen to their own mothers? Afterwards some of the students who had sat silent through it all came over to apologize shamefacedly not only for what had happened but for their own lack of courage in staying silent.

A measure of just how bad it was that night was highlighted by the *Leicester Mercury* the following night. It contained a space empty except for the statement that it had been reserved for a report on the debate but that the proceedings had been too obscene to publish.

At the end of it all I was totally exhausted. But, as so often happens, good came out of it. Malcolm Muggeridge rang me a few days later and, hearing the tiredness in my voice, asked what was the matter. After I had explained he said to me, 'Mary, what are we going to do for these young people? How can we mobilize the cohorts and demonstrate our faith and belief? We must have a great festival of light,' he said. And that was when the idea which finally blossomed in the great Festival of Light demonstration in Trafalgar Square in 1971 was born.

But I have to say that the just-about-annual opportunity to debate in the Cambridge Union is one which I have always valued and enjoyed. Perhaps the most memorable was in November 1971 when I debated against Richard Neville of *Oz* magazine. This was televised by London Weekend's *Aquarius* and was covered by Jeremy Paxman writing for the university magazine.

'Yes, I'm a student.'
'Bet you have a pretty good sex life at university.'
'Oh, er, yeah, man, you bet.' And winking a knowing eyelid he disappears to his lonely bed. Or to the Union debate on pornography. Those who can, do; those who can't, talk about doing. In this case the discussion centred on doing in public and private and the effects of one upon the other.

But unfortunately something went wrong. They were all there, the pro and anti porn marketeers, right through from Richard ('they don't like pooftas in the outback') Neville, to

Mary ('they're going to love this in Kidderminster') White-house, and the stage seemed set for the Union's main claim to attention this term. London Weekend Television was there, and reportedly there were representatives from every national newspaper present.

In all the preparations one thing was overlooked. The audience. The *Observer* appeared to find the display of juvenility indulged in amusing, admitting in passing that 'the Cambridge Union was always a bit of a joke'. Quite what that remark was meant to mean is not apparent. It sounds nice anyway. What in fact we were treated to on this occasion was a display of juvenility, ignorance, arrogance, bad manners and stupidity, to which the final vote, inaccurately reported in the *Evening News*, bore no relation whatsoever.

Those lucky few who did manage to get through the hallowed portals and past the assorted blimps with price tags on their lapels displayed what Cambridge and most student bodies are famous for – complete intolerance and triviality. The Union loves nothing more than a show. The whole debating process having been reduced to the level of cheap personal aggrandizement, I suppose there's not much else left. On this occasion, however, there was a genuine chance for some kind of constructive opinion forming, without the usual degradation to the level of pig-pen party politics.

But no, Neville came in with his arm round a friend from Oz or somewhere, whose black cat-suit, naked navel, cosmetics and yellow dahlia did everything possible to reinforce the prejudices inculcated by third-rate vaudeville a few years ago. It was a cheap trick, and the audience loved it, rising to its feet in a display of admiration for Neville's bravado in scandalizing the establishment.

You could, however, credit Neville with some degree of authenticity. The same could not be said of Dr Martin Cole or John Mortimer, with their self-conscious use of words like 'hang up' and 'turn on' dropping like pebbles into a pond from their middle-aged mouths. Who was it said in the early days of the youth movement, back in the sixties, 'Don't trust anyone over thirty'? Of course he was wrong, and it's too easy to divide it up on generational lines. But trust does enter into it, and if you suspect someone of not being true to themselves, how can you believe in the truth of their ideas?

There can hardly be a greater condemnation of the so-called liberal students at the Union than that they all collapsed into paroxysms of laughter when Mary Whitehouse inadvertently gave a Harvey Smith. Like giggling at the guy in drag, it betrayed a veneer of liberalism which cracked like the make-up around the mouth of a sixty-year-old roué.

The description of the pro-porneteers as 'pillars of the alternative establishment' proved only too apt. Neville received a standing ovation for a speech which contained one point of significance . . .

And if we consider the real issues at stake in the pornography question it becomes apparent how much of the stand taken by the trendy liberators, and not least by people like John Mortimer (oh-so-clever with words), is purely a question of fashion. For the fundamental arguments in the debate, on the side advanced, strangely enough, by Messrs Whitehouse and Longford, are very much in tune with the liberal sentiments so vigorously espoused by the counter-culture, and which are in turn taken up by the majority of the student body.

It was Lord Longford who said he didn't care what the audience thought of him or anyone else on his side personally; he was asking them to base their decision purely on the case. Sadly the Union proved him wrong. Like a group of middle-aged Conservative Party housewives confronted by placard-waving demonstrators, they found it too easy to say who was right and who was wrong without even listening.

Mary Whitehouse came closest to the philosophy of the counter-culture when she talked of the commercialization of sex, a point which the pro-porneteers found it easy to disregard, and which most of the audience probably didn't hear amidst the laughter at the swinging skull lowered from the gallery. The point is, in fact, obvious enough to need no further comment. It is a manifestation of a senescent capitalism and there is really little difference between the exploitation of people in the pre-Factory Act world, and the exploitation of their personal identities and bodies in blue movies. It's funny, I thought we were trying to get away from commercialism and exploitation nowadays. But then if we were all totally well adjusted, we wouldn't need to buy *Oz* and look at the pictures.

Another point made by Mary Whitehouse was that pornography depersonalizes sex. No matter how much more open we may be about sex. No matter how much more group sex we may have, it still remains a personal matter, for it is still the method by which we affirm our identity, and is one of the most available methods of self-annihilation, through which, again, we find ourselves. And, if in all our moral righteousness, we spend our time putting down depersonalization in other fields, then why not in pornography?

'Talk about events going full circle!' I said to myself when the BBC let it be known in July 1992 that it would dramatize *Lady Chatterley's Lover* in the spring of 1993. The prospect was tantalizing. What motivation lay behind the decision? Either, I thought to myself, it's a calculated attempt to demolish, once and for all, the standards regarding taste and decency under which the Corporation is supposed to operate, or else, far more likely, they'll have to 'clean up' the notorious text but bank on the viewing public being attracted by the scandals attached to its title.

However, the possibilities were intriguing and I reminded myself of the substance of the legal action launched by the Crown against Penguin Books in 1960, the result of which opened the floodgates of obscenity throughout the years that have followed. Perhaps the Judge's summary of the book will be of interest to those who may not recall the details of the case, but wish to be in a position to comment on the wisdom of the BBC's decision.

The story of a woman who first of all, before she married, has sexual intercourse and then, after marriage, when her husband has met with disaster in the war and has become confined to a wheelchair, paralysed from the waist downwards, after marriage. She, living with her husband in this dreary place of Wragby, commits adultery on two occasions with somebody called Michaelis while her husband is downstairs in the same house, and then proceeds to have adulterous intercourse with her husband's gamekeeper. And that is described . . . in the most lurid way, and the whole sensuality and passion of the various pieces of sexual intercourse is fully and completely described.

The fact that the then Bishop of Woolwich, the late Dr John Robinson, stood as a defence witness was in itself extraordinary. For him to state, as he did, that Lawrence had tried to present the adulterous relationship between the woman and the gamekeeper as 'in a real sense something sacred, as in a real sense an act of holy communion' shook the Church of England and a great many people to their foundation.

The late Malcolm Muggeridge joined in the widespread concern about the effect the result of the *Lady Chatterley* case would have upon society at large. Having referred to the way in which 'in our sort of society eroticism is abundantly, variously and ever more intensively exploited . . .', he went on to say that this state of affairs 'is ignoble, tiresome, decadent, and ultimately self-defeating, in that the appetites thus excessively stimulated lose their true zest, and grow like diseased plants away from the light. Pornography', he went on, 'is as habit forming as benzedrine.'

'Auntie is right to be coy about Lady C', read the *Sunday Times* headline on 26 July 1992, of Janet Daley's piece on the BBC's plans to transmit a dramatization of D. H. Lawrence's novel.

'Well, that title's something of a shock, too,' I thought. Janet Daley has not, over the years, been our most ardent supporter. Indeed, in the article she begins by asking whether the BBC has 'finally been bludgeoned into playing it safe' and whether it has 'finally succumbed to prudery'. What perhaps interested me most about Ms Daley's piece was the way in which her views and mine have gradually coalesced. Many is the time that I have made the point, as she does in her article, that to read something in a book is a totally different experience from watching it on television. In the case of the printed word we, as individuals, interpret the words in terms of our own experience and imagination whereas, said Ms Daley,

> the effect on the impressionable is of a different order altogether from the effect of a written text. Which is why even a sadistic or violent literary work is admissible but the filming of it is not. To see the acts being done is to make the doing of them thinkable. The mere fact of people actually having behaved in this way widens the bounds of what is acceptable in a way that no piece of fictional prose can.

So visual media such as film and television must operate under a very different set of moral rules, not only because seeing is believing, but because a book – even a cheap slasher 'novel' – requires active participation. Reading fiction involves constructing in your own head the images that the words convey.

Watching (or being exposed to) a film or video can be a completely passive experience (which can even be inflicted on the young or impressionable without their consent). Like the real world, events simply appear spontaneously with complete verisimilitude. And they arrive, as Lawrence's sex scenes would in the most ill-advised 'faithful' adaptation, without the mediating internal voice of a human heart.

Wonderfully put, I thought.

CHAPTER FIVE

THE LAST TEMPTATION

'For church leaders to criticize the film [*The Last Temptation of Christ*], without any firm grounds for doing so, is a pretty dreadful thing to do,' said James Ferman, Director of the British Board of Film Classification, in August 1988. He added that he was 'shocked that they should depend on hearsay evidence – any criticism based on that is very dodgy'. He went on to claim that the said churchmen were causing distress among sincere Christians who felt that their deeply held beliefs were being mocked.

It took Ronald Butt to point out in *The Times* on 18 August that year that James Ferman was tarred with the same brush he was using on the bishops, MPs and others who had expressed concern about the film. He himself had not seen the film when he declared that 'from hearsay and hearing about this film it suggests that the film does not offend against the law on blasphemy'. *Et tu Brute.*

The advent of the film brought many expressions of concern but none were more aptly worded than Ronald Butt's own:

> There is something deeply wicked about imposing on an image of goodness which has upheld people for 2000 years, such weakness as using his carpenter's trade to make crosses for Roman crucifixions and the fantasies of the brothel. Its only purpose, even if it is a subconscious purpose, is to undermine and that, so to speak, is the work of the devil.

In spite of all the efforts made to stop the transmission of Martin Scorsese's blasphemous film *The Last Temptation of Christ* it was shown in the cinema in 1988. It caused a tremendous furore, as witness Paul Johnson's article in the *Daily Mail.* He drew attention to what he termed 'the insatiable desire of directors and writers to achieve notoriety and draw attention to themselves by shocking, horrifying and outraging people'. As he pointed out, the film portrays Jesus as saying, 'I am a liar. I am a hypocrite. I am afraid of everything. Lucifer is inside me.' Jesus is depicted as weak, fearful and confused, not knowing the difference between the voice of God and that of the devil. He is shown hallucinating on the cross. The devil comes to him in the shape of a beautiful girl masquerading as a guardian angel. He fails to perceive the deception and follows her.

The film depicts Jesus making love to Mary Magdalene, to whom he is married, but Mary, the sister of Lazarus, is also pregnant by him, and Martha, too, has had his children. Jesus is shown to be an adulterer.

However, our concern about the possibility of the film being shown on terrestrial television channels and the breaking of new barriers which would inevitably result was very real. National VALA wrote to the Director of Public Prosecutions on 31 December 1990, drawing his attention to the nature of the film and stating that 'while we were well aware that action under the present blasphemy law would be unlikely to succeed, we understood that broadcasting was now covered by the new (1990) Broadcasting Act' and pointed out that under this legislation 'it would be an offence to (as far as possible) "transmit programmes which offend against good taste and decency, give offence to public feeling or incite to crime and disorder" '.

The DPPs reply, dated 4 January 1991, was, to say the least, unhelpful. The Director 'accepted that the film may cause offence to some members of the public, but was of the opinion that there were no grounds for prosecution, including prosecution under the Obscene Publications Act 1959'. There seemed little else that we could do.

It was a call from a national daily newspaper on 21 August 1991 that brought it all back. 'BBC2 is going to show *The Last Temptation of Christ* as part of its autumn schedule,' said the journalists. In one way incredible, in another not the least surprising, knowing the urge to 'push back the boundaries' which clearly exists in the breasts of some of those with the most programme power in the Corporation. I rang the office of Alan Yentob, head of BBC2, to enquire if the press had got it right. Apparently, yes 'but, of course, we shall have to be sensitive to the timing, and maybe there will have to be cuts'. In other words, don't worry.

ITN was first to call – they came to the office to do an interview which we thought went well – 'dignified and unemotional' especially when seen against some of the news shots from the States, one of a man slashing a screen, another showing the moral majority calling for the film to be burnt – too near to the activities of the Nazis and the Inquisition for my liking. The media were in touch all day and before it ended the Pope had called on all Catholics to support a ban on the film while the Earl of Halsbury and Lord Nugent had written to the Home Secretary to ask him to prevent the film entering the country. The editors of the *Church Times* and *Baptist Times* were in touch, but media interest suddenly swung from *The Last Temptation* to the arrival in Britain of Sylvester Stallone for the launching of *Rambo* – just a year to the day from the dreadful Hungerford massacre. And that gives some indication of the pressure under which we worked – one minute *The Last Temptation* with its blasphemy, the next *Rambo* with its violence.

Next morning saw me picked up at 5.45 a.m. to get to the BBC Television Centre by 7.30. Back home the phone never stopped: the *Washington Post* rang, so did *The Times* and just about every other paper. BBC Northern Ireland, Solent Radio, IRN, a United States Television company, BBC *Nine O'Clock News*, and along with all this the pressure was building up on the British Board of Film Classification on whom the ultimate responsibility lay. Would they or would they not give *The Last Temptation* a certificate?

We thought that it would be illuminating to discover what steps *had* been taken by the Chairman of the Independent Television Commission, which is responsible for standards on satellite as well as terrestrial programmes, before the film was transmitted. He told us that the film had been previewed by, among others, 'the then Head of Religious Broadcasting who advised that there was no reason why the film should not be shown'. What can one say? Only that to show the film on BSkyB is one thing, to show it on the BBC quite another!

Quite how firm the Corporation's decision was to screen the film in spite of its claims that 'no decision had been made' was illustrated by a letter sent on 29 September 1991 on behalf of Alan Yentob to anxious viewers. 'It is true, as has been reported, that we intend to screen *The Last Temptation of Christ* on a date yet to be arranged.'

However, following intense pressure from viewers, MPs and the Church, Duke Hussey, Chairman of the BBC Board of Governors announced on 2 November that 'There are now no plans for the BBC to transmit this film.'

What a relief! And what an indication of how the broadcasting authorities will fulfil their obligations if the pressure is great enough. It does, of course, beg the question of how and why the Corporation should have decided on the screening of the film in the first place, and why the powers that be should have so lamentably failed in the legal duties laid upon them. Someone, somewhere, should be held responsible. I should say that a question central to many of the telephone calls which came in at that time was, would I take out a private prosecution for blasphemy as I had successfully against *Gay News*? My reply was the same in each case. No, I would not. I had re-established the validity of the blasphemy law and now, I felt, it was for the Church to take the initiative.

'They don't give an inch, do they? They *know* what's in the guidelines, but they don't take any notice of them!' said a member of National VALA's staff on reading the reply of John McCormick, Secretary of the BBC, on behalf of Duke Hussey, Chairman of the Governors, in response to our complaint about a blasphemous sketch in an edition of *Something for the Weekend* in June 1989.

We had received complaints immediately following the programme, and again the following morning expressing amazement, disquiet and anger at an episode in which Abraham is seen to throw a custard pie in the face of Isaac to the accompaniment of the singing of Psalm XXIII. The sheer puerility of the 'humour' was almost unbelievable. It was not only Christians who were deeply distressed by the sketch: so were Muslims. I think their feelings must have been accurately reflected in a letter, a copy of which I received, sent by a prominent Muslim leader to Mr Hussey.

20th June 1989

I was surprised to the sick joke made during the above mentioned programme when Prophet Abrahim covered face of Prophet Isaac with Custard Pie with the singing of 'The Lord is my Shepherd'.

This indeed was done in a very bad taste, which is offensive to all those who believe in Prophets of Books, including Muslims. We have not yet solved the *Satanic Verses* affair and in view of sensitive nature of jokes like this, we would urge you to ask the authors to be more careful in future. They must show some respect to the Holy Books and Prophets of Books and refrain from making irresponsible jokes about them.

Yours faithfully, etc.

We wrote to Mr Hussey again, supporting the Muslim leader's letter which we felt to be 'very responsible' and worthy of 'sympathetic consideration', and we pointed out also that:

ill-considered gratuitous blasphemy is by no means uncommon in BBC programmes, as witness the documentary *Changing Places* (20 June 1989 8 p.m. BBC1). The use in the programme of 'Jesus Christ' and 'Jesus' as loud gratuitous expletives is a recent example, but such blasphemy is by no means unusual.

Indeed it is not. The constant stream of complaints which come our way about such blasphemy makes that very clear.

I had thought that because this particular complaint originated in Muslim concern this might mean that it would be more carefully considered than are those from Christians particularly in view of the anger aroused by Salman Rushdie's publication of his *Satanic Verses*. But no, it brought the usual soft justification. We were told by John McCormick, then Secretary of the BBC, that 'the joke was aimed not at the Prophets themselves but at a particular style of acting and film making'. How stupid we were not to realize that.

Mr McCormick said that the language used 'demonstrated the passion with which the artist approached his work', that it was a 'natural part of his speech and not intended to cause offence and that its inclusion in the finished documentary was justified on that basis'. Quite extraordinary – except that such justification has been used so many times that it has become routine. The BBC incidentally, considers someone's right to his 'natural speech' – no matter how offensive or blasphemous – more important than the offence it undoubtedly gives.

Reading over this exchange of correspondence I am struck by the defensiveness and lack of humility on the part of the BBC. We are 'sorry that *you feel* [my italics] that the sketch was offensive' not 'we are sorry that we transmitted a sketch that offended you'. The onus, of course, is on us.

Blasphemy is widespread, the use of 'Jesus', 'Christ', commonplace, and nowhere more obvious than in the late-night films on both BBC, Channel 4 and ITV. Often associated with obscenities it demonstrates an insensitivity totally out of keeping with the 'creativity' which apparently justifies it.

The unacceptable – culpable – silence of certain leaders and sections of the Church in the face of such denigration and fouling of the name of Jesus has underlined more powerfully than anything else its abdication in the face of the intellectual/humanistic control of the media and of broadcasting in particular over recent decades. 'Where were you when they crucified my Lord?' Busy counting the collection and signing the latest petition in favour of easier divorce or abortion?

CHAPTER SIX

A LOT
OF MAN HOURS

Some days, in my far from boring life, are more exciting than others. As I wrote in my diary on 15 May 1991,

> Well, I really can't get over it – I've been invited by one of the cable companies to broadcast to 40,000,000 teenagers in twenty-seven countries! I will be interviewed for ten minutes and will then take questions from Russia, Germany, Israel, the USA, Asia and goodness knows where else! No problem about language.
>
> Then I got a call from Channel 4 about the O for Obscenity slot in the *A-Z of Censorship* which I had agreed to do and which was being transmitted every evening during the screening of the Channel 4 *Banned* series of films (April/May 1991). No sooner settled that than into Colchester to do a fifteen-minute chat with the BBC about our work, its origins and aims, etc. Back home to do a TV interview for Barry Norman's *Film 91* about the Japanese film *Al No Corrida* (*In the Realm of the Senses*) which until now has only been allowed to be shown in cinema clubs. It contains scenes of unprecedented sex and violence and ends with a woman being arrested carrying – for pity's sake! – the severed genitals of the lover she has just murdered. The decision by the British Board of Film Censors – after a year's hesitation – to give the film an 18 certificate, was the point of the interview. I was asked what advice would I give James Ferman, Director of the BBFC. 'He's a very nice man,' I said, 'but I think he should take a rest!' I said it with a smile so I hope it didn't sound too offensive.

And I finished my day's entry with this thought, 'It really is quite amazing the way in which the Lord is using me even though, physically, because of my back injury, I'm not capable of travelling around as I did. In fact, if I *had* been dashing around the country I would not have been so immediately available to do these things.'

'It does lead to a lot of work/man hours etc., – films are taken out and reviewed against your monitoring reports. I'm not sure we can devote similar amounts of time in future if reports keep coming in!' So said what sounded like a rather exasperated John McCormick, Secretary of the BBC. He was returning National VALA's telephone call to enquire when we would receive a reply to letters we had sent over several weeks during January 1990 individually to the governors of the BBC. These contained detailed monitoring of a number of its late-night films including *Uncommon Valour, Legal Eagles, Prizzi's Honour* and *Salvador,* transmitted over the Christmas holiday period, all of which contained unacceptable obscenities and blasphemies.

Such conscientious attention to our complaints was not something we were used to! We had no doubt that it was not unconnected with the fact that many of the MPs to whom we had also sent the reports had replied expressing themselves as 'horrified' and 'appalled' and indeed 'amazed' at their contents, and stating their intention of 'taking up the matter' with the Home Secretary and the BBC. This is no place to give details of the language used. Suffice to say that the best known, if I may put it that way, of obscene four-letter words was used countless times, sometimes in an unbelievably blasphemous as well as obscene fashion, linking it to the name of Jesus Christ Himself.

Of course it wasn't only the BBC which was giving offence with such films. So was ITV, with, for example, its *Hollywood Shuffle* and *OUT.* It has to be said, in fairness to the BBC, that the response from George Russell, Chairman of the IBA, was, to say the least, defensive. Mr Russell felt that 'to write down a list of swear words is not the best test of whether the film is offensive to public feeling'. That could well be, but at least it's a start and in any case a précis of the plot – if discernible! – was given in every case. To hear the same four-letter word in all its various applications used over and over again can only desensitize the viewer and make nonsense of the obligations 'not to offend against good taste and decency' laid down in the Broadcasting Act under which ITV is supposed to operate. And there really is no reason why members of the IBA, as it was then, should not also be subject to the same bombardment as that applied to the BBC.

One of the biggest monitoring projects we had undertaken for years was carried out in the latter part of 1989 and in the early months of 1990, in which we covered late-evening films on BBC, ITV and Channel 4. Our approach to films shown by Channel 4 and ITV was essentially different from that to films shown by the BBC. Because advertising finances independent television, we made a note of the firms whose advertisements appeared during these films and, after writing to them enclosing the appropriate monitoring report, we received some very concerned replies.

The Rt Hon. the Lord Jenkin of Roding, Chairman of Friends Provident Insurance, in his reply to me (dated 26 April 1990) following his receipt of our detailed monitoring of the film *Semi-Tough* wrote,

> Let me say straight away that it is recognized on all sides that *Semi-Tough* was an unsuitable environment for our advertisement. Had our agents known of the amount of bad language and obscenity contained in the film, they would have made every effort to have our advertisement moved to another slot. . . . It is, of course, perfectly true that the preview described the film as a '. . . rough-tongued comedy'. However, this gave no indication of the extent of the foul language used and, to our agents' certain knowledge, Channel 4 did not transmit any warning regarding the language used in the script for this film. In our view, therefore, Channel 4 were at fault, both for not making it clear to advertisers just how much foul language was to be used in the film and in failing to give a warning to viewers that they might find this offensive. Had they done so, it is quite probable that our agents would have sought to withdraw our advertisement and move it elsewhere. None of us here consider that 'rough-tongued' is a sufficient description of the script in this case.
>
> Your letter has, therefore, given me the opportunity to

impress on our advertising staff and, in turn, on our agents that, as a company with high ethical standards, we do not wish to be associated with entertainment of this kind and that we will expect the agents to make greater efforts to avoid embarrassment. For this reason, I am very grateful to you for having drawn the matter to my attention.

We had written also to Fiona Kendrick, Marketing Manager of Findus about the film *Suburbia* with its violence and bad language, and received an equally concerned reply,

Unfortunately, as a documentary there was no Board of Censors' Certificate as in the case of cinema films. We have expressed our disapproval to both our advertising agency and in turn to Channel 4 and we are now actively seeking methods to avoid this recurring.

Lord Alexander, Chairman of the National Westminster Bank said in his letter,

The agencies who buy television air time on behalf of the Bank are already aware that we do not wish to have our advertisements shown within programmes that are likely to offend the majority and they are being reminded of this again. I know you will appreciate, however, that we often need to book a package of slots and, within certain agreed parameters, the timing decision sometimes has to be left with the television contractors. Please be assured that the appearance of one of our advertisements alongside that sort of programme you describe does not mean that we condone that programme.

It has to be said that Channel 4 was by far the worst culprit. The sadistic violence involving women, the gross obscenity and blasphemy were, in some cases, almost beyond belief. One typical film *Broken Mirrors* carried a sequence in which a naked man, with his face in the crotch of a prostitute hanging on a cross, shouted, 'Hail, Mary, full of grace.'

As the IBA had clearly shown itself either unwilling or incapable of controlling such excesses, we wrote to a total of ninety-five firms whose advertisements appeared during these films. The response from George Russell, Chairman of the IBA, to whom we also sent the reports, justified the films as appealing to 'tastes and interests not generally catered for by ITV'. Nothing in the Broadcasting Act which controls ITV permits such blasphemy and obscenity because they appeal to what one can only describe as perverted tastes!

As I said at the time, 'The purpose of this research into the incidence of bad language on television has been to discover what, if any, effect the undertakings given by the broadcasting authorities have had upon the quality of programme standards. Mr Duke Hussey, Chairman of the BBC said [on 24 February 88] that he had given "the Home Secretary an undertaking that the BBC will take firm steps to eradicate unnecessary and gratuitous violence, sex and bad language from our programmes". In its Annual Report [dated February 1991] the ITC stated, as had earlier reports, that "Many people are offended, some of them deeply, by the use of bad language, including expletives with a religious connotation. It is therefore important ... to avoid any gratuitous use of language likely to offend." '

All our monitoring for the report had been of films transmitted after 9 p.m. but to demonstrate how the problem of bad language was permeating more and more programmes we referred to the new BBC programme *Chalkface*, transmitted in family viewing time, in which the word 'shit' was used several times by a teacher as a matter of course. A couple of weeks later the same programme had teachers using equally if not more offensive language.

The Times headed its leader 'Language Most Foul' and made the point that 'Television confers legitimacy upon words which would otherwise never be heard in most homes, and which few people want heard there.' In its editorial the *Daily Telegraph* quoted Eric Partridge, the well-known lexicographer who defined the most famous of swear words as 'an expletive used by people for whom aesthetics mean little or, rather, nothing' and finished by claiming that 'restricting the use of such words on television is not a serious infringement of free speech, but one of the conditions for the rehabilitation of our language' – interesting, and how true. It was very encouraging to see how so many commentators criticized the bad language from the point of *quality* of writing – and no one accused us of being oversensitive!

I couldn't help but think how, in all our years of campaigning, no issue had aroused such unqualified support from the press and indeed within broadcasting itself. A change of heart? A realization that more was at stake than 'just a matter of personal taste' as has so often been the defence? Rather, perhaps, an indication of a new mood of responsibility which accepts that broadcasting has incalculable power and that the 'ordinary' viewer and listener has an important role to play. That thought lifts my heart.

And the House of Lords debated it, too.

Lord Nugent of Guildford asked of Her Majesty's Government: 'What further action will they take to check the use of obscene and blasphemous language in television programmes?'

The Minister of State, Home Office (Earl Ferrers): 'My Lords, the content of individual programmes is a matter for the broadcasting authorities. But the Government have recently established the Broadcasting Standards Council and have extended the Obscene Publications Act to broadcasting.'

Lord Nugent of Guildford: 'My Lords, I thank my noble friend for that factual answer. However, it does not meet the point with which I am concerned. Is he aware that last month a report was published by the National Viewers' and Listeners' Association, which regularly monitors the programmes of BBC1, BBC2, ITV and Channel 4, which finds that the number of obscenities and blasphemies in programmes has increased three-fold over the past three years? The incidence is about forty a week. [It is now commonplace to have forty obscenities in one programme.]

'My noble friend played a distinguished part in placing the Broadcasting Act on the statute book. That Act states that nothing likely to offend against good taste and decency or to offend public feeling should be transmitted. Does he acknowledge that further action is now needed? Will he ask the authorities to take action to restrain their producers from this increasing use of debasement of language?'

Earl Ferrers: 'My Lords, I understand my noble friend's anxiety. Very often the use of bad language is completely unnecessary and adds nothing other than to give offence to the viewer. However, that is a personal observation. The Government have to remain separate from the issue. The broadcasters have to be constitutionally independent of government. Arrangements have been made for satisfactory programmes to be made and to be monitored. If people have cause to complain, they can complain either to the BBC or ITC – the regulatory bodies – or to the Broadcasting Standards Council. But it would not be right for the Government to interfere in such cases.'

Viscount Tonypandy. 'My Lords, while we understand the independence of the broadcasting media, is it not also a fact that by raising the matter today the noble Lord, Lord Nugent of Guildford, has served notice on those who seem to believe that the media belongs to them, that their influence upon standards in this country is too great for them ever to feel so independent that nobody has a right to put a brake upon them?'

Earl Ferrers. 'My Lords, the noble Viscount makes a very good point. I believe that some people feel that they are sufficiently independent that they can do what they like. The television companies do not belong to the producers but nor do they belong to the Government. All that the Government can do is to set up a regime in which standards can operate and through which people may make complaints if they feel that standards are not upheld. Let us remember this. If a licensee does not keep to certain standards, the Independent Television Commission has the right to reprimand him and fine him 5 per cent of his net advertising revenue. A company which earns £200 million can be fined £10 million and its licence revoked.'

Lord Molloy. 'My Lords, we understand the difficult problem that faces the noble Earl. But does he not agree that if some of the language that we hear on television were uttered on the streets, those who make such foul utterances could be arrested for using bad language?'

Earl Ferrers. 'My Lords, I understand that those who use such language do so because they believe that it is the language that people use on the streets.'

Lord Elton. 'My Lords, does the Minister agree that the Government's duty to stand back makes it all the more important that opinions should be expressed publicly in this House? Having read the report to which my noble friend, Lord Nugent, referred, does my noble friend the Minister accept that much of the language reproduced in it would have been startling and shocking on the lips of a trooper twenty years ago, let alone on the lips of a fishwife? Is it not regrettable that the change of standards that has occurred over that period should now be influenced by an authority which has exercised a downward pressure over the past three years?'

Earl Ferrers: 'My Lords, my noble friend is quite right. Although the Government may not be in a position to dictate what should or should not be broadcast, as he knows too well, it is perfectly right for concern to be expressed. But I was a little anxious if he felt that a fishwife's language was rather worse than a trooper's. My experience is that it would be the other way round.'

Baroness Birk: 'My Lords, none of us appreciates gratuitous use of bad language. However, is the Minister aware that according to the latest 1990 Attitudes to TV survey published by the Independent Television Commission (which covers ITV and Channel 4) there has been a significant decrease in the offence caused to the public by bad language? Is that not a more accurate index than simply counting up the incidence of certain words in late-night films, as the survey did to which the noble Lord, Lord Nugent of Guildford referred? Monitoring by a count was the method used by the National Viewers' and Listeners' Association in a mathematical calculation of how many times such words were used. I thought that was horrifying.'

Lord Elton: 'My Lords, the point has been made very neatly. The broadcasters have an enormous effect on national standards. It is regrettable that those standards should be lowered.'

Earl Ferrers: 'My Lords, I am sure that my noble friend is quite right.'

The Earl of Halsbury: 'My Lords, does the noble Earl accept that the function of swearing and bad language is, like all aggressive displays, to substitute psychological or verbal violence for physical violence? Does he further agree that the more commonplace its usage the less effective that prophylactic is?'

Earl Ferrers: 'My Lords, I certainly agree with the second part of the noble Earl's question.'

Reading through the Hansard report I could not help but think how the contribution of Labour's Baroness Birk stood out like a sore thumb among the contributions from the government side of the House.

It was more than interesting to see how the debate increasingly featured in serious discussion, in the press particularly. *The Times* of 19 July 1991 carried as its top centre-page feature Janet Daley's piece 'Brutalizing ourselves to death' in which she suggested that concern about the use of four-letter words sprang from prudery but went on to talk about the brutalizing effect of screened violence, with which, of course, I profoundly agreed. Her piece was linked to the newly published Broadcasting Standards Council's report which, she said, 'revealed yet again how much more the British complaining classes are concerned about obscene language than about the depiction of violence, sexual or otherwise', and went on to point out that 'By far the largest number of complaints to the Council come under the priggish heading of "taste and decency".' I was stirred to write a letter to the editor and delighted to see it published as the first letter a few days later on 23 July.

In it I expressed a conviction which has grown in my mind over a number of years, namely, that the normalizing of foul language is by no means unconnected with the increase of violence in our society. The more normal such language becomes the less it is likely to be used in exceptional circumstances to express anger, so that fists, feet, anything rather than words, become the automatic vehicle of outrage. And it should never be forgotten – in assessing degrees of offence – that the essential element of broadcasting is that it is heard and seen in the home. I pointed out that 'Television is not cinema and viewers have a right to try to uphold standards which they feel important, not only in their own homes but to the quality of our culture generally. That is not a triviality.'

Quite how desperate the situation in relation to the use of obscenities on television had become was revealed by the publication in November 1991 of our second 'Debasement of Language' report.

> In our first report (May 1991) on the Debasement of Language we revealed that the incidence of bad language on television had more than doubled in the two years between 16 April 1989 and 31 March 1991. This second report

reveals that the incidence of bad language has more than doubled in the first nine months of this year.

In some cases, as with the F word, there has been more than a six-fold increase from 15 instances per month in the first quarter of this year to an average of 101 per month in the second and third quarters of this year. The S word was transmitted at the rate of an average of 59 per month in the first quarter of this year, 70 per month in the second quarter and 100 per month in the third quarter of 1991.

Blasphemous language has increased from an average of 19 per month in the first quarter of 1991 to an average of 46 per month in the following second and third quarters. Swearwords and blasphemous expression totalled 2,340, an annual rate of 3,120.

We would emphasize that this research covers only films shown after the 9 o'clock watershed. Were all programmes on radio and television to be covered the overall volume of swearwords and blasphemy would be very much greater.

The TV team from the USA assured us that this report was 'quite unique in the history of broadcasting'. News of it, they told us, had been transmitted worldwide. We had thought that the blasphemous obscenities alone would make it difficult for our report to be carried by any newspaper sensitive to the feelings of its readers!

We had felt that because of the publicity surrounding the Monmouth by-election on 16 May 1991, the increasing unemployment figures, the question of whether the Chancellor would or would not reduce interest rates, and the possibility of an imminent general election, not to mention the bidding for the ITV franchises, we would get very little coverage of our monitoring report. How delighted we were to be proved wrong! The second leader in *The Times* of 17 May and in the *Daily Telegraph*, plus various other publications, mightily reassured us that all our hard work – two years of it – had not been wasted. To hear it reported on Radio 4 news as one of only four stories worldwide at 6 a.m. and in succeeding bulletins, for me to be interviewed from 7.15 a.m. right through the morning, by LBC, BBC Wales/Scotland/Northern Ireland and, so it seemed, just about every provincial and local radio station, was to realize how even the most hardened of broadcasters had been bowled over by the content of the report.

I have to say that I found the use of the expression 'Jesus f . . . Christ' and 'God f . . . damn' almost beyond belief and they have never lost their power to shock and distress me. We *all* need forgiveness for that.

Within a short time of our publishing that report, on 24 October the Broadcasting Standards Council published *A Matter of Manners*, its report on viewers' reaction to the use of bad language on television. The Council had compiled a list of 'unacceptable' words and sought reaction to them, in terms of their power to shock, from 300 viewers. At his press briefing Lord Rees-Mogg, Chairman of the Council, disclosed that 'the C word came top followed by two American-derived graphically sexual terms of abuse, the M phrase and another C phrase.' The F word ranked fifth. I realize that by identifying words or phrases simply by their first letter will probably leave many readers unable to interpret them – several foxed me until I found them defined fully in the BSC report. I imagine that most would prefer to be left in ignorance.

At his press conference Lord Rees-Mogg disclosed his belief that the F word was losing its power to shock. The newspapers asked me how I reacted to this and I told them that 'the tragedy is that he is probably but regrettably right. Constant use of such language desensitizes people. To reduce the act of love to an ugly obscenity is to demean the very essence of love which lies at the heart of human life and the family.'

We were, and remain, concerned by the BSC's apparent lack of concern over the possibility that as a society we will come to accept such language. However, we were grateful for his lordship's claim that 'There is a feeling that broadcasters are taking away the right of parents to teach their children what is appropriate about bad language.' Hear, hear, to that!

The battle against obscene language in broadcasting is an endless one but sometimes something happens which brings it to the forefront of public attention. Such was the transmission on BBC1 of the programme *A New Life*, at 8.45 p.m. on a Sunday evening (11 August 1992). I did not watch it but complaints about the use of four-letter words started to come in first thing next morning leaving me in no doubt as to the nature of the film. I rang Duke Hussey's office and also that of John Birt, Director-General designate, and passed on to them the anger – 'Sunday evening, too!' 'My children were watching!' and 'We were totally unprepared for such language at that time!' – which had been expressed to me. I felt quite a lot of sympathy coming down the phone.

I wrote in my diary a couple of days later

Points of View this evening quite extraordinary – the very first item was, to the best of my knowledge, an unqualified apology for the screening of *A New Life* on a Sunday evening at that hour. The BBC apparently received 153 phone calls and those responsible had issued a statement to the effect that they greatly regretted what had happened. Viewers were told that there were two versions of the film – one had been 'cleaned up' but apparently the wrong one had been shown. Anne Robinson, the compère, kept her face straight but I must admit we couldn't resist a smile! I hope it wasn't cynical but I couldn't help but ask myself if this was another barrier down – deliberately or otherwise.

CHAPTER SEVEN

YES,
PRIME MINISTER

We were greatly honoured, of course we were, to have Duke Hussey, Chairman of the BBC, Lord Rees-Mogg, Chairman of the Broadcasting Standards Council and John Tusa, Managing Director of the World Service of the BBC, all together at one of our functions. This was the presentation in May 1992 to Mr Tusa, on behalf of the World Service, of National VALA's Annual Award. This Award has been made over the years in recognition of the high quality of television programmes. Especially, in this case, because Terry Waite and other hostages had been so grateful to the World Service for giving them great 'courage and comfort' during their ordeal in Beirut.

Terry Waite himself had originally agreed to make the presentation, but a letter came from his public relations officer to say that he had now been ordered to rest and could not, therefore, accept. However Lord Rees-Mogg enthusiastically agreed to do so and in his address said:

> The idea of the Broadcasting Standards Council was first suggested by Mrs Mary Whitehouse. Previously people had to appeal direct to the broadcasting authorities against decisions made by broadcasters, who had set those standards themselves. There is now the opportunity to complain to an independent body and to people who have no connection with the work put out. I believe that public rights are concerned here. We are in the position of being a statutory body with our own point of view. We are there to respond to the public and try and act as a channel in which public complaints can be effective. It seems to me that good work has been done, and we have been able to establish a relationship with the public and the broadcasters. This enables us to put

forward what the public really feel about the problems of sex and violence, pornography, obscenity and problems of taste so that the broadcasters are fully aware of public opinion.

John Tusa's appointment as Managing Director of the BBC World Service has been more than amply justified as it is one of the best appointments made by the BBC. On this occasion the Award is going to the World Service, which I believe is 'the jewel in the crown' of the BBC.

I believe that one should not approach journalism unless one is prepared to make truth-telling its central point. The standards of truth in the World Service of the BBC are probably the highest in world broadcasting. It is inevitable that a great deal of this work is unknown to the British public. It is, therefore, only occasionally when a crisis occurs that other nations become aware of this truth-telling. I remember going to Greece shortly after the regime of the colonels had fallen, and more than half the population relied on the World Service for their information about the country's affairs. In all those countries where regimes are hostile to truth the World Service has been, and is, the resource for telling people the truth. Whenever regimes of tyranny have been overthrown the World Service, not by propaganda against the regime but by the process of offering truth, has played a crucial part in the changes to society. If you look at the whole of Eastern Europe and the Soviet Union, when their regimes fell they had to go through the process of *perestroika*. Through the BBC World Service they were exposed to challenge and the Service played a great part in all the events of Eastern Europe.

In responding John Tusa said that his work with the World Service had given him the best six years of his life. It was an extraordinary organization. The work they had done to relieve the plight of the Beirut hostages represented but a small part of what they had been able to do for the countless listeners in the world whose condition was very similar to that of the hostages and whose need is very great.

We believe we talk to the weak and to the strong, that is the strength of the World Service. What is less often said is what the BBC World Service brings to Britain. It brings credit to

Britain – it has an international place. It reflects the way it sees British life and society and British politics. It broadcasts for Britain and in a particular sense to Britain. Our supporters matter very greatly to us – people like you and people who pay for them, the British tax-payer. This gives us confidence that they matter at home because of the work they do in Britain and on behalf of Britain.

The inspiring student uprising in Peking in 1989 made the world hold its breath, and the terrible punishments meted out afterwards by the authorities, cut off China from the rest of the world and for how long no one knew. The presentation of National VALA's Award in 1989 by His Excellency Ji Chaozhu to Tim Slessor, Executive Producer of Documentary Features at the BBC, was a very special occasion. *The Yellow River* was made jointly by NHK Japan, CCTV China and the BBC, whose teams filmed the river from its source as it looped and twisted its way through 3000 miles to the Yellow Sea. They were the first outsiders to traverse some of the forbidding terrains and to record the lifestyles of the people who live in the river's vicinity.

From the marvellous presentation edition of *The Yellow River* published to celebrate the screening of the programme and given to me by the Ambassador, I learnt that the 'Huanghe' is a powerful symbol of the mythology of China. It is the dragon of Chinese legend, the country's historic heartland. Within its huge basin, spreading across one of the world's great civilizations, bones from the Paleolithic era – a million years old – have been found. Over five thousand years ago neolithic people settled by its shores to grow crops and to fish; their painted pottery is still admired for its symmetry and the beauty of its execution. Since then it has overturned the great dynasties of China, the Shang and Zhou, the Qin, Han, Tan and Northern Song. But back to the day itself. Because the Ambassador was to attend, the police were notified and were in touch with us several times as a demonstration of Tibetans was expected to march past All Souls' Church, Langham Place, where we were holding the presentation. There was some anxiety that His Excellency's arrival might coincide with the march which could result, we were told, 'in an international incident'. We arranged for him to be taken in by a side door and all was well.

One unexpected but most welcome guest was Mr Tagawa, Executive Producer, Documentaries, of NHK Japan, producer of *The Yellow River*, who had flown unexpectedly from Tokyo to be present. Speaking in Japanese, translated by Shozo Ueda, head of the NHK Bureau in London, he spoke of the 'strong friendship of brotherhood' which had developed between the Chinese and Japanese teams as they 'travelled together from the source to the mouth by car, horses, rafts, cows, et-cetera, with the co-operation of the Chinese people'.

The presentation of the Award has, over the years, covered just about every type of programme:

1971	Sir Adrian Boult (Music)
1972	Cliff Richard (Music)
1973	Independent Television News
1974	*Sam* (Drama, Granada)
1975	*Softly, Softly* (Drama, BBC)
1976	*Tomorrow's World* (Science, BBC)
1977	*Jim'll Fix It* (Children's programme, BBC)
1978	not presented
1979	*Songs of Praise* (Religious, BBC)
1980	not presented
1981	*Today* (News and Current Affairs BBC Radio 4)
1982	BBC and ITN for coverage of the Falklands War
1983	*Yes, Minister* (Comedy, BBC)
1984	*Right to Reply* (Topical, Channel 4)
1985	*Blue Peter* (Children's programme, BBC)
1986	*Crimewatch* (Public Response, BBC)
1987	Frank Bough (services to broadcasting)
1988	*The Yellow River* (Nature, BBC2)
1989	*Survival* (Nature, Anglia)
1990	*Challenge Anneka*, BBC
1991	World Service of the BBC

All had a special quality so that it is invidious to pick out any one of them but true to say that some remain more vividly in the memory than others. Take *Jim'll Fix It*, for instance. I wrote in my diary that night:

It was all very happy – an inspired idea to have so many children and there really was a great deal of fun. Jimmy spoke very kindly about our work and he was very touched by the 'We've fixed it for Jim' medallion which we had specially made for him. The team responsible for the show is quite obviously committed to something way beyond just the production of a programme. Some of the stories they told about the way in which they get involved with the children were very moving, like the one about the little girl Jimmy said he was going to marry and they got engaged with a huge cuddly toy just a few days before she died.

Jimmy, wearing a track suit and running shoes, said he believed the programme 'reflected good times, happiness and dreams. It goes to show that happiness can exist in even the most difficult situations', and added 'While Mrs Whitehouse possibly wouldn't agree with my personal lifestyle, it is through organizations like hers that there is some semblance of decency.'

Well, I don't know anything about Jimmy's lifestyle and, in any case, it's no business of mine. What I do know is that, as the years have gone on, so Jimmy has continued to make his highly acclaimed contribution to those in need and for that one continues to be grateful. His knighthood reflects the respect in which he is held by everyone.

In 1979, in her own inimitable and delightful way, Thora Hird announced as part of her acceptance speech of our award that British Rail was going to name one of its new engines *Songs of Praise* and that she had been invited to participate in the ceremony. A well-deserved honour to her and to one of the most consistently popular religious programmes.

I prayed on the morning of the presentation that it would be a joyful day and indeed it was, made so not least by the presence of Dr Robert Runcie, then Archbishop of Canterbury, who was full of fun. He spoke of how he had been in the full glare of public life for only a short time but it had made him realize the kind of pressures we had been under. He had never known until now of this positive side of our work and had looked upon us more as a 'moral watchdog'. He added that he felt there was a 'certain significance' to this lack of publicity for our Award. So did we! I recorded in my diary:

The BBC team led by Andrew Barr, the producer of *Songs of Praise* was very appreciative and the ceremony ended

by him asking me to name my favourite hymn. I turned to
Ernest to ask him which it should be. ' "Fill Thou my Life,
O Lord my God" – our wedding hymn,' he said, whereupon
the Archbishop gave a note, and Bill Cotton, and the rest
of us all joined in. What a lovely way to finish the day!

But it didn't really finish there because, as the
formalities ended, Dr Runcie turned to me and said that
he'd accepted our invitation to make the presentation not
only because he wanted to support *Songs of Praise* but
because he wanted to meet me personally, and tell me that
he now had a good many reservations about 'the
permissive sixties', not a few of which were influenced by
the kind of stand which we had taken and by our courage
in doing so. That was wonderful too.

Looking at my entry for that really quite remarkable day I read
that 'Bill Cotton kissed me as he went' and that I said to Ernest
afterwards, 'Sir Hugh Greene [the then Director-General of
the BBC] would have had an apoplectic fit with the idea of this
Controller of BBC1 kissing me or even talking to me for
that matter!'

We were intrigued to hear from a senior BBC man present
that plans had been afoot to abolish *Songs of Praise*, but that
the choice of the programme for the Award and the Archbishop's high praise for it had changed all that. And, of course,
the programme has gone from strength to strength.

The Award presentations have always been delightful
occasions but seldom noted by the press. There was one outstanding exception. In 1984 Mrs Thatcher, as Prime Minister,
made the presentation to the production team and cast of the
famous BBC series *Yes, Minister*. Her enjoyment of it was well
known but we were thrilled and surprised that she was willing
to devote the best part of a Friday morning to the presentation.
Quite how much time she devoted, though, we had yet to
discover!

We held the presentation in the Conference Centre at All
Souls' Church next door to Broadcasting House. When I
arrived I found the Prime Minister's personal assistant waiting
for me. She took me on one side and told me that late the
previous night (around midnight, I gathered), the Prime Minister had called her to her room. She had written a short *Yes,*

Minister style sketch – with help from her husband – for inclusion in the morning's proceedings. 'We are, however,' she said, 'still awaiting clearance of copyright from the BBC, but in the meantime,' she said, 'Paul Eddington and Nigel Hawthorne are in the gentlemen's lavatories learning their parts!'

We didn't have to wait long for the BBC to give clearance or for the press to catch on to what was about to happen. Or for the arrival of the late Stuart Young, the then Chairman of the BBC, who brought with him John Howard-Davies, then the Corporation's Head of Light Entertainment. When Paul Eddington and Nigel Hawthorne appeared they both said how nervous they were, 'never having done anything like this before, and doubting we ever would again!'

Stuart Young roared with laughter – as he did many times during the proceedings that followed – when I said that if anyone had told me twenty years ago, almost to the day on which we launched our campaign, that 'all this would be happening in the presence of the Prime Minister and the Chairman of the BBC, I would have thought they were hallucinating!'

The TV cameras, the photographers and pressmen made the most of the occasion with accompanying editorials. The *Daily Telegraph* even printed the whole of the sketch with a huge photograph on its back page, writing up the story with great enthusiasm.

Mrs Thatcher [it claimed] had chosen the best part for herself, that of Prime Minister, and the way in which she made the hapless Minister and his civil servant writhe and squirm had the audience in fits. In the sketch, she managed also to fulfil, or at least set in train, what is plainly one of her profoundest ambitions – the abolition of all economists. In her preamble to the performance of a lifetime, she described *Yes, Minister* as 'truly my favourite programme. Its closely observed portrayal of what goes on in the corridors of power has given me hours of pure joy. I therefore wondered how, on behalf of millions of viewers, I might show my appreciation of the superb acting and writing which goes into the programme. I'm afraid that for Paul Eddington and Nigel Hawthorne my idea will involve a little work. But I'm sure they won't mind. They are so professional. What I have in mind is that we might perform a little sketch in the Prime Minister's study. I know, *Yes, Minister* has never identified the Prime Minister of the day for the very dubious reason that they thought I might be replaced by a man. O ye of little faith.

'So with apologies to Anthony Jay and Jonathan Lynn (the scriptwriters) I have arranged for the world première of *Yes, Prime Minister.*'

And this is how it went. Re-reading it now I realize, with a chuckle, how prophetic it all was!

PRIME MINISTER: Ah, good morning, Jim, Sir Humphrey. Do come in and sit down. How's your wife? Is she well?

JIM HACKER (*puzzled*): Oh yes, fine, Prime Minister. Fine. Thank you. Yes, fine.

PRIME MINISTER: Good. So pleased. I've been meaning to have a word with you for some time. I've got an idea.

JIM HACKER (brightening visibly): An idea, Prime Minister? Oh, good.

SIR HUMPHREY (*guardedly*): An idea, Prime Minister?

PRIME MINISTER: Well, not really an idea. It's gone beyond that, actually. I've given it quite a bit of thought and I'm sure you, Jim, are the right man to carry it out. It's got to do with a kind of institution and you are sort of responsible for institutions, aren't you?

SIR HUMPHREY (cautiously): Institutions, Prime Minister?

JIM HACKER (*decisively*): Oh yes, institutions fall to me. Most definitely. And you want me to set one up, I suppose?

PRIME MINISTER: Set one up? Certainly not. I want you to get rid of one.

JIM HACKER (*astonished*): Get rid of one, Prime Minister?

PRIME MINISTER: Yes, it's all very simple, I want you to abolish economists.

JIM HACKER (*mouth open*): Abolish economists, Prime Minister?

PRIME MINISTER: Yes, abolish economists – quickly.

SIR HUMPHREY (*silkily*): All of them, Prime Minister?

PRIME MINISTER: Yes, all of them. They never agree on anything. They just fill the heads of politicians with all sorts of curious notions like the more you spend, the richer you get.

JIM HACKER (*coming round to the idea*): I see your point, Prime Minister. Can't have the nation's time wasted on curious notions, can we? No.

SIR HUMPHREY (*sternly*): Minister.

PRIME MINISTER: Quite right, Jim. Absolute waste of time. Simply got to go.

JIM HACKER (*uncertain*): Simply got to go?

PRIME MINISTER (*motherly*): Yes, Jim. Don't worry. If it all goes wrong I shall get the blame. But if it goes right – as it will – then you'll get the credit for redeploying a lot of underused and misapplied resources. Probably get promotion, too.

SIR HUMPHREY (*indignantly*): Resources? Resources, Prime Minister? We're talking about economists.

PRIME MINISTER: Were, Sir Humphrey, were.

JIM HACKER (*decisively*): Yes, Humphrey, were. We're going to get rid of them.

PRIME MINISTER: Well, it's all settled, then. I'll look forward to receiving your plan for abolition soon. Tomorrow, shall we say? I'd like you to announce it before it all leaks.

JIM HACKER (*brightly*): Tomorrow, then, Prime Minister.

PRIME MINISTER: Yes. Well go and sort it out. Now, Sir Humphrey – what did you say your degree was?

SIR HUMPHREY (*innocently*): Degree, Prime Minister?

PRIME MINISTER (*firmly*): Yes, Sir Humphrey, degree. Your degree. You have one, I take it – most permanent secretaries do – or perhaps two.

SIR HUMPHREY (*modestly*): Er, well, actually, Prime Minister, a double first.

PRIME MINISTER: Congratulations, Sir Humphrey, but what in?

SIR HUMPHREY (*weakly*): Politics – er . . . and er . . . economics.

PRIME MINISTER (*soothingly*): Capital, my dear Sir Humphrey. You'll know exactly where to start.

SIR HUMPHREY (*bleakly*): Yes, Prime Minister.

Exit JIM HACKER *and* SIR HUMPHREY.

As the sketch ended to enthusiastic applause, Mrs Thatcher added: 'Modesty forbids me to say how the plot works out in the end. But I can give you another clue – the economy perks up as it is doing now.'

First to the microphone when Mrs Thatcher had finished was one of the script-writers Jonathan Lynn. 'We would congratulate the Prime Minister on taking her rightful place in the field of situation comedy.' Anthony Jay, his co-writer said, 'Under the new reciprocal arrangement I am looking forward to taking Cabinet and Jonathan will be answering questions in the House!' That was a day I shall never forget not least because, contrary to the image built up by certain sections of the media, Mrs Thatcher was, as so many people said, so friendly, so natural and so kind as she mixed with the audience for over an hour before she left. One pressman went further: 'Never before in the history of the world', he said to me, 'has a head of government, prime minister, president, or whatever, put their reputation at risk by appearing before the press, the TV camera in an unrehearsed sketch like this!' Anyway, she did, and it was an unqualified success. As was borne out by the television coverage on every news bulletin that night.

My own appreciation went even deeper. Her aide had sought me out to say that the Prime Minister would like me to join her in a 'little quiet chat' on the platform. Trying to negotiate the steps onto the platform I slipped and caught my shin across the edge of one of the steps, sending my plate of sandwiches from the buffet lunch flying across the floor with a crash. But what amazed me – and still does – was the speed with which the PM put herself between my agony and the hovering press, pulling other people close to make a barrier. And as we sat together like two old friends she said, in what I thought was a most generous gesture, 'When you and I, at our age . . .' – and I am fifteen years older than she is! She refused to let me go to the door with her when she left soon afterwards and I sat there thinking how very privileged we had all been.

The 1990 Convention was another very successful occasion. Among the guests were the Earl of Halsbury and the Marquis of Donegal as well as the kind man who, completely out of the blue, sent us £2000 towards expenses. The Award was presented to Lord Buxton, the founder of the *Survival* series and, until recently, Chairman of Anglia TV. He was most appreciative and Magnus Magnusson, presenting the Award, reminded us all of an event long hidden in National VALA's history. He told us that it was our objections to the crudity and obscenity of a programme *Casanova* on BBC1 which had caused it to be removed from the schedule in 1972 and replaced by *Mastermind*, formerly shown late in the evening on BBC2. And we all know what a huge success that has been!

In his tribute to Lord Buxton, Magnus Magnusson said:

This Award, which I am privileged to make to Aubrey

Buxton, is, of course, not just to Aubrey, it is for what Aubrey stands for and what the programme with which he has been associated with for so long stands for. If I look at it professionally, as a television person myself, *Survival* is the most stunningly brilliant form of sheer programme-making that I can imagine. The camera work marvellously meticulous. The production skills required to get these programmes together, I can assure you, are breathtaking – and the editing, the thing that you never really notice, which really puts the stamp, the pace, the rhythm, the style to the programme, that is quite impeccable. It's become the world's longest running and most successful sales programme abroad that we can imagine. There have been nearly seven hundred of these programmes since 1961 – twenty-nine years he's been at it!

In his reply Lord Buxton said that he was:

> . . . very proud and privileged to receive the Award from the Association, it has been earned by a magnificent team of people. *Survival* has in fact won a great many awards around the world but there's nothing so exciting as getting one at home and nothing more rewarding or marvellous than getting one from viewers, and therefore I think that the award from your Association will have pride of place, quite apart from its magnificent appearance, in our array of awards, and I cannot tell you how grateful I am to receive it on behalf of all the cameramen and one camera girl dotted around the world, and on behalf of the production team at home under Mike Hay who is our Executive Director and runs the base.
>
> I can't tell you therefore what an encouragement it is to people producing our sort of shows to be recognized by your sort of people representing as you do such a vast body of opinion in the country.

Each one of our presentations has had a quality unique to itself and certainly the 1991 occasion bore that out. Listening again to our tape-recording of the speeches, I felt that they called for rather special treatment, so I trust you will feel that this verbatim report justifies the space it fills. Incidentally, we wrote to King Michael of Romania to ask if he would do us the great honour of presenting the Award to the BBC for its showing of the Anneka Rice programme on his country. He wrote back, regretting that his commitments would make it impossible for him to do so, but suggested that we might invite his daughter Princess Helen, which we did.

First of all, my opening remarks:

I am going to ask you a question first. May I ask how many of you saw the Anneka Rice programme on Romania? Quite a lot! I saw it twice and I think it was one of the most moving, wonderful programmes that I have ever seen in all my life. You talk about the good things television can do, there you saw it in action. And so we decided that we would this year give our Award to Mr Tom Gutteridge who is the Managing Director of Mentorn Films who made the programme and we are very grateful and honoured in having Princess Helen of Romania to be here to make the award.

Princess Helen was obviously touched by our gesture and very happy to make the presentation. What she had to say, coming from someone so deeply involved, made a great impression:

I would just like to thank everybody for inviting me here, it is a great pleasure to be here amongst you all.

I went to Romania for the first time last Easter and as you could imagine it was a very traumatic and emotional time for me as it was the first time I had ever been there, as my father was forced to abdicate at the end of 1947, and we have all lived in exile since that time.

It shocked and distressed me very deeply to see the plight of not only the people and the children of Romania, but the whole of the country which is so dilapidated and so sad. I feel the children of Romania have not been abused in a pornographic way, but have been abused in the sense of their whole freedom and liberty, by being herded into the most squalid and disgusting conditions that I have ever seen. I know that in some European countries there are a lot of difficulties and a lot of poverty, but nothing can compare with this European country, Romania. The squalor that these children live in – and having said that, it is not just the children that are herded into institutions, it is also the older people who are just left because nobody can look after them.

Romania is a very beautiful country. I was there last in October hoping to find some orphanages that I could help on a long-term basis with my Trust 'The Princess Helen Trust'. It was a most beautiful sunny day in October, the leaves were turning and the sky was very blue, and having seen that it made me feel that one day Romania will become a great country again and will take its place in society and in the rest of the world as it should do. But, obviously, there is a very long hard task in front of us to rebuild Romania to become that sort of a country.

That brings me back to everybody in Britain. I would like to thank everybody very sincerely first from myself and also for my family for all that you have done for my country. It means a tremendous lot to me and moves me very deeply that everyone has taken such a lot of care for that poor upset country. That again brings me to the programme which you [Tom Gutteridge] made with Anneka Rice in helping Romania by refurbishing this orphanage. Those children, thank God, have now got a better standard of living and will live in comparative comfort compared to a lot of the others, and it means so much to me that people have gone out there and worked very hard to bring some happiness to these children. And on that note, I would like to present this to you and thank you again.

Tom Gutteridge thanked us

. . . very much indeed for this, which is much more attractive than a BAFTA Award! It is extremely attractive, I can see it follows a distinguished list of programming that you have honoured over the years. I apologize for the fact that Anneka herself cannot be here, she has a long-standing engagement, she is filming in Northern Ireland and simply couldn't get across in time.

It is a great honour for all of us in the company, which is an independent company, entering Kenneth Baker's brave new age of broadcasting and indeed trying to become a broadcaster as well. It is a great honour for us all and in particular for the production team who made the programme.

I think it proves that entertainment programmes can actually achieve something as well as simply being sources of entertainment and it proves something which we set out to achieve through the programme two years ago when we first started it. That under certain circumstances the power of television can be harnessed for the common good. Our series was designed to attempt to achieve some lasting benefit to the community using the resources of the community. The fact that 12 million viewers watched the programme, of course, is a bonus!

In the case of Romania there are no resources at all, therefore, we were forced to take out hundreds of workers. The material we were faced with was an appalling sight, an orphanage that had no plumbing, no heating – it stank. It was impossible to walk through the door without vomiting, it was in an appalling state and in four days the place was transformed by the most wonderful workforce who came from all over the country as a result of Anneka's appeal and all the firms who donated nearly £2 million-worth of resources and equipment in that short space of time.

I just want to pay particular credit to two people, both of whom are with us this morning. The Associate Producer of the programme, the person who really produced the programme, Janine Waddell.

We decided to do the programme three or four weeks before we actually did it. We have a planning period of only three or four weeks from the time we got the letter from the charity, it was Janine's responsibility working with just one other person to organize all the planning and the permissions. Romania at the moment is a bureaucratic nightmare, and quite understandably, and to organize nearly two hundred people to get out with equipment, supplies, food and a convoy of twenty-five lorries crossing Europe and they all had to be there at the same time and arrive safely was a logistical nightmare. And that was something that Janine co-ordinated.

And then Martin Hawkins, the cameraman. I said it was impossible to walk into the orphanage without vomiting, it became a bit of a standing joke, I have to say, with Martin, as to how he would survive, because basically he brought you those pictures, he was the person behind the camera lens! They are extraordinary pictures throughout the programme and he is, in my view, one of Britain's finest cameramen. It was a great privilege to have him working with us again and I would like to think that the programme was one of his finest productions.

Once again I must apologize that Anneka is not here but in a sense she is here, live on tape, if we can get that piece of machinery to work.

Thank you all so much, and we will treasure it through our year of tenure.

Because Anneka Rice was not able to be present personally, she had made a video which contained personal expressions of appreciation from her as well as her own feelings about the making of the programme. It also included coverage of her return visit to the orphanage and illustrated the progress which had been made since the filming of the programme.

We all valued very much the obvious lengths to which the production company and Anneka herself had gone to express their appreciation of our Award. Certainly these have given us personal contacts with professional broadcasters which we were very pleased to have.

CHAPTER EIGHT

BATTLE
FOR EASTENDERS

This Temple of the Arts and Muses is dedicated to Almighty God by the first Governors of Broadcasting in the year 1931, Sir John Reith being Director-General. It is their prayer that good seed sown may bring forth a good harvest, that all things hostile to peace and purity may be banished from this house and that the people, inclining their ear to whatsoever things are beautiful, and honest and of good report, may tread the path of wisdom and uprightness.

Foyer of Broadcasting House

Nothing more vividly illustrates the harsh reality of the fight to 'banish' all things 'hostile to peace and purity' than the one that raged around *EastEnders* in 1989. It is, I think, important to record just how prolonged and intense that battle was and remember that it remains as a watershed to the establishment and maintenance of 'family viewing time'. Lessons were certainly learnt and for that we must all be grateful.

I wrote a letter to *The Times* on 6 June 1989:

'What do you want me to do? Carve up his arse into slices on a plate?' I do apologize to you, Sir, and to your readers. But, then, surely inappropriate, totally, for the ears of countless children watching BBC's *EastEnders* last Thursday evening?

I am moved to write out of desperation. Letters to and meetings with the Chairman, Mr Marmaduke Hussey, have had little if any effect. 'Bitch', 'bastard', are commonly heard in the midst of the endless trouble and strife which characterizes the series. We were all told (2 May) that Kathy Beale 'could not wait to get her knickers down' so that she could be raped. And in spite of the BBC's own warnings to producers against the use of 'domestic objects' as weapons of violence, we watched (23 May) the crazy Sue madly smashing the glass jar from her baby's grave, cutting her own wrists with it, then threatening bystanders with its jagged edges. Bitter and violent fighting with chains and fists, grippings round the throat as well as the striking of women are by no means unknown.

In his piece 'Who regulates the regulators' [*The Times*, 31 May 1989] Brian Wenham refers to the way in which, following his appointment as Chairman of the BBC, 'Duke Hussey set about his stable cleaning with full reformist zeal . . . yet 30 months on the new BBC displays the full virtues and vices of the old'. Indeed. Perhaps your readers would have ideas as to how this bi-weekly violation of the sensitivities of us all, and of the BBC's own guidelines, could be halted. Short of sacking the producer concerned, I have come to the end of mine.

It wasn't published. I wasn't surprised.

'Do you know what's arguably the worst aspect of that storyline?' I said to the friend who watched the *EastEnders* rape episode with me. And I answered my own question. 'Many of the children watching at half past seven in the evening might wonder whether that's what Dad does to Mum and they wouldn't be able to ask. So the horror of it, however deeply buried, could well create fear and anxiety and Dad would never know what had gone wrong.'

But, of course, the youngsters weren't only brought face to face with the explicit horrors of rape in this so-called 'soap'. They were treated, as the series progressed, to attempted suicide, arson with the intention of burning a man to death, threats to kill, from a daughter to her mother and a son to his mother (paper knife and kitchen knife in hand), abortion (leading to the break-up of a marriage), obscene gesture (delivered in front of a child), promiscuity, homosexuality (£200 offered for sexual favours), foul language, blasphemy, lying, cheating, endless argument, sinister Mafia-type undercurrents, throw-away lines like 'he tried to get into her knickers, not for the first time'. All typical, one would have thought, of the BBC's late evening *Wednesday Play* or of Channel 4's notorious 'red-triangle' films.

Just how powerfully television can affect human behaviour was never more vividly illustrated than by the episode in March 1986 in which the character Angie who had had a row with her dissolute husband Den was seen, in the last shot, throwing a handful of sleeping pills into her mouth and swilling them down with a bottle of gin. It seemed to us so highly irresponsible that we rang Stuart Young's office and that of the Director-General in the hope that the sequence would be cut when the episode was repeated the following Sunday. Mercifully, and I use the word advisedly, bearing in mind the letter which appeared in *The Lancet* a couple of weeks later, the offending sequence *was* cut but the impact of the initial transmission was devastating. The text of the letter follows:

Soap May Seriously Damage Your Health

Sir

On Sunday March 2, the omnibus edition of BBC Television's soap opera *EastEnders* showed the character Angie taking an overdose. In the following week we experienced a 300 per cent increase in the number of patients attending the accident-and-emergency department at the Hackney Hospital in East London for deliberate overdose. This was the straw that nearly broke the camel's back. As in other hospitals in central London the number of our medical beds has lately been reduced and our bed state was critical. On Sunday night we were putting up beds to cope with the influx. The following week a 'yellow alert' was declared, resulting in the cancellation of routine admissions.

In the week after the *EastEnders* programme 22 patients attended the accident-and-emergency department having taken an overdose. During the previous ten weeks the average had been 6.9 ± 3.4 (SD). During the previous ten years the average for the week in question was 6.7 ± 1.6 (four years' figures unavailable). Perhaps the long spell of cold weather contributed to the increase in overdoses in Hackney, but the close temporal relation with the screening of an overdose on a programme which is widely viewed and purports to reflect real life in our part of London makes a causal relation seem likely.

In these days when cash limits are rationing care, is it unreasonable to ask the BBC to contribute towards the extra cost they have caused the City and Hackney Health Authority? Do the BBC programmers consider the likely consequences of screening self-destructive behaviour that is likely to be copied? Next time, could they please arrange for Angie to take an overdose in the summer when our bed state is not so acute?

Simon J. Ellis   Department of Medicine
Susan Walsh   Hackney Hospital
                                                London E9

This was not the only hospital to receive such patients. A coroner in Hampshire, speaking at the inquest on a nineteen-year-old, one of three young people in the district who had taken overdoses and died as a result, declared that 'It seems highly probable that a lot of young people watched the regrettable suicide scene in *EastEnders* which gave the impression that, if you think you will be found in time (as Angie was), it is safe to take an overdose.'

Doctors at a Midlands hospital revealed that in the week following the episode forty people were admitted after overdosing. An inquest on a twenty-three-year-old man found that he killed himself the day after the programme in what was reported as 'a copycat drink and drug cocktail' after a row with his girlfriend. That coroner, too, was highly critical of the BBC, not least because the story-line gave the impression that, even though Angie swallowed the tablets, she was full of life in the next episode, apparently unharmed.

How did the BBC react? Jonathan Powell, Head of Drama Series and Serials, who had given his personal approval to several of *EastEnders'* most controversial episodes, apparently responded by asking for statistical and clinical proof, claiming that this had not been given. What was particularly disturbing was that, to the best of my knowledge, the BBC made no apology – which would have amounted to an admission that television *can* affect how people behave. Imagine the implications of that for everyone concerned in producing programmes.

We were aware of the continuing story in *EastEnders* of

homosexual Mark, son of Arthur and Pauline Fowler, but were nevertheless startled to read a lengthy item on the front page of *The Times* (20 November 1991) to the effect that a copy of Alex Comfort's *The New Joy of Sex* would be 'bought as a Christmas gift' for him 'in the Boxing Day episode'. The story went on to say that *EastEnders* producers had sought clearance to use the book from its publishers, who could barely contain their delight 'that as many as 20 million viewers will see the book. Reed, which expects a significant surge in sales, is pleased with its Christmas present. Richard Charkin, its consumer books chief executive, said that *EastEnders* will have helped the company to increase the book's sales by about 25,000 during the holidays.'

Considerable controversy had surrounded Comfort's earlier book *The Joy of Sex*, so I went out and purchased a copy of its sequel. I suspected it was a totally inappropriate book to be given such publicity at any time, let alone in family viewing time – and as a present, for pity's sake, off the Christmas tree!

It was only a few days before Christmas so I knew I had to work quickly. The BBC's Chairman was already on his way north but his secretary told me that she would telephone him. The Director-General was involved in a meeting, but his secretary said she'd give him my message when he came out.

Now, it was just a matter of waiting to see what happened on Boxing Day – and credit where credit is due! – there was no sign of the book in the programme. If it had not been *The Times* who had first so prominently carried the story I might have wondered how accurate it was.

Which brings us to the question of judgement. Precisely who is prepared to transmit and defend such a travesty of accepted standards? In a letter to me of 15 July 1988 Paul Fox, BBC Television's then newly appointed Managing Director, justified everything: 'We continue to believe that it is the proper concern of *EastEnders* to reflect responsibly all manner of social and personal problems within contemporary life.' No mention of any limitation which might be set because of the timing.

'Reflect responsibly' . . . well, how about this for a 'responsible' storyline? It was shown on 16 July 1988. The chap who owned the wine bar over the road, Wilmot Brown, was pinching Den's clientele and had also raped one of Den's customers, which provided the excuse for Den to fling a petrol bomb into Wilmot Brown's premises, with the declared hope and belief that he's inside and 'will burn to death'. The smile on Den's face at that thought is one of the most memorable moments of the episode. After all, one of his pals had encouraged him to 'fix that bastard one way or another' and no one's going to let on who did, for they all join in the chorus of 'I hope he burned to death!' Even the hapless rape victim fervently joins in with the same hope – after all, the 'bastard could have given me VD'. It was repeated between 2 and 3 p.m. on the following Sunday afternoon. The moral of the story for young viewers was, if someone makes you angry set fire to his house in the belief, and hope, that he's inside.

Looking back now it is difficult to believe that all this happened as I recount. But it did. Week after week we sent in specific complaints and week after week they seemed to have little or no effect. But, in the end they did. And we weren't the only ones involved. The press, politicians, and other concerned organizations joined in the battle.

Mr Peter Dawson, General Secretary of the 43,000 strong Professional Association of Teachers at its Annual Conference in August 1989 described *EastEnders* as 'projecting, as normal, highly deviant forms of behaviour . . . homosexuality, bad language, crime, infidelity and drunkenness . . . *EastEnders* is a very good soap opera – brilliantly acted and superbly scripted. That is the problem. It conveys the impression that this is what real life is like. It packs together in a highly concentrated manner all the extreme forms of behaviour.' He went on, 'The whole nation is totally drugged by *EastEnders*.' He claimed that parents' ability to make moral judgements was undermined by television: 'What are parents supposed to say to their children about sex before marriage? They watch television and see that this is the norm in our society,' and speaking about the need for adults to set a good example he asked whether they themselves 'respect authority, practise courtesy, deal honestly, live uprightly and talk cleanly?' Very good questions which really go to the heart of the matter, and an assessment of the content and impact of *EastEnders* which reflects almost exactly what National VALA has said so many times, and so many different issues, over the years.

It wasn't only the Professional Association of Teachers that expressed its concern. Peter Baldwin, Vice President of the National Association of Head Teachers, on the eve of his 1989 Conference spoke about the way in which foul language and violence is 'polluting youngsters' minds' claiming that 'programmes like *EastEnders* are affecting children as young as five'. He said that when he took up his position as head of a primary school in Chorley, Lancashire, eleven years ago, the problem did not exist. Now 'children from good homes, with hard-working responsible parents, use four-letter words at the slightest provocation'.

And if one seeks an answer to the question 'Why?' one needs to look no further than the words provided in the *Sunday Telegraph Magazine* of 30 August 1987, of the producer at that time, Julia Smith. She declared that 'nobody in the hierarchy of the BBC has ever suggested a single change to any of [her] plots and characters'. She had tackled head on, she said, some of the most disturbing and controversial issues of our time – unemployment, mental illness, prostitution, single parents, suicide and homosexuality – and had 'always been conscious of the moral element' in everything she had done.

'At last we're getting somewhere!' I thought. I had received a letter dated 7 July 1989, from John McCormick, the Secretary of the BBC, writing on behalf of the Chairman, telling me that 'Following the recent episodes to which you refer, the producers of the programme *EastEnders* have been reminded that many viewers do find this language offensive and their attention has been drawn to the general guidelines.'

Perhaps a suitable epilogue to the chapter would be this quotation from the House of Lords' Hansard, 25 July 1989.

Lord Nugent of Guildford: My Lords, I thank my noble friend for that not very informative answer. Is he aware that in an episode of *EastEnders* shown during family viewing time at 7.30 in the evening of 12th July there was a scene with a girl, who had been raped, reporting at a police station which breached all standards of good broadcasting? Is he further aware that the Commissioner of Police of the Metropolis has already complained to the BBC that the portrayal of the police officer in these very sensitive circumstances as rough and unsympathetic was quite damaging to all that the police have tried to do in recent years? Is my noble friend aware that a complaint was made by Mrs Whitehouse of the National Viewers' and Listeners' Association about the fact that showing a scene of sex and violence during family viewing time is very offensive? Will he please expedite the setting up of the Broadcasting Standards Council to deal with such offences.

It is, perhaps, fair to say that the BBC in persisting with the excesses of *EastEnders* had been its own worst enemy. After all, the idea of a Broadcasting Standards Council has been and still is an anathema to most broadcasting personnel but since November 1991 has been established by law.

Julia Smith's troubles did not end with *EastEnders*. She also produced the opening episodes of *Eldorado*, the BBC's £10-million soap which in the summer of 1992 saw its viewing figures slump from over 8 million to around 2 million within a matter of weeks. I certainly wasn't surprised. There aren't many programmes on television that I can't *make* myself watch but *Eldorado* quickly became one of them – so tawdry and silly. The situation was so bad that Verity Lambert, the programme's executive producer, flew out to Spain to take over after the departure of Julia Smith in an 'exhausted' condition. According to the *Sunday Times* of 9 September 1992 'an allegedly Titanic row' had occurred between Smith and Lambert, 'the former wanting the soap to remain true to the gritty realism that made her name, the latter preferring a slick American approach!' – though exactly where the 'gritty realism' came in was beyond me.

CHAPTER NINE

THE CANCER
IN OUR CULTURE

One of the functions of the privacy of sex is to reinforce the incest taboo: if you de-privatize sex and make it a public thing, then I think you are more likely to get sexual abuse of children, because an initial safeguard curtain has been removed.

Lord William Rees-Mogg,
Chairman, Broadcasting Standards Council,
The Times 10 July 1992

I am well aware that many other groups and individuals were involved in the campaigns which led up to the creation of new laws and the team work we did with them was much appreciated. I refer particularly to the Protection of Children Act 1978, the Indecent Displays Act 1981 and the Video Recordings Act 1984. The Protection of Children Act, introduced by Cyril Townsend, MP for Bexleyheath, as a private member's bill, reflected the increasing sense of revulsion, nationwide, against the sexual exploitation of children by pornographers. As with all of our campaigns leading to legislation, we launched a petition: over 1½ million people signed our ABUSE petition with a mere 1 per cent refusing to sign. The public support for action to control child pornography was and remains overwhelming, though as time has gone on the problems, such as shortage of police manpower, have meant that questions about the effectiveness of this bill, as expressed by people like Sir Bernard Braine, MP, and Michael Allison, MP, have, sadly, been vindicated, and the present availability of increasingly obscene and cruel child pornography is not only a challenge but a shame to us all.

It needs to be said that it was the Labour benches in both

Houses that opposed these bills. Lord Houghton, the humanist Labour peer, referred to the Protection of Children Bill as 'conceived in hysteria' and he fought it to the bitter end.

According to my diary (27 October 1978) the *Daily Mail* rang to ask if I would be prepared to go into Soho to see what effect the newly passed Indecent Displays Act, for which we'd fought so long and hard and which came into force that day, had already had on the sex-shop displays there. 'So long as there's no attempt to photograph me against a background of pornography or naked ladies,' I said. I wrote later that I was 'glad that I went, though whether I shall be after I've seen the paper tomorrow is another matter!' But I was 'appalled at the way in which the sex industry had taken over Soho – the electronic displays day and night are terribly aggressive. The huge photos of girls spreadeagled with a black cross over their private parts were ludicrous and were quite as bad – if not worse – in their concentrated impact than anything I have seen in Denmark. Incredible that the situation should have been allowed to deteriorate to this extent. "Home of the free". "Bastion of Christian civilization", I don't think!'

Superintendent Peter Kruger, then head of New Scotland Yard's Obscene Publications Department, told me the next morning that he felt the article in the *Daily Mail* was very helpful and that his men were going out into Soho that morning 'to seize right, left and centre', and would be making a charge, under the new Act, relating to one particular poster I had mentioned. Looking back now and seeing the transformation not only of Soho but of other hotbeds of licentiousness there can be little doubt that the Indecent Displays Act has been effective.

The universities, too, were playing their part. After many years of unsuccessful debates, the results of often hectic occasions began to go into reverse: for the first time on 30 January 1981 I won a debate at Oxford by a margin of 15 votes against Victor Lowndes and his associate. Then the Cambridge Union rang: they'd heard 'what a marvellous debate it was at Oxford', would I *please* come and repeat the performance for them? At first I said no, but when I heard that three Christian students from Cambridge had committed the great undergraduate sin of appearing at Oxford to hear the debate and support me, I changed my mind. And what a night it was! *The*

Times in its twenty-column-inches report next day made the most of it: I had apparently 'soundly thrashed' Mr Lowndes at Oxford and very tongue-in-cheek the report went on:

> Mrs Whitehouse, a veteran campaigner against pornography, appeared in a flowing green gown with gold trimmings which would not have looked out of place in the pre-orgy scenes from the film *Caligula*. She was supported by the Bishop of Norwich, the Rt Revd Maurice Ponsonby Wood, in a fetching purple two-piece outfit with matching silver jewellery. While the party of Mr Lowndes, the former Chairman of the Playboy Organization in Britain, was predominantly in velvet, fashioned into bow-ties or frocks, depending on the sex of his undeniably attractive entourage.

At the end of what was, without doubt, a memorable evening the packed debating chamber voted for 'the forces of light' by 357 votes to 191!

The ongoing controversy over video 'nasties' figured prominently throughout 1983 and Prime Minister Margaret Thatcher took a public stand against them. Incidentally, of all the prime ministers who have held that position throughout the years we have been campaigning, Mrs Thatcher has been the only one prepared to speak out publicly in our support, though John Major has shown himself supportive in correspondence with us.

As part of our campaign against the sadistically violent and grossly obscene video 'nasties' which in some cases involved animals as well as men, women and children, in the spring of 1983 we wrote to every MP (over 600), pointing out the inadequacy of the current film classification system, calling for new legislation and pointing out that even liberal Sweden had now introduced it. By courtesy of Dr Brian Mawhinney, I spoke to a meeting of parliamentarians in the House of Commons and showed some examples of the type of material we were concerned about. Several got up and left the room, which indicated, we were later told, that they felt too sick to see any more.

A careless rush across the patio brought me low at around the same time and threatened to inhibit my activities just when our video nasties campaign was coming to a head. A general election had been called for 9 June and, clearly, we should try to make legislation to control them a key issue. Walk about I could not, but our good friends Roy and Polly Bennett lent us their comfortable and well-equipped caravan. I would also need a team for our planned 'hustings' tour.

Steve and Kay Stevens rang to say that they were willing to help however they could and happily agreed to join me. We had posters made to stick on the outside of the van and a seat built so that I could speak to the crowds through its open roof – I'd be even more visible there than I would be standing on street corners. Our 'Children at Risk' campaign was launched.

With my physical condition being far from what is necessary for the heavy programme we envisaged, I wrote in my diary: 'Lord, you know everyone's heart. As true today and for ever, as when the disciples prayed together in the Upper Room. Especially I need to be sure of and rest in that truth at this time.'

We set off on our tour of the East Midlands and East Anglian towns and were immensely grateful for all the help we had from the various police forces while the local press, who obviously thought we were a one-off, gave us tremendous publicity. One of the most delightful occasions was our visit to Luton. As we stopped in a lay-by at the edge of town there was a knock on the caravan door. Who should be standing outside but our old friend David Atkinson, MP for Bournemouth South. He had come to speak on behalf of Graham Bright, the local MP, from whom we had a most sympathetic hearing and a promise – which we sought from all the candidates! – that if he was successful in the parliamentary draw for private members' bills he would introduce a bill to control video nasties.

It was by no means all solemn and serious and certainly the reporter from the Cambridge *Evening News*, who, like many other journalists, joined us on our way, caught something of its atmosphere. He produced a half-page piece enlivened by a photograph of me waving one of our Children at Risk posters as I stood half-way through the caravan roof. Under the headline, 'Hold my legs! she said . . . I didn't dare', the reporter told of how he had 'spent part of yesterday afternoon trying to push Mrs Mary Whitehouse through a hole in the roof of a caravan', and how he had 'tried and tried . . . Not that she was too fat, but the trouble was that the hole was too small. Only about a foot square and really meant for ventilation.'

I was sitting at the top of a set of decorator's steps, screwed on to the floor by one of our sons who had also stuck some upholstery to the top of the steps for me to sit on once I'd got my body through the hole.

The reporter made the most of the story, explaining how he and Kay Stevens inside the caravan could only see

> her [my] brown-trousered legs poking through the ceiling. While she communicated by loudspeaker to the outside world, we inside the caravan had problems communicating with her. She filled the hole so completely that there was scarcely any room for our voices to get through.
>
> In the end, I acted as a sort of messenger between her and Steve Stevens, shouting up at her past her midriff or applying my ear to the gap so I could hear her.
>
> Thus we progressed through central Cambridge and into the Market Square. 'Your children and families are in great danger,' declared the amplified Mary. 'Vote for the candidate who will fight for decency. I suggest you ask all your candidates for their policy on decency, video nasties, pornography, media violence and cable TV.'
>
> She was well received, particularly by young people who smiled welcomes. 'More and more young people are agreeing with what I've been saying for years,' she said.

And what an extraordinary sequel there was to Graham Bright's promise! Following the election the draw for the private member's bills took place in the House of Commons and whose name was drawn first by the office out of the hundreds of names in the ballot box? None other than that of Graham Bright. And within a year his Video Recordings Act was on the Statute Book. How grateful we were! But, as time went on, we came to realize, reluctantly, that those Acts deal only with the tip of the iceberg.

There were other signs of cheer. The change in public – even sixties liberal – opinion was quite vividly demonstrated in a *Times* interview of 11 March 1988 with the writer and broadcaster Bel Mooney. Having admitted that she would once have 'defended' the activities of Hugh Hefner of *Playboy* and

Bob Guccione proprietor of *Penthouse,* Mooney admitted that she now thinks that the well-known page 3 girl phenomenon 'is possibly, potentially more damaging than hard-core porn because it is as ubiquitous as sliced bread, and it's bad for you. If young men are forever seeing images of women as commodities, as dolled-up things, can we ever hope to create a society in which men do not regard women in that way, and as fair game?'

When asked whether any pornography at all should be available, even in adult-only specialist shops, Mooney said, 'I don't know, I just don't know. As a novelist I don't have opinions, I'm raising issues and values . . . but I do believe in my heart of hearts that every society has to have taboos, which are an essential part of civilized life; that there is a point beyond which you do not go. I'm just afraid that people who say no to censorship are not actually seeing what's lurking there, they're living in Cloud Cuckoo Land – and I think I did, and I don't any more.'

The story of Mark, which was published in the *Times Educational Supplement* of 21 October 1983, is one that I have quoted time and time again, and it never loses its impact either on me or anyone else. It is as true now as when I first read the story, that Mark's sufferings alone should be enough to move us, not only to profound pity – and guilt – but to action. And, of course, he is by no means alone.

Mark was a frail-looking boy of thirteen from an unsettled home whose father was 'violent one day, passive the next'. Mark had seen his mother beaten. His father bought a video recorder and joined a video club, 'regularly bringing home for family consumption the latest XX-rated video films'. The boy watched an increasing number of these films with his father until well into the night, often seeing the 'best bits' repeated in vivid slow motion. Consequently, he found it hard to sleep. When he did he had nightmares. When he got up, he would watch the video again instead of having his breakfast, and he would often rush his supper in order to watch again. The effect of all this upon his state of mind and body was appalling, though predictable. Dark patches under his eyes became a permanent feature. He lost weight. His school work suffered because he was too tired to concentrate. He couldn't take in new work, and his handwriting became illegible. His

voice and his hands would shake and he would 'laugh ner-
vously and become easily excited' as he talked about the latest
film he had seen, the violence of which he would describe
almost incoherently.

In the words of his teacher:

> All aspects of Mark's academic, emotional and even physical
> development were affected. His writing focused on describ-
> ing the latest tale of horror; his art work became a disturbing
> visual rendering of a mind which was obsessed with violence,
> with drawings full of torn bodies, blood and individuals kill-
> ing one another. His emotional stability had notably deterio-
> rated: he was aggressive, moody and tearful, and had become
> withdrawn and pallid.

The teacher who acknowledged that while Mark's behaviour
could not be blamed entirely upon watching violent videos
also said that it had made a considerable contribution to his
marked deterioration. Apparently, this had also been noted in
one of his friends who had only been exposed to such material
for a weekend.

The school intervened to ensure that Mark no longer had
access to such films, and his condition improved, but, as the
teacher asks, 'How much permanent damage has been done
to a child who was already emotionally disturbed?' May we
be forgiven.

The BBC transmitted a programme about video nasties
(*Open Space* BBC2, 22 June 1984) in which John Smyth, QC,
and I participated. Among those in the audience was a father
who spoke of an experience within his own family. One Saturday, his twelve-year-old son went to spend the morning with a
friend. When he came home he was not interested in his
lunch, nor later in his tea. His parents concluded that he was
probably sickening for something and got him off early to
bed. About midnight they were awakened by dreadful noises
coming from his bedroom.

When they rushed in to see what was the matter, they
discovered their son kneeling, screaming beside his bed, bang-
ing his fists upon the floor. He went on and on, unable to tell
them what was the matter, so they took him into their bed,
and held him until he eventually fell asleep. It was several

weeks before he was able to sleep alone again, and even then he would sometimes shout and cry in his sleep. Bit by bit, the full horror came out about the video nasty he had seen at his friend's house and, in the telling, a certain healing took place.

It was obvious, from the appearance and manner of these parents (both of whom were on the programme and spoke to me afterwards), that they were deeply caring people who would never have had such videos in their own home or knowingly allowed their child to see one.

An eleven-year-old boy took his mother's tranquillizers after watching video nasties (*Daily Telegraph*, 26 April 1984), while another eleven-year-old lived in such fear of a mutilated corpse bursting from his bedroom cupboard that 'he locked his wardrobe, hid the key and refused to go into his bedroom'. According to the Wolverhampton *Express and Star* he was still, eight months later, 'too afraid to sleep in the dark'. It was also reported that the boy was one of more than 150 children aged between ten and eighteen who regularly watched X-rated films at a local cinema club.

It took Mary Kenny's piece in the *Sunday Telegraph* of 21 May 1989 'Jason and the Churches' failure' really to bring home to me the terror of young Jason's death: asphyxiated during a homosexual orgy. He died, so the report said, 'with a tear running down his cheek'. Half the jury were apparently in tears too. Mary Kenny described how, listening to the report on the car radio, she 'had to pull up for a few moments just to weep'. She went on to castigate the silence of the Churches, and for that matter all of us, when we hear of the scandal of the little 'rent boys' who prostitute themselves for cash, living and, as in Jason's case, dying in the most appalling circumstances. Four men bought Jason for a homosexual orgy and, at the end of it – or maybe only in the middle – he was dead.

The degree to which children have suffered and continue to do so in our so-called permissive society was never more vividly illustrated than by a piece which appeared in the British press in September 1989. The story was told at the launching of the National Children's Homes drive to raise 14 million to care for abuse victims and their families.

A man who sexually abused his three-year-old son at bathtime deliberately dropped the little boy in boiling water so that his cries of pain would be attributed to scalding rather than to the father's abuse. Apparently the mother was deceived. This story only came to light because when the boy was eleven, he contacted the telephone child counselling service Touchline by ringing from a public call box and he continues to do so. Linda Whittaker, co-ordinator of the charity, said that the boy did not give his name because he is 'afraid of what his father would do, whether his mother would stand by him and because of his fear of splitting up the family and losing his brothers and sisters'.

Jonathan Dimbleby, the television presenter who chaired the charity launch, said, 'Child sexual abuse is such an unspeakable horror that most of us feel unable to do anything but avert our gaze from it.' How true. Nothing else could account for the fact that stories like these are losing their power to shock. We should be shouting our anger from the roof tops and demanding until we obtain it legislation to outlaw the pornography, so widely available, which stimulates the sex drive of unbalanced, immoral or uncaring adults.

'There is nothing referred to in that piece of film which is not already available in this country,' said the senior police officer from New Scotland Yard. He was speaking at one of National VALA's fringe meetings at the Tory Party Conference in Blackpool in 1987. The film in question was a video extract from the tape sent to us by Dr James Dobson, a member of the US Attorney General's Commission on Pornography (1986). In the film Dr Dobson, Chairman of 'Focus on the Family' made reference to

> one particular film of a little boy who had been abducted by a molester and then the molester took his picture and then those pictures were confiscated when they caught him. This little boy was nine years of age. He had blonde hair and kind of cute little haircut. In the first picture he was alive and clothed and for some reason was smiling. In the second picture – I will never forget it – he was nude and dead and had a butcher's knife in his chest. These videos are out there being sold.

Dr Dobson went on to say:

> Billions of dollars are made by selling pornography to kids.

Not just magazines. Are you aware of pornographic lyrics in rock music? Have you really taken time to listen to these lyrics, to get a feel for what your kids are listening to?

Prince. Do you know about Prince? He parades back and forth on the stage when he is giving a live concert and masturbates the neck of his guitar and ejaculate flies out of the end of it. 'Sugar Waltz' was number one. Do you know what 'Sugar Waltz' is? It is the waltz of the vagina. The song 'Like a Virgin' from Madonna says: 'feels so good inside'. Judas Priest sings 'Eat Me Alive' which deals with a girl being forced to perform oral sex at gunpoint. In '10 Seconds to Live', Motley Crew croons about intercourse in an elevator. This is what our kids are listening to and they are buying it by the millions.

It was in November 1989 that a team from the BBC's Radio Arts and Education features editor came to Ardleigh to talk to me about the School Kids *Oz* trial of 1971. Now that it was nearly twenty years since that notorious case they wanted to look again at the issues it had raised. This was one of a stream of obscenity trials beginning with *Lady Chatterley's Lover* (1960), through *Last Exit to Brooklyn* (1967), *Nasty Tales* (1973) and *Inside Linda Lovelace* (1976). Because of the ineffectiveness of the Obscene Publications Act (1959), all of these cases resulted in 'not guilty' verdicts, creating a situation where the police were powerless to act against obscenity.

I brought a private action in 1974 against the film *Blow Out* given an X certificate by the then GLC film viewing committee. It was about four professional men who decided to eat themselves to death, expressing a gluttony which had to be seen to be believed. The sex in the film was sadistic and explicit. I lost the case. Not because the film was not obscene – the magistrate declared it to be so – but because the cinema was not classed as a 'public place'!

The failure of the office of the Director of Public Prosecutions to produce prosecution witnesses in case after case was little short of a public scandal, and the high costs in these 'Not Guilty' cases meant that public funds were being used, albeit indirectly, not to protect the public interest but to finance the pornography industry. And there was no end to the battle. In the autumn of 1987 our campaign against the transmission by Channel 4 of Tony Harrison's poem 'v' with its stream of four-letter words was occupying our minds. We didn't even have to wait for the transmission of Harrison's poem for its effect to be seen, of all places, in the leader page of *The Times*. Bernard Levin – who else? – took the opportunity to quote from the poem. I'm tempted to do so too. After all, if *The Times* can . . . but no. Asterisks will act as a compromise.

> Aspirations, ... , folk on. . . . . dole
> 'Ave got about as much scope to aspire
> Above the . . . . . they're dumpted in, ...
> As coal aspires to be chucked on t'. . . . .
>   fire.

That's enough to make the point. Mr Levin's encouragement to his readers to listen to 'a poet of such talent read a poem of such quality' was more than a little sick-making. But he was put in his place by Ronald Butt, *The Times* political commentator, who referred to the way in which Levin had 'denounced as scent-hounds or book-burners anyone who objected to the broadcast and had condemned as part of a "campaign" the opinions of those who took this view as though his own article was not likewise part of a contrary campaign'. As Mr Butt said, Bernard Levin 'clearly despises anyone he thinks might be shocked and is determined that they should accept his definition of what is sayable and writable'.

The *Independent*, determined to show how independent it was, joined in the controversy by printing the whole of 'v', while *The Times* showed how fair it was by publishing my letter in the top of its correspondence column. Even several years later I can't help but feel I hit the nail on the head, certainly to my satisfaction, when having mentioned the IBA's obligation, under the Broadcasting Act 1981, to ensure that 'nothing is included in programmes which offends against good taste and decency', I went on: 'By agreeing to the poem's transmission, members of the Authority tell us that obscene four-letter words, piled up at a speed and with a force that magnifies their brutality, do not offend their individual standards of decency and good taste.'

And I wrote in my diary later that day:

> Now that *The Times* and *The Independent* have given *the* four-letter word an aura of respectability it will be very difficult

to challenge it elsewhere, including on television. Does this matter? I ask myself. Is it just a matter of fashion, of established taboos? Clearly there is no intrinsic 'badness' in the juxtaposition of four individual letters, the objections lie in the combined harshness and crudity of their sound combined with the coarseness of their usual setting – tenderness has no part in them – they have an intrinsic violence.

The controversial transmission on Channel 4 of 'v' provided a classic example of how some of those who work in the media live in their own Cloud Cuckoo Land. Reality to them is the script, the studio floor creating a close, incestuous atmosphere in which the viewer in the home has no reality and is afforded therefore, little consideration. The degree to which a broadcaster's 'right to transmit' has become sacrosanct, and to which all other considerations are secondary was clearly demonstrated by this transmission. Whatever Tony Harrison's justification for writing the verse – and his anger at seeing his parent's grave despoiled by such obscenities is surely well understood – the decision to transmit on television his rendering of 'v' was quite another. It raised many more profound issues than ever it resolved.

Did anyone, from the Chairman of the IBA down, involved in the decision to transmit the reading of the poem ask themselves what would be its effect on broadcasting as a whole? If a torrent of four-letter words are deemed acceptable at 11 p.m., the arguments for not using them at 10 p.m., 9 p.m. had surely been weakened irretrievably. Within days of the 'v' controversy National VALA wrote to each of the Governors of the BBC about the homosexual element in an episode of *EastEnders*, following it up with another letter about the same series two days later – Charlie Cotton tries to flog packs of cards, '52 pairs of different tits'. Cheap humour at any time, I told them; during family viewing time, 'unforgivable'.

A letter came from a Cheltenham man, a complete stranger, to support our stand against pornography and the findings of the 1991 Rochdale inquiry which had concluded that the Satanic rites described by a six-year-old boy were fantasies fuelled by watching horror videos like *Nightmare on Elm Street* and *The Evil Dead*. I'd never heard it better put.

He said that:

> While not blind to the good in our society, I am constantly depressed by the sheer scale of the evil in it – of which pornography is just an example. It is a corruption and debasement of the human spirit. It defiles and poisons the mind. It promotes the degeneration of one's attitude towards the dignity, rights and feelings of fellow human beings. It does not reduce us to the level of animals, since that plausible phrase is an insult to animals. It is evil in a way animals cannot be.

Nicola Tyrer writing in the *Daily Telegraph* in March 1991 referred to the evidence which showed that youngsters well below the age of eighteen are seeing X-rated films. She said that in *The Evil Dead* 'five young people spend a weekend in a haunted cabin. One by one the friends turn into homicidal monsters with green flesh and pupilless eyes, laughing maniacally as they set about chopping the hero to pieces. In self defence he kills them all in one of the bloodiest one and a half hours that I have sat through.'

Ms Tyrer goes on to say that *Nightmare on Elm Steet* contains 'scene after scene of terrified teenage girls being stalked, graphic mutilations and sickening images'.

Two or three days later the *Daily Telegraph* published a letter from me in which I said,

> Reading Nicola Tyrer's most timely and perceptive article 'Nightmares in every street' (March 15) one is tempted to say, 'We told you so, in and out of season for many years' – not out of pride but out of anger that children should still be paying such an awful price for our unwillingness to face up to the cost of ineffective obscenity laws.
>
> It does not matter a jot whether the cost is to the pockets of pornographers, or to the arrogant pride of those who are so sure that we are all incorruptible, no matter how gross and perverted our indulgences. The result is the same.
>
> At last people like Nicola Tyrer have smashed the façade behind which, in this country as elsewhere, fortunes have been made out of the hideous suffering of children. As long ago as 1986 the Conference of the International Association

Above, left: Aged two and a half – and not always as good as I look here, so I was told.

Above, right: Chester 1939, just before our wedding and the outbreak of war. Ernest and I are with (*left to right*) my mother, cousin and sister and a patch of cat mint, cuttings of which we have grown in each of our gardens since.

Below: Lichfield Road School, Wednesfield, Staffordshire where I held my first teaching post in 1931. I am pictured on the far right of the bottom row.

Above: In National VALA's office, which was created out of a room in our home in Essex.

National VALA's activities resulted in the presentation to the Prime Minister of 1,350,000 signatures for the upholding of public decency in 1972.

Above, left: Packing up the car in preparation.

Left: The crowds who accompanied us in delivering the petitions to 10 Downing Street.

Below, left: With Lord Longford who supported us. The campaign culminated in legislation to control indecent displays.

Above: Debating against Victor Lowndes, head of Playboy Clubs International, at Oxford University in 1981. We carried the motion that 'A licence for pornography is a denial of freedom' by 15 votes. (*New Standard*)

Below: Touring the marginal constituencies with Kay and Steve Stevens during the 1983 General Election. (*Leicester Mercury*)

The work with National VALA has allowed me to meet many interesting and famous people such as Pope Paul VI at Castel Gandolfo in August 1971.

Before addressing his officers I talked with James Anderton, former Chief Constable of Manchester.

A confidential chat with Cliff Richard during the presentation of the National VALA Award to *Blue Peter* in 1985.

Douglas Hurd popped in for a cup of tea during the setting up of the Broadcasting Standards Council. (*East Anglian Daily Times*)

Right: With Sir Harry Secombe, warming up on the *Highway*. (*Simon Butler*)
Below: Lady Thatcher's version of *Yes, Prime Minister*, which brought the house down in 1984. (*Daily Express*)

Magnus Magnusson presenting the National VALA Award for 1989 to Lord Buxton, Chairman of Anglia Television, for *Survival*. (*Anglia TV*)

Spitting Image. (*Central Television*)

The calm before the storm. Preparing to be gunged by Noël Edmunds. (*BBC Photo Library*)

Me whispering in the ear of Lord Hill, newly appointed Chairman of the BBC! (*John Jensen*)

I don't think Douglas Hurd and William Rees-Mogg saw me as such a threat at the launching of the Broadcasting Standards Council, but none the less it's one of my favourites. (*The Times*)

How does my garden grow? I always need Ernest to make sure it does!

of Democratic Lawyers was told that 'one million children, some as young as three or four, are traded on the international pornography market every year. Many never reach the age of 15: they either die of illness, commit suicide or are murdered in the so-called "snuff movies".'

And there was the recent case of the ten-month baby whose genitals had been bruised and torn beyond recognition by a man stimulated by pornography. Surely this is impossible to live with.

Dear Mrs Whitehouse

For some weeks now I have been looking for an address to write to you and in tonight's local paper there is a letter from you.

I also, like you, feel very strongly about pornography. In November last my husband left me and my 15-year-old son for someone else after 32 years of marriage. He left behind a lot of things in the garage and when my son started to sort it out he found a briefcase with these terrible books and magazines with pictures and stories and also in another box was a lot of dirty filthy letters from girls who he had been corresponding with and a lot of photographs that he had bought and I am sure he had taken some of them, he was interested in photography and they were terrible. I just didn't know such things existed. He never had them sent to his home address but to a friend's who keeps a shop and my son-in-law is sure that they were selling them but we can't prove that.

It is so distressing to think that you have lived with a man like that for so long and never knew what he was like and for my young son to have found them was disgusting. Now I know why you have made a fuss about it and why my husband thought you were interfering in things that didn't concern you.

The daughter of the woman he is living with is now 15 but she knew about her mother's affairs with my husband before anyone did, as she found letters from him when she was 12 and also she has just told her grandmother that she had found dirty books and photographs that her mother had, and it has affected her so much over the last two years that she is suffering from the slimmer's disease and she doesn't want to grow up.

It was the visit of Mr Alasdair Milne, one-time Director-General at the BBC, to our house in April 1993 which took my mind back to one of the most intense battles we had fought. He had come with the producer to talk to me about the late Sir Hugh Greene for a programme they were making about him. 'We didn't feel it would give an accurate picture of him without some references to you,' they said with knowing smiles.

Inevitably meeting Alasdair Milne again took me back to our battle over the showing of the film *Scum* which was made for the BBC, but as Director-General Mr Milne refused to allow it to be shown in 1978 in the *Play for Today* series, and was courageous enough to explain his decision on television. The film contained scenes of kicking in the genitals, a coshing using a sock full of billiard balls, an attempted braining of someone with an iron bar, an attempted drowning in a wash-basin and a homosexual rape.

His decision caused an outcry from the 'anti-censorship-at-all-costs-lobby'. However, Mr Milne stuck to his ground. The film was shown in the cinema with an X certificate, which meant that no one under eighteen could see it. However, Channel 4 started to take an interest in screening the film. The officer with special responsibility for films at the Independent Broadcasting Authority, remembering the earlier controversy, decided to view the film along with his colleagues on the film committee.

After the screening they sent a memo to Colin Shaw, then Director of Television at the IBA, now Director of the Broadcasting Standards Council, which read,

> We have grave doubts about allowing it to be shown. It contains a lot of violence and bad language, but even that could be defensible were it a film of any merit. In our view it is not. It is essentially an exploitation movie with stereotype characters appealing to the baser instincts which we feel would be difficult to defend.

National VALA decided to apply for a judicial declaration which was finally heard in the High Court on 13 April 1984.

Lord Justice Watkins declared that 'having regard to the IBA's statutory duties and to the history of divergent opinion as to the propriety of the film *Scum*, the Director committed a grave error of judgement in failing to refer it to the IBA for its decision as to whether it be shown'. He concluded by saying that I, as a licence holder, had 'sufficient interest to entitle her to seek and to obtain relief by way of declaration . . . I grant it, as I have already indicated, because I feel it is outstandingly important that so powerful a thing in our lives as television be carefully controlled.' His lordship went further, saying that the IBA itself was 'in breach of its duties' in not instructing the Director-General in what circumstances he should refer a programme to the IBA before it was shown. I was granted costs.

I was delighted by the result, feeling that it not only vindicated the action we'd taken but also because I felt it had underlined the rights of the ordinary citizen when faced with the power of a mighty Authority. The case would also, I felt, have a great impact on television standards in the future because the IBA would have to exert its authority more.

It's strange how things seem to go in waves – and it was a large one that struck our office early in November 1992, following the publication of our second Aids report: the decision to study the role of television in 'normalizing' casual sex followed the publication by Harvard University of a report dated June 1992 which predicted that, by the year 2000, 25 million people would have Aids and that up to 120 million would be HIV positive.

This appalling – and immeasurable – threat to human health and happiness is of great concern to us all, not least to those involved in television and film making. By reversing their acceptance of casual and promiscuous sex they could, we felt, help to turn the tide towards a more responsible social climate. The first step was to assess the size and nature of the problem by discovering how far permissive lifestyles characterized television programmes.

During the middle two weeks in September fifty-six of our monitors watched the 143 transmitted programmes between 6 p.m. and midnight which we felt might be relevant to the project. The results were striking. Reports back showed that in adult viewing hours (9 p.m. to midnight) 70 programmes contained characters who were faithfully married while 141 portrayed characters engaging in extramarital and promiscuous sex, 11 contained homosexual characters and 48 contained dialogue which took for granted sexual activity outside marriage. Grounds for concern, we felt. What was, perhaps, even more disturbing were the reports on the content of the 81 programmes shown before the established 9 p.m. family viewing time watershed. In this group 69 programmes portrayed characters as promiscuous, living together outside marriage and, in three cases, as homosexual. This was more than the number of characters shown as faithfully married.

On 8 November, the day of our Aids report publication, my phone rang at 7.20 a.m. Could the journalist concerned arrange to do a recorded interview with me in half an hour? 'Certainly,' I said and that started a stream of enquiries and eighteen recordings for press and radio right across the country including one for the BBC's World Service and another for Reuters. We took the phone off the hook at 5.30 p.m. by which time my voice had given out. It was encouraging that few of the journalists who interviewed me showed any of the antagonism so prevalent in the past. That was Monday. Tuesday was a sort of recovery day but Wednesday saw the publication of the Broadcasting Standards Council's *Annual Research Review into Sex and Sexuality in Broadcasting* and it all started again.

I thought the best thing to do was to put out a statement to the Press Association, which always deals very fairly with us. I said that the Review 'very much echoed our stand on violence and bad language but that as far as the treatment of sex on television is concerned, it depends what you mean by sex – it can be anything from a kiss to the portrayal of rape!' And that, I felt, invalidated that section of the report.

Among the radio interviews I did was one for Radio Glasgow who had also included a trendy producer, whose name now escapes me, and Colin Shaw, Director of the Broadcasting Standards Council. During the battle that ensued I referred to the link between foul language and violence saying that 'if foul words (four-letter ones, for example) are normalized through consistent use then that reserve of abuse for extreme cases of anger is removed and the use of actual violence in moments of anger become even more likely'. To my amazement – and gratitude – Colin Shaw, considering his previous attitude to our work, agreed with me.

The battle over *EastEnders* was intense but limited and in the years that have followed shown to be effective. And credit for this must go not only to our membership but also to the press and perhaps most importantly to those BBC professionals who, in one way or another, brought the change about.

But there has been and there remains another battle which has been on our agenda from the very beginning of our campaign thirty years ago – the battle against TV violence. As we fought it we found ourselves facing an implacable enemy, composed chiefly of so-called liberal academics and the 'freedom-at-all-costs' lobby – who have throughout the years denied the existence of any evidence demonstrating a link between media and social violence.

Many, many times, as we have debated the issue in the press, in universities and elsewhere, we have found that our opposition has depended upon twisted and percented statistics to make their case. Always very professionally and indeed cleverly presented.

Now times are changing. Concern about social violence – not least as it affects children – grows almost daily and it is essential that this, so far hidden or denied, be squarely assessed and the evidence acted upon. Over the years we have collected much of this evidence and I thought that now was the best and the most timely opportunity to itemize at least some of it for reference.

CHAPTER TEN

DANGEROUS VIOLENCE

But within nation states, or at least within our nation state, which is what matters to me, we have chosen the path of reason, to establish that civilized order is liberty under law, and government by consent.

Of late that civilized order has been increasingly threatened by unreason and lawlessness, violence and terrorism. Television may well have been, if not the cause, a contributing influence. By reflecting, television may have inflamed. By depicting, television may have magnified. By projecting, television may have incited. By accentuating, television may have encouraged.

Robin Day
Day by Day, William Kimber, 1975

20th September 1989

Whether or not there exists a clearly established relationship between violence on television and in society, the BBC believes it is prudent to assume there is one.

Yours sincerely

Henry Campion
Chief Assistant, Management Resources
Policy and Planning Unit
BBC

There is now a greater explicitness of violence being portrayed with excellent special effects and with sound, giving tremendous visual impact, and there is a greater explicitness in sexual encounters being shown in films, videos, and magazines. Although pornography has been present since humans could express themselves in drawings, it is only in the last 10 years that great advances in explicitness and quantity have been made in this country to the very worrying level we now find ourselves dealing with.

Although violence has long been a factor in life, the diet of violence now portrayed in films and television has reached a level where stronger control and a lessening of the confusion of the definition of obscenity is required. Whilst the family as a whole is being subjected to the obscenity in films, magazines, etc., there is a more stealthy intrusion into family lives through child pornography. Child pornography is now thriving and includes sexually explicit photographs, slides, magazines, films and video cassettes, audio cassettes and handwritten notes. This material is used for the sexual arousal and gratification of paedophiles.

In some cases coming to the attention of UK police, the arousal and fantasy fuelled by the pornography is a prelude to sexual acts with children.

> Superintendent Michael Hames, Head of New
> Scotland Yard Obscene Publications Department,
> speaking at one of National VALA's fringe
> meetings at the 1990 Tory Party Conference

It was the story of the thirteen-year-old boy who came before the court having committed unbelievable atrocities against a fourteen-year-old – he whipped, burned and beat him unconscious – that made me exclaim in desperation, 'What will it take, and how much more suffering will there have to be before the broadcasting authorities, video and film producers finally accept their responsibility for the situation?'

It moved me to write a letter to *The Times*, which was published on 13 August 1992, in which I said,

> One accepts that there cannot be a single cause for such decadent ferocity but it surely does reflect our society's obsession with violence. And when one has the situation which now exists when film, video and television all set out to entertain with cruelty and wickedness, often of a most tortured kind, how can we stand on one side and point the finger of horror and shame at lads who have grown up in a world in which sadism is good box office?

I went on to refer to a BBC2 programme *Q – The Winged Serpent* in which 'viewers were treated to the sight of the body of a totally flayed man lying on a bed, a man skinning another man's face with a large knife, another seen slitting a man's chest with a knife and digging out his heart'.

A couple of days later I received a letter agreeing 'that broadcasting is a major factor in society's violence today' from a professor in medical oncology who enclosed a copy of a letter published two years previously in *The Times* (24 July 1990) from Richard Reddy of Arizona, USA. I think it worth quoting at some length. He spoke first of how he had lived and worked for five years as manager of engineering for an oil company, among the various island peoples of Micronesia and the northern Marianas where each island group had its own distinctive culture. Having referred to the financial aid given to the islands by the United Nations, he went on,

> The island of Kosrae is characterized by gentle people. Five years ago there was no crime of any kind, the culture strictly controlled by the chiefs and extended family system.
>
> They decided to use their funds to become 'progressive' and develop commerce. Along with that came television, video cassette recorders and video tapes. As the local entrepreneurs responded to market demand, and the market, after seeing a few violent tapes, insisted on more of it, violent films began to dominate the videos.
>
> Within a short time violent acts began to appear in what used to be a peaceful population with no history of civil disorder. In addition to interpersonal violence and that against property one particular incident stands out: a group took exception to a decision that the attorney general made, broke into his house, tied him up, urinated on him and then burned his house down.
>
> On another island, Yap, a teenage boy was killed when two youths jumped out of the jungle and attacked him as they were, according to officials, acting out a horror movie.
>
> In contrast, the people of Ulithi atoll, about 2,000 of them scattered across a number of islands, about 100 miles from Yap, have decided to maintain their traditional culture. They ban violent and pornographic videos and they have no violence or deviation from their traditional sexual norms.

They help each other with the same community spirit that used to dominate Kosrae.

When one wants to determine the effect a particular outside stimulus will have on a particular society, one locates smaller simpler societies and studies the effect that stimulus has on these less complicated 'models'. Kosrae and Ulithi are both part of the same country with common ancestry, but each made a different decision regarding violent videos. Violence displaced Kosrae's traditional peace within a two-year period. There is still no violence on Ulithi.

'Is he really frightened that his children are going to turn into slashers?' was the apparently flabbergasted Michael Winner's elegant response to Prince Charles's outspoken criticism of television violence and sex when he opened the Museum of the Moving Image on the South Bank in London on 16 September 1988. Having become accustomed to Mr Winner's patronizing and arrogant dismissal of any views which might call into question his own judgement and activities, I was not surprised. After all, he was responsible for *Death Wish I, II,* and *III,* some of the most violent films ever seen in the cinema.

The response to the Prince's remarks by Steven Barnet, senior research fellow of the Independent Broadcasting Research Unit, was arguably even more offensive. 'I would much rather have the views of experts in the field than the subjective views and prejudices of people whose only qualification is as a parent.' Unbelievable. Apparently even a prince should not so far forget himself as to question the infallibility of researchers.

My own immediate reaction to the Prince's words was not only of gratitude but also of unreality, almost of disbelief. They echoed the words we had used up and down the country and far beyond throughout the previous twenty-five years:

> They say [said the Prince] that all you have to do if you don't like it is to switch the television off. And if, as parents, you complain that a diet of freely available and insensate violence is likely to influence the way some people behave and relate to others, then you are told there is absolutely no proof that violence on TV has any effect on people's behaviour. But that, as we all know, is palpable nonsense.

And within minutes of his speech that is precisely what he was being told.

The answer to whether or not they – in this case the BBC – take seriously all their avowed concern about the possible effect of television violence, and all their codes intended apparently to control it, could not have been more effectively answered with a powerful negative than by their repeated showing of *Fort Apache, The Bronx* first in September 1985, then in July 1987, and – Hungerford or no Hungerford, and promises or no promises to the Home Secretary by the Chairman – in May 1989. As one of our monitors reported:

> The film *Fort Apache, The Bronx* was about the rough, tough life in the Bronx, a district of New York, and portrayed the daily routine of the New York police in dealing with drugs and vice rackets in the area. It opened with a sequence of two 'rookies' – inexperienced police officers – sitting in their police car. A woman approached the car and without any warning drew a pistol from her handbag and fired all its shots into the officers, who were both killed outright.
>
> The woman who killed the police officers was a 'junkie' and was also involved in a prostitution ring. She solicited a man who was changing the wheel of his car, then led him to a warehouse where she proceeded to sexually arouse him before slashing his neck with a razor blade.
>
> Later in the film this same woman, in a drug crazed state, took a razor blade from her bra strap and slashed a man's face with it. He took out a flick knife and stabbed her in the stomach killing her and then two men rolled her body in a carpet and took her in the boot of his car and dumped her in the municipal rubbish tip.

As I said in my speech at our first public meeting in the Birmingham Town Hall in May 1964, 'If violence is constantly portrayed as normal on the television screen, it will help to create a violent society.' The story of broadcasting in the years since then vividly highlights the power of those who have access to the media, and to television in particular, to make nonsense of the lessons of human experience. The words were uttered, not as some profound, newly discovered, philosophical concept, but as a piece of plain and obvious common sense.

The historical truth of the matter is that throughout the centuries people have communicated, through hieroglyphics, through the spoken and printed word, through pictures, through still and moving film. These media have been the foundation of our culture, the basis of exchanged ideas and philosophies. Now, in the second half of the twentieth century, we have been invited, and in some cases persuaded, by the advocates of 'artistic freedom' to believe that television has no effect upon viewers' values and behaviour, even though the late Sir Hugh Greene, while Director-General of the BBC, once described television 'as the most powerful medium ever to affect the thinking and behaviour of people'. We forget that truth at our peril. But what we must also assess, if we are to keep our sanity, is the measure to which we have been deliberately misled, conned and exploited by those within the broadcasting industry who have consistently ignored not only their professional obligations but also the wealth of human experience now available.

It rapidly became perfectly clear that common sense was not going to be allowed to stand for its own sake. People, like ourselves, who challenged the accepted 'cant' that there was 'no evidence' that television has been a strong influence in creating the increasingly violent nature of our society, had to be discredited and proved wrong. In the face of persistent shouts of 'no proof' and 'censorship' – that most terrible of all accusations! – we had to produce academic as well as common-sense argument to support our case. We turned first to the publications of the broadcasting authorities.

The message of the codes on the treatment of violence published by both the BBC and the IBA is straightforward and, one would have thought, not open to misinterpretation by honest minds. It has been open to being ignored, not once, but constantly and – how could it be otherwise? – with the connivance of the people who published the codes in the first place. One of the BBC's most enlightened publications dealt with the treatment of violence in fictional programmes and was published back in 1959!

Having referred to the difficulties posed by what it describes as 'the fashionable cult of the anti-hero', it goes on:

The distinction between heroes and villains has become blurred and conventional morality may be replaced by a tacit acceptance of brutality as a necessary part of 'winning'. But makers of action/adventure series and of single plays need to remember that violence is subject to the law of diminishing returns. Excessive violence may rob the audience of its capacity to concentrate on anything else in the programme either at the time of its use or later. Any competition between directors in the use of violence for effect could eventually result in its dramatic point being lost. 'To go one better', may produce the opposite effect.

In 1950, the Home Office published its report on *Children and the Cinema* and as I browsed through a copy I could hardly believe my eyes!

The harmful moral effects attributed to 'bad' films are commonly centred on the exhibition and glorification of crime, violence and sexual licence, the latter nonetheless deplorable because it is often coated with a thin layer of conventional morality. Films of this latter class often pay lip service to morality in their dénouements, while flouting propriety throughout the greater part of the story and its contributory episodes. That many films do contain sequences that are brutal, anti-social or licentious is undeniable. Some of these sequences will pass over the heads of the youngest children, and it may be that only a few films err seriously in these ways; but these few must, on grounds of ordinary human experience, be accounted bad influences on the minds of those who see them. We have no doubts at all about such films. We think they are bad and we should like to see them banned altogether to children . . .

If that is true of the cinema, how can anyone deny its truth when applied to television, not to mention video?

In order to make our own research as comprehensive as possible we studied the work of internationally respected psychologists and social scientists like Leonard Berkowitz who, writing in the *Scientific American*, in February 1964 concluded that 'filmed violence is potentially dangerous . . . [it has] increased the chance that an angry person, and possibly other people as well, will attack someone else.' Still in the USA and reflecting growing public anxiety about social violence, President Johnson's Commission on the Causes and Prevention of Violence, 1969, concluded that: 'Violence on television encourages violent forms of behaviour and fosters moral and social values about violence in family life which are unacceptable in a civilized society.'

Two years later the US Surgeon General's Report decisively confirmed that view, and the strength of the evidence presented in the report forced all three major US television networks to concede that their previous insistence that the case against television violence had not been proven, 'was no longer tenable'.

In 1975 Dr Michael Rothenburg appealed for 'an organized cry from the medical profession' against violence on television and its effects on children. A child psychiatrist working at Seattle's Children's Orthopaedic Hospital and Medical Centre, he stated that '50 studies involving 10,000 children and adolescents from every conceivable background all showed that viewing violence produces increased aggressive behaviour in the young.' He went on to suggest that 'immediate remedial action in terms of television programming was warranted, and that every doctor's office and health clinic should have available guidelines for children's programmes'.

Dr Rothenburg underlined his claim by stating 'that the average American child, by the time he is 18, will have watched 15,000 hours of television, witnessed 18,000 murders and countless highly detailed incidents of robbery, arson, bombing, forgery, smuggling, beating and torture'. He declared that 'there is an average of six times more violence during one hour of children's television than there is in one hour of adult television.'

Just how little impact such information and advice has had upon programme content is tellingly illustrated by the following letter, published in the *Sunday Telegraph*, on 16 March 1986, which tells its own story.

Having read Alexander Chancellor's article [of 23 February 1986], 'Who cares about TV violence?' I was moved to do a small survey of my own, because I, and others, do care about television violence.

I am a primary school teacher, working with four-, five-

and six-year-olds, in a very 'middle-of-the-road' school in Hampshire. Since I started teaching 10 years ago I have seen a marked decline in the social behaviour and attitudes of the small children I teach. This has become apparent to many of my colleagues throughout the county. Children's play has become more aggressive; the incidence of bullying is commonplace and there are frequent complaints by children and parents about rough, hurtful play.

Over a four-day period I asked the children in my class what they played in the playground at morning break, and tabulated the results. It is quite clear, from this, that television *does* influence children's play. Out of 21 games, 13 are directly taken from television programmes. It explains to me the kicks, punches, deliberate 'roughing up' – in other words, violence – which occur during playtime when the children are imitating those television characters, recognized for their violent tactics.

I question whether these programmes are suitable for small children at all, but as they are screened at children's viewing time should not their content be scrutinized and their value assessed in the light of their audience? Since television has such a strong influence, then please let that influence be for good, not bad.

Dr William Belson's report *Television Violence and the Adolescent Boy* (1977) was based on six years' research at the London School of Economics and concluded that

serious violence is increased by long-term exposure to: plays or films in which close personal relationships are a major theme and which feature verbal or physical violence; programmes in which violence seems just thrown in for its own sake or is not necessary to the plot; programmes featuring fictional violence of a realistic kind; programmes in which the violence is presented as being in a good cause; Westerns of the violent kind.

Dr Belson found, for example, 'that teenagers exposed to violent programming committed 49 per cent more violent and anti-social behaviour than those in matched low exposure'. Dr Belson's report was specifically praised by Professor George Comstock of the University of Syracuse in his book *Youth Vio-*

lence, (Pergamon Press, 1986). He described it as 'the most substantial survey on the topic of TV violence and anti-social behaviour yet published'. Here in Britain it was largely ignored by the broadcasting media and was attacked by intellectuals like Professor Bernard Williams of Cambridge, who has been in the forefront of the lobby to protect the status quo.

It is chastening to recall what Dr T. R. Gurr said in his revised book *Violence in America.* He put the current wave of violence in the Western world in proper context:

> Historically, war has been the most obvious correlate of all the great crime waves in Britain and in the States. However, since the mid 50s almost all western societies have experienced a massive wave of crime and violence simultaneously. Although the US and Canada have the highest actual rates of murder and theft – with increases of 400–500 per cent – England has experienced 1100 per cent increase in violence due to its starting at a much lower level . . . The mass media saturated a whole generation with violent entertainment. It is plausible to argue that the 1960s saw a significant reversal in the long secular tendency towards restraining and not condemning violence.

This statement challenges us to lift the argument far above a 'matter of taste' – 'If she doesn't like it she can switch off.' We are confronted here with the question of our common quality of life for many years to come.

Worldwide, there are over 850 scientific studies and reports which leave no doubt as to the harm caused by television and film violence. These studies, compiled by the International Coalition on Television Violence (ICAVE) chaired by the American psychiatrist Dr Thomas Radecki in 1983, reveal an overwhelming consensus 'that violent entertainment plays an important and major role in teaching a culture of violence and distrust, to viewers of all age levels, social classes, ethnic backgrounds and intelligence levels'. Dr Radecki emphasizes that factual non-glorifying documentaries have been found to increase rather than decrease sensitivity to violence but goes on:

> However, when the purpose of the violence is to entertain or excite the viewer, or portray violence as a successful way

to resolve a conflict, the results have been quite harmful. Research shows that the most common effects are major increases in anger and irritability, loss of temper, increased verbal aggression, increased fear and anxiety, and a desensitization toward violence. Increases in fighting, distrust and dishonesty, decreases in sharing and co-operation, increases in depression, willingness to rape, and actual criminal behaviour have all been repeatedly found.

The research carried out by ICAVE has extended beyond television to books, not least because many violent books are made into violent films. It has studied bestseller fiction published from 1905 to 1988 and revealed that 'there has been a dramatic 61 per cent decrease in the number of positive or pro-social themes since 1966 when compared to the first half of the twentieth century'. During the same period, the research showed that sensationalistic, violent themes in bestselling novels have increased by over 300 per cent. Just how violent some of these books are is illustrated by a count of 509 acts of violence in *Red Storm Rising* by Tom Clancy, followed by *The Matarese Circle* by Robert Ludlum with 330 acts of violence. But back to television.

These studies have had little effect, losing out in the unscrupulous battle for ratings. 'Children see 80,000 horror scenes,' shouted *Today*'s front page headline on 4 October 1989. This was a reference to ICAVE's two-year international research into television violence and related to the number of scenes of violence seen by British children before they are eighteen. Dr Radecki had come to Britain to announce the results of his project to which we in National VALA had contributed by taking all programmes on all four television channels for two weeks per channel in September/October 1988 from 7 p.m. to 10.15 p.m.

CHAPTER ELEVEN

MORE DANGEROUS VIOLENCE

Quite how far violence has permeated our society was high-lighted by a 1988 advertisement for the National Society for Prevention of Cruelty to Children which included a photograph of a child being smothered, under the headline: 'It can take more than a minute to suffocate a five-year-old. Luckily, Jenifer's mother lost her patience again.' The no-doubt well-meaning advertisement went on to say that the mother then 'switched her method of attack to beating the terrified child with a length of plastic tubing.' All this was intended to arouse the compassion of people so that they would support the NSPCC. But it wasn't long before the complaints began to be heard.

Patricia Guinan, district clinical psychologist at the Blackburn, Hyndburn and Ribble Valley Health Authority, claimed that the explicit nature of the advertisement was 'capable of resulting in imitative behaviour in certain circumstances'. Indeed. After consulting medical experts the Advertising Standards Authority upheld her complaint. It found that 'it would be widely held among psychiatrists that the picture was likely to be provocative to anyone with murderousness in himself and could be an unintended goad'.

As Lord Deedes writing in the *Daily Telegraph*, said,

> Only one of two conclusions can reasonably be drawn from this, the first being that ASA and its psychiatric advisers are mistaken and have done the NSPCC a grievous injustice. If, on the other hand, there is substance in Mrs Guinan's complaint, then those who repeat like parrots that no proven link between television violence and crime in society exists are called upon at least to reconsider their arguments.

Because of National VALA's long-standing conviction that television plays a big role in the increasingly violent nature of British society, and our equally strong belief that television is the one contributory cause of social violence which, given the will, could quickly and effectively be dealt with at source, we have carried out monitoring projects to assess its incidence in programmes. The first two projects were carried out in 1985 and 1986 and the third – previously arranged – within three weeks of the Hungerford tragedy in 1987 which highlighted public concern about televised or film violence.

Our research showed that something like a quarter of all programmes on all four channels contained violence and we were highly critical of the broadcasting authorities in their failure to deal with televised violence in the months which followed Hungerford, and did not hesitate to say so.

The BBC had taken something to heart following our report but not much. '*Performance*' boasted a pre-screening announcement for 7 July 1991 on BBC 2: 'Its extremely violent and sexual content may be offensive to some viewers.' I hope that everyone intending to watch was already settled down because otherwise the warning would have been missed. In any case, nothing in the obligations under which the BBC is supposed to operate gives licence to the screening of such material. The film contained much gripping by the throat, the sight of a man being gagged before being tied to a car over which acid had been thrown, and, as just one example, a man is held down, his shirt ripped off and repeatedly lashed on his back with rope. The incidents of gross brutality proliferate again.

'What sort of person throws acid into the eyes of an elderly widow?' asked the banner headline. What indeed. The case came up at the Oxford Crown Court that week when two young men aged twenty-three were sentenced respectively to ten years in prison and nine years in a young offenders' institution.

It was the callousness of the exercise which was so appalling. Before calling on the seventy-five year-old widow, one told the other, 'She's lonely – on her own. She's got lots of money. All you have to do is to chuck the stuff in her eyes and knock her over.' The 'stuff' they chose was a bottle of kettle descaler which carried the warning 'Very corrosive, causes severe burns'. They also bought gardening gloves, presumably to protect their own hands. The old lady was punched and her glasses removed. The descaler was splashed in her face and eyes. Her attackers stole 320 cigarettes, half a bottle of rum and a tray. Their victim spent four months in hospital and, at the time of writing, her sight is still impaired.

My anger, when I read the story, made me ask how in a supposedly civilized country, such an outrageous thing could happen. Of course, one must never forget the responsibility everyone has for his own actions, but my exasperation went deeper than that. Had not these young men grown up in a society which has not only come to terms with violence, but turned it into entertainment in the films, videos and television programmes, which have, a little at a time, desensitized us all? Of course, I told myself, and then again asked 'Why are film makers, television programmers and video producers, not prepared to sacrifice the viewing figures, the hard cash which is their reward? And when – if ever – will those in positions of final authority, in government, broadcasting and the courts, make a reality of the obligation laid upon them?

'We lost!' said the senior police officer referring to a recent obscenity case involving a rock and roll record, 'And, to tell the truth, I think we have now reached the situation where matters are totally out of hand and there is nothing that we can do to control it.'

'Well, what about this one? Surely *this* is actionable?' I said, referring to a song broadcast on Radio 1 called 'Skin her alive' which goes on to tell of the 'pleasures' of killing a female victim. No, he didn't think so.

Peter Mullen, writing in the Yorkshire *Evening Post*, to whom I'm indebted for the above, went on to say:

Now isn't that just lovely? Other bands such as Obituary and Cannibal Corpse sing much worse songs – yes, there is worse, but I won't quote them here. Just what the hell do we think we're playing at, allowing this sort of thing to be published and even broadcast on the BBC? Don't we have enough rapes and murders without glorifying them on the music stands and over the air waves?

A victim himself? An eighteen-year-old St Austell youth admitted at Truro Crown Court (13 April 1992) that he had killed a twenty-one-year-old girl whose mutilated body was found trussed up in a bedspread and dustbin liners in the attic of a house in St Austell. Adrian Smith, alias Chaffe, who lived in the same block of bedsits pleaded not guilty to murder but admitted manslaughter on the grounds of diminished responsibility. That plea was not accepted by the Crown.

Prosecuting, Mr Neil Butterfield, QC told the court that Chaffe had killed Angela by cutting her throat, almost to the point of decapitation, after having hit her sixteen or seventeen times with a lump hammer. He had returned to her flat the following day and mutilated the body, probably with her electric carving knife after he and his girlfriend had watched videos which included scenes of horrifying violence and mutilation. Chaffe told police officers that he had burgled her flat during the day and decided to return the property he had taken. He killed Angela, he claimed, when she surprised him on her return from work because she would have recognized him.

Dr Randle Thomason, a consultant forensic psychiatrist, told the court that at the age of seven Chaffe had been referred to a consultant child psychiatrist and an education psychologist because of his aggressiveness and dishonesty. At a children's home he had smashed up the dining room, carved graffiti into a toilet door, cut the bathroom curtains to ribbons and attacked the swimming-pool liner, causing considerable damage. Dr Thomason added that Chaffe's lying in his witness statement, his limited capacity to feel emotion, the destructive violence of the killing, the subsequent mutilation of the body and his 'obsession with knives were all evidence of a major personality disorder'. Perhaps that is the answer to the media's obsession with violence and our own acceptance of it. I wonder if society as a whole can suffer from 'a major personality disorder'?

The public outcry here in Britain which followed the murder of two-year-old James Bulger had worldwide repercussions not least among the boffins of the film and television world. One of America's most powerful TV moguls, Howard Stringer, who heads CBS, declared that his network would be cutting back on shows which were 'hurting American society by portraying rape, murder and violence. When things are as rough and tough as they are on the street, we have a responsibility to assess violence in programming.'

Whether or not it was the result of genuine concern, or fear of the effect of such a move by its main rival CBS, NBC declared its intention to change its emphasis to include more 'adventure stories, comedies and dramas with family-orientated themes'. Its president, Warren Littlefield, declared, 'We found our shows were a little too dark, a little too much centred on crime,' while the Chairman of Federal Communications Commission, James Quello, warned, 'The US is nearing the time when it should consider laws creating "violence-free safe harbours" during evening programming.' His view has been backed by a newspaper survey showing that 72 per cent of viewers thought there was too much violence in entertainment programmes, although some accepted it in news or 'docudramas' on law enforcement. Mr Quello added: 'Writers and producers must be encouraged or directed to use their creative juices for more constructive purposes, to fashion meaningful drama that inspires, excites and entertains.'

American playwright Arthur Miller joined in the condemnation of television and film violence saying it was responsible for youth crime and claimed that ' Britain was only at the start of a violent crime wave.' The author of *Death of a Salesman* and *The Last Yankee* said America was in the grip of a crime wave where murders like the Bulger case happened every day. In a message to Great Britain, he said:

> I come from a place where what you have just witnessed happens about 20 times a day. The single major cause of death in the US among black teenagers is guns, gun shots. I think it is an unravelling of the social fabric. You are probably at the beginning of it and we are in the middle of it.

So what's to be learnt and when will we learn it? I believe it's true that no outcry following any other murder has been comparable to that which followed the discovery of Jamie's body. However soon we outsiders are able to forget, his family never will. The challenge to us as viewers is immediate, specific and for ever: pens to paper, phones – no matter the ongoing cost – at the ready, visits to MPs' surgeries, letters to the Minister of the Arts and the Prime Minister.

Plenty of evidence is available, although there has been some improvement at 'family viewing time', that the type and amount of violence shown on all channels – Channel 4 being the worst culprit and BBC the least culpable – is now far in excess of anything seen in, say, the eighties.

The *Daily Mail* was one of a number of national and provincial papers which carried out its own monitoring of televised violence after Jamie's death in March 1993. Its researchers watched all programmes between 3 p.m. and 1 a.m., including four satellite stations, during one typical week covering the whole spectrum of broadcasting. They found, 'There were more than 400 killings, 119 woundings and 27 sex attacks on women. Vicious weapons were wielded, foul and abusive language reverberated.' It was a comprehensive piece of monitoring and covered every programme and trailer from news and comedy to drama and films. The newspaper went on to point out that:

> At the very least, these findings provide statistical proof that the Government is more than entitled to question the ethical approach of the television companies.
>
> It is a common defence of British broadcasters that what they show on our screens simply reflects life. Yet this hardly bears scrutiny. According to the latest official figures, there are 14 killings in Britain in the average week.
>
> In the week when we monitored the eight channels, 401 people were sacrificed in the name of entertainment. And that figure does not include deaths where the actual moment of killing is not seen by the viewer.
>
> There is no doubt that satellite television is more violent than terrestrial. In the course of a week, there were 193 killings on Sky Movies Plus and 96 on the Movie Channel.
>
> A typical example is *Friday, the 13th* Part III, with 19 deaths. Victims are variously butchered . . . All the killings are accompanied by exaggerated sound effects. . . . Incidental music is used to quicken the pulse of the watcher.

We were, of course, quite unaware that the publication of our second report (*Murder and Mayhem*, 21 October 1991) would coincide with the riots which broke out in Cardiff, South

Shields, Oxford and Birmingham in the late summer of 1991. We had reported on the violence in twenty-seven late-evening programmes and claimed that 'the crude and sadistic violence in many late-night programmes meant that the BBC governors and the controlling bodies of ITV and Channel 4 were failing in their duty', and had set out in some detail the type of violence to which we were referring: 74 shootings, 19 incidents with knives, swords, razors, etc., 29 episodes of violence involving women and five incidents of arson as well as numerous car crashes. Two episodes in Alan Bleasdale's drama *GBH* were included as well as films like *The Untouchables*, *Extreme Prejudice* and *Manhunter*.

As we made clear at the time the report showed that there was not necessarily more violence but that it was more explicit and sadistic, pointing out that the violence shown on some of Channel 4's *Banned* series had, without doubt, 'opened the floodgates'.

However, the *Independent on Sunday* (6 June 1993) carried a full page feature headed 'Hollywood: when the killing had to STOP' with the sub-title 'This summer, family entertainment takes the place of celluloid gore. Have we seen the last of the action hero?' We were told how Arnold Schwarzenegger, producer of blockbusters bristling with machine-guns and flame-throwers, 'was not pleased' when he saw the prototypes of his latest film *The Last Action Hero* with 'its murderous robots and blood-spattered scenes'. He, along with other film-makers, has apparently had a 'change of heart'. The films he made in the eighties contained, according to one assessment, between 35 and 148 violent acts an hour.

And he is not alone. Apparently film-makers everywhere are increasingly accepting the power of filmed violence to undermine the social and moral health of society and seeing the importance of the preservation of family values. How wonderful that is! – if true.

CHAPTER TWELVE

WHAT A LIFE!

Looking back I can see how every year in our now nearly thirty-year campaign has been different. Each one interesting, challenging and full of the unexpected opportunity, but perhaps the twelve months between the summers of 1987 and 1988 can lay claim to have been among the most exciting, varied but also tragic.

In August, after a crazed gunman ran amok in Hungerford – '*Rambo*-style killings', the papers said – my own life was threatened in copy-cat style. I appeared, and much enjoyed the experience, on the *Dame Edna Everage Experience*, while the Government announced the setting up of a Broadcasting Standards Council. That autumn the worst hurricane for a couple of centuries played havoc with our garden and countless others; Channel 4 transmitted Tony Harrison's four-letter word poem 'v'; the Governors of the BBC invited me to Broadcasting House for the first time to attend a seminar on television violence, and a few days later Ernest and I were guests of Mrs Margaret Thatcher at a reception at No. 10 Downing Street.

In the space of a few months the Home Secretary, Douglas Hurd, announced that the government intended to bring broadcasting under the 1959 Obscenity Act, something else National VALA had long worked for, while at the same time Marmaduke Hussey, Chairman of the BBC, assured the Home Secretary that 'violence, sex and bad language' would be curbed, as public and parliamentary pressure against violence on television grew with almost every passing day. No longer were we the lone voices that some had always claimed we were. But just how well, or otherwise, the Chairman's intentions translated into programme content is another story – see Chapter 8. *EastEnders* constantly made headlines with its arson, bribery, homosexuality, and rape, even though it is transmitted in family viewing time. (It has to be said that much 'cleaning up' has taken place since.)

I debated in the Cambridge Union and preached at Rugby School, wrote to President Reagan about the programme *Air-base* and received a personal reply, did some heavy gardening and fractured my spine. That little exercise destroyed my mobility for months or, rather, years, but left me free to write, do telephone radio interviews, and television producers came to see me instead of the other way round. Extraordinary: I'd never been more handicapped, yet rarely more in demand!

Prince Charles attacked sex and violence on television, Mrs Thatcher backed him up and National VALA wrote him a letter of thanks. I gave a fourteen-minute talk on the BBC World Service and reviewed Joan Collins's book *Prime Time.* The *Reader's Digest* published a poll on the public's attitudes to violence on television, relating it specifically to our work: 43 per cent supported us, 36 per cent were against, 25 per cent didn't know. Not bad at all, we thought. National VALA was invited to answer a questionnaire on sex, violence, and bad language on television, for consideration by the Broadcasting Standards Council. We invited Lord Rees-Mogg, the Council's Chairman, to be the guest speaker at National VALA's 25th Anniversary Convention in March 1989 and he accepted. I agreed to be interviewed by Boy George for the *Tatler* magazine. We made a special appointment to see Duke Hussey, about *Rumble Fish* with more than seventy obscenities including many four-letter ones. My diary reminds me that 'during the meeting the film was strongly defended by John McCormick, Secretary of the BBC, but not by Mr Hussey himself.'

An unforgettable year, but let's take it a little at a time . . .

Sixteen people dead at the hand of a crazed gunman. Ordinary people going about their normal everyday life suddenly confronted by a *Rambo* style killer. A sixty-six-year-old man, who threw himself across his wife's body to save her, was shot dead, as was the kind-hearted taxi driver who looked after pensioners, the mother picnicking with her children, a man walking his dog, an elderly couple having a cup of tea in their kitchen, and the rest.

Because our concern about the link between televised and social violence was so well known we held our fire for a few days and left the platform to others. How well it was filled. Prominent public figures, editorial writer after editorial writer, linked the event to the glorification of violence on television. But to what effect? The BBC axed the film *Black Movie* due to be screened the same weekend and also withdrew *Body Contact* from the September schedules, but ITV screened an episode of *The Equalizer*, with its trigger-happy shootings and killings, the following evening. Although an episode of *The Professionals* and the violent western *Nevada Smith* were cancelled, an episode of *The Bill* went ahead. This, even though the programme opened with a mad gunman on the loose. The possibility of sudden death became personal to me through threatening letters which resulted in day and night police protection and a warning to keep away from the windows for several months.

Just how far ratings – and therefore hard cash – ruled the thinking at Thames TV in those days was vividly illustrated by a spokesman for the company who said, within a week of the Hungerford shootings, 'We have an episode of *The Bill* being shown that includes a hostage shoot-out situation which has echoes of Hungerford but on a smaller scale. We looked at that very closely two or three times and decided that there would be nothing wrong in showing it.' He went on, 'Programmes may be dropped from the schedules within a day or two of the tragedy out of natural respect for the dead but that obviously is not going to last for ever.' Incredible.

Not that TV moguls were alone in their insensitivity. Following complaints from passengers, some of them with children, about the showing of Michael Winner's *Death Wish III* on a National Express coach on the night of the Hungerford shootings, we wrote to the coach firm's managing director to tell him that this film had 'a body count of 60, many of them police, which worked out at one killing every ninety seconds'. The firm moved promptly to ensure that such films would not be shown again on its coaches, which reassured us that good sense still prevailed in some quarters, at least.

One of the most controversial programmes of the year was the screening on 1 March 1988 by the BBC of its play *Airbase*, described by Lord Rees-Mogg, then Chairman of the Broadcasting Standards Council and a former Chairman of the BBC's Board of Governors, as 'straight anti-American propaganda'.

Criticism of the play was widespread: it was described as 'a ludicrous misrepresentation of American airmen in Britain' in which US servicemen and women were shown injecting themselves with drugs freely available over the canteen counter, drinking heavily and eventually precipitating a world war.

Maybe my generation, which remembers the decisive support given to the Allies in the 1939–45 war and in the difficult years that followed, when my own children were small and were therefore beneficiaries of the Marshall Plan, will be more sensitive to insults to our friends. I felt so ashamed of that play that I wrote a personal letter to President Reagan apologizing to him for the insult to his forces who were, after all, our guests.

In his personally signed reply, the President said that my letter had 'confirmed the warm relationship between our countries and our people particularly the latter. The bond between us is treasured, I'm sure, by the great majority of our two peoples, and I'm also sure we both pray it shall always be the same. Again my heartfelt thanks.' I treasure that.

Not quite all was trial and tribulation, however. In July, Ernest and I drove down to London to take part in a recording of *The Dame Edna Experience* in which I was to be the first victim of a new series. Having met Barry Humphries in Australia a few years earlier, and enjoyed it – I still have the koala bear he gave me – I didn't feel too overwhelmed, though it certainly was a once-in-a-lifetime experience. And the transmission of the programme in September provided considerable and much-appreciated light relief. Amazing, the number of people, especially men!, who stopped me in the street afterwards to tell me what fun they thought it had been. The 'gladdy' bulbs which Dame Edna gave me blossomed happily the following summer, a cheerful souvenir of a one off night to remember – not least because of what happened to 'Dr Kurt Waldheim'! Each of the guests, Cliff Richard, Sean Connery and myself, entered the set through a curtain on to a small platform, and then walked down several flights of steps before being welcomed with a great flourish by Dame Edna. Sean Connery, I wrote in my diary next day, was 'surprisingly shy but rather endearing', while Cliff very kindly rejected a suggestion from the Dame that maybe I was something of a prude – or words to that effect. 'Not at all,' said Cliff who made it clear that he supported our work.

Then with the greatest flourish of the lot 'Dr Kurt Waldheim' was announced. In he came, bowed to the assembled audience, then stepped briskly down the first flight of steps before the floor opened and he disappeared. What a chorus of dismayed cries – and both Cliff and I rushed across the platform believing it really *was* the doctor! Then, realizing that we had witnessed a very clever stunt, a roar of laughter brought the house down.

There were areas of encouragement. The concern about the link between televised and social violence highlighted by the Hungerford tragedy was not just a five-day wonder. Increasingly in parliament, from the pulpit and in the press, pressure upon the broadcasting authorities grew. And in spite of the rearguard action by certain broadcasters and film-makers – notably Michael Winner – the nature of the society in which we live and the role of television within it came under increasing scrutiny. Words were not minced.

The idea so beloved by commentators and practitioners that 'television reflects society' and that such a notion is sacrosanct and can justify almost anything, began to be treated with less than total approval. Common sense was being allowed, albeit very, very slowly, to raise its head again. I couldn't help but recall how a quarter of a century earlier at our first mass meeting, we had said what was to us a matter of obvious fact, that, 'If violence is shown as normal on the television screen it will help to create a violent society.' How we were laughed to scorn.

Well, I suppose I ought to have had more sense. Everyone said so anyway – 1987–88 had been a dreadful winter, very wet, and I, following threats to my life, under orders from the police not to go near the windows even to *look* at the garden, let alone work in it. No weeding done at all. Then came the day early in March when I was free again and could go out to deal with the great clumps of dock growing deep in the heavy wet soil. I dug up some of them and needed to clear them away to the compost heap. Fetch the barrow, was my first thought. Too much trouble – it's right down the garden, came the second, so I leaned down, heaved up as much as I could and carried the heavy load across the lawn. 'Big doors swing on little hinges,' they say and certainly that short walk radically changed my life for years to come.

I'd fractured my spine and when I saw the X-ray – straight

down so far, then off at an angle of 45° – there was no argument about that. 'Irreversible,' said the specialist with a cheerful smile, 'but after about a year you should be in less pain. However, you mustn't fly, travel by train, stand, or sit on an upright chair.' Oh, well, at least I could walk and drive in a car so long as I was well cushioned. I could still talk, write, do radio and television interviews and, after some weeks spent more or less flat on my back, I did.

And then there was the miracle. Following a CAT scan, I was called to see the consultant who had first attended me. He apologized for 'all the anxiety' he must have caused us over so many weeks but he told us that both he and the other consultant he'd brought in from the hospital 'had been convinced' by what they saw in the X-rays that I had cancer of the spine. But now he told us 'there was no sign of cancer in my spine or any other organ of my body'. How grateful I am to all those who have prayed so faithfully for me at this time.

I recorded in my diary that 'I had said to Ernest on our way to see the specialist that morning that I was sure that if the Lord had further work for me to do, he would make me physically fit to do it – if not then I was in his hands and I was content to leave myself there.' There were certain limitations, however, that I had to accept. My spine, I was told, was 'paper thin' and I must be very careful. It was bent with the fractured and compressed vertebrae and that, I was told, was irreversible. But five years later, I am amazed – and profoundly grateful – for the way in which I have been enabled to carry on.

It would be less than honest of me to give the impression that this has been an easy time. Travelling, speaking, not only all over the country but abroad, had tuned my body and mind into the challenges – and pleasures – of an active life. Having watched the transmission on Channel 4 on 20 October 1988 of an interview with me filmed as I sat in the garden the previous summer I wrote in my diary:

> Struck with the difference between the picture I
> represented on Channel 4 yesterday – peaceful, happy
> and full of faith – with the way I feel now, lonely,
> frustrated and lacking in the joy that faith gives. When
> I'm not, as now, involved in initiatives, with activities, with
> the travelling and meeting people that that involves, then I

do feel isolated, and for the first time I find myself anxious about growing old and lonely . . . Come on, Mary, snap out of it. Self pity suits no one. 'Walking on the water is easy to impulsive pluck but walking on the dry land as a disciple of Jesus Christ is a different thing.'

And certainly, there was no shortage of events to keep me busy as, for instance, the repeat of *The Singing Detective* in June and July 1988 in spite of a record 652 letters of protest and in spite of Duke Hussey's promise to the Home Secretary that 'the BBC will take firm steps to eradicate unnecessary and gratuitous violence, sex or bad language from its programmes'.

The summer months are usually quieter than the hectic autumn and winter ones. But not in 1988. August that year was dominated by the controversy over the blasphemous film *The Last Temptation of Christ* which had already opened in the USA and was expected to open here in September.

The week following my eighty-second birthday in 1992, which had been exciting enough, wasn't exactly a usual week, but it was a very interesting one. It began with a visit from my old Australian campaigning friend, the Revd Fred Nile MP and his wife Elaine, also an MP, followed later in the day by a journalist and photographer from *The Times*. Next day a feature writer came from the East Anglian *Daily Times* and the BBC rang. They intended to do a television *Desert Island Discs* which they're calling *On the Mantelshelf*, basing the interview on the objects displayed upon it! I wrote in my diary, 'Tickled by the BBC chap's description of me as an "icon" – been called some things in my time but never that before! He said that he so described me because I was so well established in the country's mythology. Well, I hope I'm not a myth or – to use Ernest's description of an icon – "a silly little metal thing!" '

Then there was the visit of the BBC's *Songs of Praise* team and the interview with me in the garden in the lovely June sunshine, ready for a programme in September to celebrate Dedham church's 500th anniversary – what a lovely building that is! Tokyo Radio rang – wanted me live on its early morning programme between 7.30 a.m. and 9 a.m. 'What time is that in Britain?' I asked. Between 11.30 p.m. and 1 a.m. came the reply. That, I'm afraid, was just not on. A few days later they rang again. Could they fax me some questions and a tape? That was fine.

A German radio journalist rang: could he come and do an interview? Well, there was no problem about that but I couldn't help but think what a blessing it is that so many foreigners speak English.

But probably the most extraordinary and wonderful event of that week was the letter I received from Kereilhouviu Kire, President of the Angami Women's Organization in Kohima, Nagaland. After paying tribute to our work she went on to say that she was writing on behalf of her organization

> because we face a situation of all-round degradation in which we have no choice but to do something in faith and defiance as we deeply care for our children and what they will become.
>
> Angamis are one of the tribes of the Nagas belonging to the Tibeto-Burmese family. We straddle the border between India and Burma. Starting from the Second World War, which we ourselves experienced when the British and the Japanese fought at the famed battle of Kohima, the turmoils of change have profoundly affected our people also as elsewhere. The resultant search for identity and direction and our inability to match the challenges of modernity has produced confusion and despair among our people. We believe the conflicts of transition are rendering our people extra vulnerable to the cheaper diversions that lead to addictive escapism. I am here referring to the virtual inundation of our society by blue videos and pornographic magazines and heroin, the last being abundantly available from the golden triangle of Ne Win's Burma.
>
> In our search for ways to meet the challenge we have felt the need to draw from others like yourself who would be able to offer advice from their experience and conviction. We shall therefore be deeply grateful if you would be in a position to share anything from all that you have done, particularly in fighting the deliberate push of obscenity and smut in video films and literature by unscrupulous members of society.

Needless to say we responded immediately!

All this verbal international activity, perhaps especially my meeting again with Fred Nile, made me realize once again that, living the kind of life I do, I never know what is going to happen next!

The summer months of 1992 could by no means be described as the 'silly season' either in relation to international monetary or broadcasting affairs. The row over the speech by Channel 4's Michael Grade at the Edinburgh Television Festival in August, in which he launched his bitter attack against Duke Hussey and John Birt, Chairman and Director-General of the BBC dominated broadcasting news for days, and left Grade looking both childish and silly. What was believed to be a long-held ambition to become Director-General of the BBC had come to nothing and thus left him, so it would appear, a frustrated man. But what a blessing, if Channel 4's output is any indication of his choice of programmes.

But there were positive responses to the controversy. Jane Thynne, media correspondent of the *Daily Telegraph*, wrote on 31 August 1992 of the intentions, outlined by Lord Nicholas Gordon Lennox, of the twelve-member governing body of the Corporation to make the BBC more accountable. They proposed: To strengthen the criteria of measuring programme success; To clarify the role of governors as regulators; To improve communication with the viewers.

When I read that I heaved a great sigh of relief. Could it *really* be that some of the main facets of our work were to come to fruition? Time will tell, but I find it hard to believe that such news would be allowed to leak if it did not have a firm foundation. And I pondered on how long – nearly thirty years – has been necessary for fundamental change to take place in long-established bodies such as the BBC: but good luck to them. I wondered how we would have reacted if we had known that in the early days of our campaign.

I asked myself another question: what role has the Broadcasting Standards Council played in this change of heart? Is the Board of Governors less motivated by altruism than by the awareness that if it doesn't do the job it is appointed to do, then the BSC will do it? Perhaps it is more likely that the Governors are waving their flag because the Charter comes up for renewal in 1996!

There was also some cheer to be taken from the announcement on 12 September 1992 by the Home Office Minister, Michael Jack, that he was considering reframing the present obscene publications legislation to provide effective control over sexually explicit 'educational' videos, and over European pornography coming into Britain via satellite.

Why only *some* cheer? Because I had to ask myself, why legislative changes to deal with only those classes of pornography? Why not go the whole hog and introduce effective legislation to replace the *criminally* weak 1959 Act? What an encouragement *that* would provide after all these years of battling to achieve it!

CHAPTER THIRTEEN

TWENTY-FIVE YEARS LATER

The 25th Anniversary on 27 January 1989 of the launching of the Clean Up TV Campaign brought congratulations from many people prominent in Church, politics and the mass media. On behalf of all those faithful folk who have campaigned with us over the years, many of whom are with us still, I quote some of the good wishes we received.

From the then Archbishop of Canterbury, Dr Robert Runcie:

> Your indefatigable work on behalf of viewers and listeners has been a fine example of voluntary enterprise in defence of Christian values throughout the last 25 years.

From the then Prime Minister, the Rt Hon. Margaret Thatcher:

> You have much to be proud of in your Silver Jubilee year and I hope the Association will have many more Anniversaries to celebrate in the future.

From Sir Peter Imbert, Commissioner of Police:

> Allow me to add my congratulations to the many you will have received. May I wish you every success and offer the hope that your half-century finds you 'not out' and still going strong.

From Lord Grade of Elstree:

> Your singleness of purpose in the face of all opposition has

been admirable and I think it wonderful that your organization has achieved so much recognition.

Mr Jon Davey, Director General Cable Authority:

National VALA's valuable role has been to put broadcasters and regulators on their mettle, to make sure that they are caused to reassess, defend or modify what they are doing. It is right that those with power and responsibility should be placed in that position. I am glad that you have been there to do it.

The media, including television, were surprisingly generous. Maurice Chittenden of the *Sunday Times* came to do an interview; BBC *Breakfast Time* rang to ask if I would like to present my own programme on 27 January. I would sit in the director's gallery talking about why we started in the first place, give examples of the highlights of our campaign and some idea of what we see for the future. I wrote in my diary that night '*Me*, functioning at the very heart of the BBC! What Sir Hugh Greene would have said beggars description!' But I managed it, with considerable help from the staff.

ITN rang to arrange an interview, as did *Wogan*, and Reuters correspondent came. I quote my diary again:

I couldn't do the ITN interview because it clashed with *Wogan* which in itself was certainly an experience! We left home at 4 p.m. and ran smack into the most awful traffic, what a nightmare that was! We arrived without time for a rest or make-up! And the show itself was an absolute free-for-all – Andrew Neil, head of the new Sky Satellite programme was, as usual, very hard and quite unrelenting in his defence of TV – wouldn't accept that there was any link between television violence and social violence, while Ludovic Kennedy supported his view without reservation – 2 to 1 wasn't in it!

Ernest said I looked very pale. Felt it, after that shambles of a car drive. No meal and certainly didn't fancy any of the sandwiches. Left by a side door pushing our way through a crowd of autograph hunters and photographers who, we were told, lie permanently in wait for Wogan's guests. What a lot – they practically climbed into the car!

Great many prayers put up for me today and so grateful that despite all the strain and stress my brain worked quite well!

My television experiences didn't stop there.

'Well, there's one thing for sure,' I said, leaning across the table. 'You go on picking your nose like that and waving a leek in people's faces, you'll never become Prime Minister!' Loud applause. It wasn't the *real* Neil Kinnock I was talking to, just his lifelike if not very flattering 'spitting image'. Next to him sat the equally unflattering images of the Princess of Wales and the Pope.

But what a strange, almost crazy day it was! Watching the programme on the TV screen gives no idea of what goes on under the table top – climbing first up a metal ladder, then a couple of boxes, sitting on a chair stacked on another box, legs hanging down inside a large hole in which the 'voices' make their contribution to the programme, complete with every kind of electronic device and a collection of gloved hands at the end of long artificial arms.

The 'Pope' was cosy and 'Princess Di' supportive, her real-life voice telling me afterwards that her script was far from friendly towards me, but when she heard how aggressive the Kinnock puppet was – 'Sex, sex, sex,' he shouted, 'that's all you ever talk about!' and I hadn't even mentioned it! – she changed her script to say how much she agreed with me, particularly, she said, my point about the puppets of the young princes: 'Terrible intrusion into their privacy,' I'd said. 'Imagine how they'll be teased by their friends at school the next morning.'

One episode I shall never forget. The producer asked me if I'd mind staying behind after the programme had been recorded and just about everyone else had gone home. 'Not at all,' I said, wondering what was going to happen next. I soon knew! A voice over my shoulder chirped up, 'Hello, Mary – it's me'. So it was, with a vengeance – 'my' puppet! There was this revolting face, 'Go on, Mary, give us a kiss' it said. 'If you think I'm going to kiss a face like that you're very much mistaken!' I replied. But at least 'it' smiled.

But that wasn't the only crazy business I got involved in. TV appearances are adventures in themselves and that certainly applied to my appearance on *Noël Edmunds Saturday Roadshow* in October 1990. For weeks he'd made some reference to my having been invited to appear and would call out in the middle of the show 'Have we heard from Mary Whitehouse yet?' And a sepulchral voice would reply, 'Not yet, Noël.' Then the day came when I did! And, of course, it was not to be an ordinary appearance. I was to be 'gunged' which, as anyone who has seen the show knows, means that the victim sits in a telephone-box-style enclosure and at a given moment the roof opens and a coloured paste-like fluid descends on their head – with a vengeance!

Before I appeared on the set my own clothes were replaced by pretty ones provided by the company. Noël was teasing the audience. Was I, or was I not, going to appear? While I was waiting the producer asked me if I would mind writing a note to be passed to Noël to the effect that 'under no circumstances would I lower myself to appear on such a low sort of show'. There was dead silence from the audience as that part was read out and then a postscript, 'Delighted to come and see you. Love, Mary' with three kisses. Noël read it out with a great flourish then bounded across the set as I appeared between the curtains and gallantly helped me down the steps and on to the seat in the 'gunge' tank. I was told afterwards that the audience sat in stunned disbelief. After a few questions the roof opened and down came the 'gunge'. I never have discovered exactly what it was made of but it hit my head with a considerable wallop, knocked off my glasses and, of course, completely ruined my hairstyle even though I'd made great play of putting on a rain-hat. As I wrote in my diary next morning:

It seemed to go on and on – what I wouldn't have given to get away from it – couldn't see a fraction of an inch in front of me. I was drenched to the skin, but quickly, off camera, wrapped around in warm towels, hurried to a bath and hairwash and then off to hospitality where everyone was most kind – apparently no one thought I actually *would* be 'gunged' though public reaction was very supportive – just one person thought it was 'very undignified', as I'm sure it was.

However the response, particularly from young people, was most kind. The programme was transmitted the following Saturday on the day of an Executive Meeting, following which we went out to dinner at The George in Colchester. They always make a fuss of us there and the head waiter, an Italian, came to our table to say the staff had watched the programme in the kitchen and they all thought I was 'beautiful'. Well, if I'm beautiful covered in 'gunge' then I can't complain!

And it didn't end there – I was invited to 'gunge' Noël Edmunds himself in *Going Live*, a children's television programme the following Saturday – but I turned down the offer. Then BBC Radio Essex rang: they had Noël on as a guest taking calls, would I like to speak to him? So I did. All great fun, really. Among the unexpected spin-offs of my appearance on the *Noël Edmunds* show were invitations to appear in TV commercials! One was to advertise Skol: 'as someone who has recently shown a willingness to send yourself up a little on programmes such as the Noël Edmunds Roadshow', my cheerily grinning face would fill the letter O on posters up and down the land! It has long been our policy not to accept such invitations – any involvement with commercials could arouse, it seemed to us, suspicions that we would be 'soft' with ITV – and the idea of meeting myself on hoardings all over the place held no attractions at all!

Another invitation came from the makers of blue rinse toilet cleanser! Well, that would have been smartly declined too had it not arrived at the height of international concern over the tragic events in Romania; the terrible photographs of starving neglected children on our screens night after night moved the hearts of everyone and, I thought, I could send any fee to Anneka Rice's fund for the children of that suffering country. However, the executive committee was split on the issue and, after much heart-searching, I declined.

Not all invitations were linked with tragedy – far from it! We laughed heartily at the latest proposition, from an advertising agency working for a well-known and highly respected bank, which made the proposal even more hilarious! I would be sitting on a table looking disapprovingly at a couple of rabbits frolicking, apparently to some purpose, because the next shot would have me looking, deeply shocked, at the sight of rabbits covering the whole of the top of the table. The third shot would be of the whole room filled with them and me – looking even more disapproving – coming through the door with a bucket of water which I was to fling over them!

By the time the story got this far I had already told my enthusiastic caller that it couldn't be done, but we had a good laugh, not least when I told him that my nickname right up to the time of my marriage had been Hutch, short for Hutcheson, my maiden name! Mind you, I never found out which bank would be interested in an advert like that! Or what its message was – unless it was intended to demonstrate how quickly interest in investments could multiply!

A tea firm rang to offer me £2000 if I'd agree to a teapot being made based on my spitting image. I told them, 'Thanks very much – but I couldn't think anyone would want to pour out a cup of tea from a pot as ugly as that!'

Then I received an official letter from Crown solicitors calling me as a *defence* witness in a forthcoming obscenity trial! My solicitor told me that a doctor's certificate declaring me unfit would save me from that (my fractured spine limits my ability to stand) and that was forthcoming without any problem. Nice things happened, too, like participating in an on-air auction to raise money for children's hearing-aids.

In the summer of 1992 I took part in a pilot programme for Terry Wogan's new autumn show. I met Cynthia Payne to discuss the motion that 'There is Too Much Sex on Television'. We were given one minute each for an uninterrupted statement followed by a seven-minute 'free for all'. I can't say I enjoyed it very much or felt that I'd dealt adequately with the matter.

However, to my amazement, a few days later I received a call from a man who introduced himself as Miss Payne's agent. He had, apparently, felt the occasion to have been 'a great success'. Would I be interested in repeating the confrontation twice a week, all over the country in universities and clubs throughout the coming autumn and winter. I would be provided with a limousine, first-class overnight accommodation and £500 per appearance! I was so taken aback that I did not decline on the spot. But did when he rang back a few days later. It was something of an eye-opener on how the other half lives!

Other funny things happen too. Coming home from

London by train one day, I noticed that the only other person in the carriage kept looking at me intently and every time I glanced up she looked away. This seemed to go on for almost the whole journey until I stood up to get out at Colchester. As I did so she said, most apologetically, 'You must have thought me very rude staring at you like that but I kept wondering if you were Mrs Whitehouse. But now I can see you properly I realize you're much better-looking!'

'Well, that's a relief anyway,' I said, keeping my face perfectly straight until the train had taken my companion on her journey. Then I had a bit of a giggle to myself and told the story with great relish when I arrived home!

CHAPTER 14

A VOICE
FOR THE VIEWER?

If pharmaceutical drugs should be carefully controlled because
they can on occasions lead to deformities, by what logic can films
and television be exempt if they too produce undesirable effects,
even if only in a few cases? All drugs now have to pass the
most stringent tests to show they do not harm even the tiniest
proportion of takers. Is violence on the screen totally
different? . . . Is it not rather up to us [the BBC] to show that
what we screen does not have ill effects, than up to others to
prove that it does?

> Sir Michael Swann
> Chairman of the BBC
> speaking at Royal TV Society Convention
> Cambridge, September 1973

We therefore recommend a public enquiry board for broadcasting should be set up, with the safeguards we shall set out, to be
responsible in the course of holding public hearings for taking
a general view of broadcast services in the public interest. The
main instrument for doing so will be public hearings every seven
years on the way each broadcasting authority has discharged its
responsibility . . . In this way, people would have an opportunity
to express their views about the performance of each
authority . . . If there was strong evidence that services were unsatisfactory, or that the remit was out of date, this could call for
action by the Home Secretary and possibly by Parliament.

> The Annan Enquiry into the
> Future of Broadcasting, 1977

'I've decided to change the opening of my speech,' said the

then Home Secretary Douglas Hurd with a smile, as he sat down in the lounge of our home on his way to give the Key Note address at the Royal Television Society Convention in September 1989. He went on, 'I'm going to say that, on my way here I called to have a cup of tea with Mary Whitehouse so that she could see my speech and tell me if there was anything she would like to see altered.' 'You never are!' I exclaimed with laughing disbelief. I could not imagine that he would say any such thing.

The biennial conference of the RTS is held in King's College, Cambridge. This event, and especially dinner in the Great Hall each night, is always special. To me the wonderful architecture, the great lights, the entertainment between courses – not least on those occasions when the King's Singers have been the guests – have made an ineradicable impression upon my mind. To shut one's eyes and hear those perfect notes floating up to the lovely ceiling is to be in, at least for me, an earthly heaven – and, in spite of all the continuing controversy around our activities, everyone was always very kind!

When we heard, a couple of months earlier, that the Home Secretary was coming to Colchester to open a new police station on his way to the Cambridge Convention, I dropped him a little note suggesting, with tongue in cheek, that as we lived only a few miles out of Colchester he might care to drop in for a cup of tea and see 'the heart of the revolution!' The idea was that his visit would be entirely informal and I did not want to exploit it by inviting any publicity. Shortly afterwards we had a call from his office to say that the Home Secretary 'would be delighted to pop in for a cup of tea'. It wasn't long before we realized that there was no way it would or could be private: police cars spied out the land around the house and policemen with walkie-talkies and sniffer dogs in every last corner of the house gave us some indication of the kind of pressure that home secretaries live under these days.

In the event it was a delightful occasion. Our visitor looked around the garden, and met the staff in our office before sitting down for his cup of tea. Sitting in the audience a couple of hours later, I could hardly believe my ears. All this was amusingly recorded by Phil Sidey, one-time Chairman of the RTS in his report on the Convention in *Talkback* in September 1989. Referring to the establishment by the Government of the Broadcasting Standards Council and the circumstances which had led to it Mr Sidey wrote:

Nevertheless, the computers ignored the really wild Downing Street card that had brought matters to such a pitch and the other wild card sitting in the hall in unaccustomed silence. Both these wild cards are women, both have tasted sweet revenge over the television world and both were linked by the Home Secretary. He addressed the television moguls in civilized, elegant, almost regretful phrases, which would not have disgraced Charles I as he indicated to some powerful noble the door to the Star Chamber.

Mr Hurd began by jovially referring to a slight delay in the proceedings as having been caused by calling in to take tea with Mrs Whitehouse in Essex on the way to Cambridge and so having to make a number of changes in his speech. The laughter which greeted this quip had within it that tiny edge of hysteria that prisoners in the dock find hard to conceal when the judge makes a light-hearted observation in court. What victory for the lady whose name doubtless will end up, after Uffington's White Horse, in *Brewer's Dictionary of Phrase and Fable*.

I have long admired Mrs Whitehouse, not for her standards of accuracy in debate or even for her powers of analysis, but for being such a bonny fighter. She took on almost the whole television world, became the butt of countless sneers and still managed to make her small band of faithful followers appear to be millions strong.

On occasion, I have suggested to Mrs Whitehouse that she should use a rapier rather than a blunderbuss and keep her targets limited in number, but I knew at the time (if I may change the metaphor a touch) it was like asking Boadicea to cut up only the nastier Romans. Nevertheless, according to her lights she has won a famous victory . . . and all without a computer.

Mrs Whitehouse, of course, had the supreme advantage of believing that without doubt she had God on her side. Sometimes I think she forgot that some of us in the trade now and then worked alongside people who believed they were God. But let us not belittle her triumph. Tea with the Minister on his way to deliver a message to the television

establishment on behalf of that other wild card, Mrs Thatcher, was an accolade indeed.

It would be impertinent to ask whether Mr Hurd had
taken tea with Mrs Thatcher earlier still. He read his speech
with mischievous relish at the beginning and end but with
apparent disinterestedness in the middle where the meat lay.
It was all much simpler when Mrs Whitehouse was the only
opposition. Perhaps we should have listened to her and so
had God on our side.

Much of the table chat over dinner that night was about
Douglas Hurd's keynote speech in which he had committed
the government to the creation of a Broadcasting Standards
Council. How strange, almost unreal, it was to hear his words,
and to realize that our efforts were coming to fruition.

It had been a long wait but I had come to understand that,
however sympathetically a home secretary might view our call
for such a body, a government finds it difficult to move unless
public opinion is ready and anxious for effective action – not
least because broadcasters and their friends in the press will
fight to the last ditch against any move which diminishes their
control and influence.

I recall how the BBC's *Panorama* got in on the act early
on. In February 1988 it speculated about the government's
intention to establish a Broadcasting Standards Council, and
to bring broadcasting under the Obscene Publications Act.
The programme amounted to a classic example of the propaganda power which lies in the hands of television journalism.
The idea of a Broadcasting Standards Council, whose purpose,
it should be made clear, was to provide a necessary and independent means through which the public could express its
views on programme content, independent of both the BBC
and the IBA, was presented as an unwarranted intrusion into
the freedom of producers to make and viewers to tune into
even the most violent and salacious of programmes.

Kenith Trodd, producer of the controversial *The Singing
Detective*, spoke of the need for producers to 'stretch the form',
which he said 'required courage', the emphasis again being
on the 'rights' of creative people rather than on the needs of
people generally and on the welfare of society. It was significant
that the only churchman taking part in the programme was

the Bishop of Durham, who seemed happy with the situation as it was and didn't support the establishment of such a Council.

The claim was made that little concern exists in the United States about violence on television. That is not true and we provided *Panorama* researchers with a catalogue of the 850 pieces of international research, dating back to the early days of film, which demonstrated in varying degrees, a causal connection between the viewing of violence and aggressive behaviour. All this the *Panorama* team chose to ignore – not exactly a demonstration of the impartiality which it is their duty to present.

The battle for broadcasting standards has waged high and wide and I can imagine that no words of his can more embarrass the present Chairman of the BBC, Duke Hussey, than those he uttered after his meeting with Home Secretary Douglas Hurd in February 1988.

> I have given the Home Secretary an undertaking that the BBC will take firm steps to eradicate unnecessary and gratuitous violence, sex and bad language from our programmes.

Little more than a year later Brian Wenham, writing in *The Times* about the BSC, had this to say about Mr Hussey, for whom I am by no means without sympathy.

> Even the most wary of bosses may come to love that which they first purported to despise. Consider the recent history of the BBC. Duke Hussey set about his stable-cleansing with full reformist zeal: a director-general fired, a new management team established, a new sleek style proclaimed. Earlier untidinesses were to end. Yet 30 months on the new BBC displays the full virtues and vices of the old. The blessing of public service broadcasting is bestowed on all programmes great or small, excellent or tawdry, major improvement is claimed where there has been at most minor change.

And it is, and always has been, the broadcasters' failure at both management and production level to put their own house in order which gave the concept of a broadcasting standards council its *raison d'être*. One hoped profoundly that the Council would be seen and accepted as a *positive* contribution to broadcasting by the public *and* the industry, otherwise bitterness and controversy would undermine the benefits which such a Council could and should bestow.

> The underlying cause of the disquiet about television was the belief, deeply held, that the way television has portrayed human behaviour and treated moral issues has already done something, and will in time do much, to worsen the moral climate of this country.

These were not the words of Mrs Thatcher announcing the setting up of a BSC in 1988, but an extract from the findings of the Pilkington Report in 1960. It was followed by countless resolutions from Church and educational bodies, women's organizations and individuals expressing their concern about the quality of the television which came into our homes and, of course, by the launching in 1964 of our own Clean Up TV Campaign.

The Annan Report of 1977 – *very* forthright – had this to say:

> In the view of most of us, the concern which people express about certain topics is justified: and the broadcasters have failed to consider seriously enough the objections raised to certain programmes. In our view people are right to object to the glorification of violence when its depiction may possibly, even probably, do positive harm, especially to the most vulnerable with the fewest defences. We agree with those who deplore the brutalization of sex and the craven disinclination to judge a sexual problem against a sense of what is right and wrong in the world. Most of us, like the nation at large, feel that the gratuitous use of bad language, which shocks some and bores others, tends to destroy the nuances of feeling which language exists to express. We do not accept as a comprehensive defence the argument often put forward by producers, writers and critics, that the action and language objected to is like life, or is artistically necessary, or that objections are at best irrelevant and at worst destructive of high art.

The Annan Report led to a debate in the House of Lords

in 1980, when its recommendation for a Broadcasting Complaints Commission was accepted. It was Lord Nugent of Guildford who encapsulated public concern when he said that the terms of reference for a Complaints Commission should include 'unwarranted infringement of the integrity of family life, in connection with the material broadcast as regards violence, indecency or profanity, irrespective of subject matter'. But many, including National VALA, felt that the terms of reference of the Complaints Commission fell far short of what Lord Nugent envisaged. Its powers were limited to questions of specific unfairness and invasion of privacy, and did not relate to standards as regards bad language and the treatment of sex and violence. It by no means fulfilled our concept of what a comprehensive broadcasting standards council could and should set out to do. There were those, ourselves among them, who believed that the BCC was established to sidetrack and remove the substance from, the demands for a full broadcasting standards council. But that it failed to do and the BSC was duly established by statute in January 1991. Its first Annual Report gave rise to much publicity directed chiefly to what the report had to say about public reaction to television programmes.

The report claimed that:

A quarter of all people are regularly 'disgusted' by what they watch on television, and seven parents out of ten claim they have switched off or to another channel because of unsuitable programmes – four in ten at least once a month.

More than 30 per cent cited bad taste on television as a reason for disgust, compared with 30 per cent who cited sex scenes, 29 per cent who cited violence and 23 per cent who cited swearing – usually considered to provoke most offence.

The fact that 1,600 people who took part in the survey were asked to identify what disgusted them, rather than less emotionally what offended them, may account for the change, the council said.

Anatomical swear words were cited as the most offensive, the use of 'God', 'Christ' and 'Jesus' as swear words ranked middling and 'hell' the least offensive swear word.

Sexual violence and rape, and the protection of children, were singled out by the Council as the two main areas of public concern about broadcasting. The research, which accompanied the Council's final code of practice for broadcasters, said most people had three motives for concern about broadcasting – worry, guilt and fear.

Worry about the effects of media on others; guilt at not being good enough parents, or at wishing away the problems associated with programmes which we as viewers may enjoy; fear about the long-term effect of broadcasting.

It was also revealed that more than half the children in Britain aged over five have a television set, but the research showed that the vast majority of parents believe in the value of a family viewing cut-off time and most parents of teenage children believe this should be 10 p.m. or later, rather than the current 9 p.m. The Council also proposed a 5.30 a.m. early-viewing watershed for children.

Lord Rees-Mogg, the Council's chairman, indicated that, with the advent of foreign satellite programmes, he would in future differentiate between pornography which involved sadism and that which did not, and he said that 'Rape and sexual violence is the big, big concern for people, and it seems to me there is a relationship between hard pornography and that which is aggressively hostile to women.'

What an extraordinary coincidence that the first complaint to go before the BSC should be BBC2's *The Mary Whitehouse Experience* on 3 January 1991, though it was not upheld. I did not figure personally in the programme – it was only my name that was blazoned forth and trailed across the screen on a large banner. This was the first edition of the TV series and its impact illustrated vividly the difference in the effect between radio and television: the radio programme of the same name had made little or no impact but television was clearly different.

People began to ring in. Having seen the title of the programme listed in the *Radio Times*, they'd assumed that it was a documentary about me and were irritated by its dubious content. Would I please complain on their behalf? Certainly I wasn't going to on my own and I didn't on theirs either.

But I couldn't help but think how times change. I referred earlier to the BBC's coverage of the official launching of the BSC. A news team had come up here to give me the opportunity to explain how, at our first public meeting in 1964 we had called for an independent broadcasting council to which the public could make complaints.

When it was established twenty-seven years later the BBC gave us the credit for its creation. How different from life in the early days of the campaign!

Nevertheless, the battle was by no means won. In its first report, the BSC rejected all ten of the complaints reported to it and the great majority of those that have followed. But this should not discourage us, rather it should stimulate us not only to use the BSC but to use it wisely.

One of the complaints against Channel 4's highly dubious *Banned* series which the BSC upheld related to *WR – Mysteries of the Orgasm*. This was described as 'a black political sexual comedy using documentary footage and fictional scenes to explore the work of the sexologist, William Reich'. Although a warning – including a specific reference to the 'masking electronically' of some of the film's more controversial moments – preceded the film, the BSC found that 'a sequence, involving masturbation even though supplied with some masking effects, went beyond acceptable limits' and the complaint was upheld.

But, as far as we were concerned, the matter went deeper than that. It was now six months since broadcasting had been brought under the aegis of the Obscene Publications Act and, if that Act had any teeth, which we knew was doubtful, now was the time to test it. We sent the tape of *WR* to the Obscene Publications Department at New Scotland Yard. Officers viewed it and agreed that its transmission could have been illegal. The Yard forwarded it to the Director of Public Prosecutions. The Director's unwillingness to prosecute – there was 'insufficient evidence' – reinforced our conviction that only a strengthened obscenity law would solve the problem. And we weren't alone in our concern. Writing in the *Daily Telegraph* about *Banned*, William Oddie had this to say:

> *Banned*, in fact, has been nothing less than the hijacking of a major TV channel for the purpose of an ideologically motivated exercise in mass indoctrination. This makes the whole operation a sustained and massive hypocrisy of the most nauseating kind.

I should be surprised if it is not worse than that. I cannot be the only one to wonder how seriously the law has been flouted over the last few weeks, as films and programmes banned here have succeeded each other, many surely contravening the terms of the Broadcasting Act and the Obscene Publications Act.

One programme in the series, *Sex and the Censors*, seemed almost to be inviting prosecution: a compendium of indecent passages cut by the British Board of Film Classification from films destined for the cinema: passages, that is, too indecent even for the very permissive X-rated category.

As with William Oddie we had no doubts about the motivation of the series. We believed this series amounted to a last-ditch stand of the self-selected élite who want to do exactly as they like on the television screen. *Banned* took Channel 4 well beyond the pale and this series deliberately cocked a snook at the existence of the BSC. Complaints against *Sex and the Censors* and *WR* were the only ones relating to that often obscene and violent series which were upheld.

In dealing with these issues it is important to be specific and I have in front of me a report sent in to the BSC, by one of National VALA's members, of BBC2's programme *From Wimps to Warriors*, which was introduced with the words, 'Some viewers may find some of the practices in this film disturbing.' How disturbing can perhaps best be judged if I quote from a report sent in to the BSC. Its attention was drawn

to sequences illustrating how the character was bullied at school. Viewers then saw shots of him being led out of a small steel mesh cage, hooded, strapped up with leather and chain 'bondage' equipment . . .

Following sequences showed him dressed in a dog costume . . . such that he is forced to stay on all fours because his ankles are chained to his testicles. Total humiliation and, in front of other people, shown cleaning the skirting board with a toothbrush or head down the toilet and flushed as punishment. Use of religious music as a background to all this was a sacrilege.

The complaints that this programme, in particular relating to the inclusion and treatment of sado-masochism, was unsuitable for broadcasting were *not upheld*.

The BSC's *Complaints Bulletin* No. 8 unbelievably reported that:

> the Council's Complaints Committee viewed a recording of the programme. The programme was part of a documentary series depicting various kinds of male behaviour. The Committee thought that the contents of the programme would have proved offensive to some viewers, but did not feel that, in the late-night slot in which the BBC had re-scheduled it and with an accompanying warning of its contents, it was unsuitable for broadcasting in the context of the series.

What on earth can one say about that? Except to add that at least some of the people who stay up to watch such a programme are themselves the most vulnerable. Television teaches. How many lessons in sado-masochistic practices were imbibed that night? Certainly, the verdicts arrived at by the BSC continue to raise the question of whether the Council, as now constituted and manned, bears much relation to the kind of council for which we had fought. Our vision was always one of a council independent of the broadcasting authorities and manned by lay people who would directly reflect the complaints and comments of the public without the council making judgments upon them. Without wishing to impugn the integrity of the present members of the Council questions should be asked as to the wisdom of appointing, for example, someone of the status of Colin Shaw whose professional life has been spent at the heart of television. For much of the sixties he was Programme Planner at the BBC; later he moved to the Independent Broadcasting Authority as Director of Programmes. He then became Director of the Programme Planning Secretariat at the ITC and is now Director of the BSC. One acknowledges that experience in the industry could be helpful but the fact remains that one is bound to question – if only from a public relations angle – the wisdom of appointing someone who has been so deeply involved in television.

The number of complaints upheld by the Council is tiny. In

September 1991 of 1071 received only 17 were upheld. Yet Home Secretary Kenneth Baker, speaking at National VALA's Annual Convention in March 1991 said that 'the adjudication on complaints from viewers and listeners will become one of the Council's *most important functions . . . the force of public opinion cannot be ignored*' (My italics).

Lord Rees-Mogg, Chairman of the BSC, was, apparently, 'mildly amused' by the remarks made by Professor Richard Hoggart, head of the joint BBC and IBA Research Unit, in which he called for the abolition of the BSC. So, I may say, was I! Not least because it took me back to our early battles with the Professor who, perhaps more than any other single person, except the late Sir Hugh Greene, then Director-General of the BBC, had done everything possible to discredit our work in its early days – and for many years afterwards.

If Richard Hoggart hasn't changed his tune, neither have we. But I think we have one great advantage. The Professor has been seen as the voice of enlightened opinion in broadcasting matters while we were presented as reactionary and illiberal. Times change. What we were saying then and continue to say about the responsibility of television in the creation of social attitudes and in the normalizing of behaviour patterns is now increasingly accepted as responsible and liberal in the true sense of those words, while the words of the Professor have an outdated ring and even a note of desperation! He described the BSC's Code on standards as 'typically Thatcherite nonsense' as though his only hope of discrediting it was to give it a party political slant. However the *Times* leader was less than enamoured of the style in which the Code of Practice was presented, referring to its 'measured mandarin prose favoured by church synods and royal commissions' (perhaps it's a bit unfair of me to wonder, tongue in cheek, whether the fact that the BSC offices lie alongside Westminster Abbey had anything to do with this!).

It went on to challenge the BSC's Code of Practice's attitude to Family Viewing Time which 'quickly gets on to marshy ground'. It picks out the suggestion that 'it may be more appropriate to think of 9 p.m. as a "fulcrum" ' and goes on to say that 'these are the accents of a progressive bishop trying to find something positive to say about marital behaviour. Limp and muddled writing like this will appeal to Mrs Thatcher as little as it will to Mrs Whitehouse'. I can only agree.

It seems to me that the Council was honest in its presentation of the public view on matters of sex, violence, bad language and blasphemy but weak in its presentation of its own position and role. I suppose, in the end, everything depends upon the degree to which the public is prepared to get involved, though the Council's rejection of so many complaints in the 1990–91 period made us feel, and say in the *Guardian*:

> This is not the body we need or wanted. What we have is an additional level of judgements instead of a body that is there to represent the consumers. The problem we have argued about since 1964 is that the public never got satisfaction about their concerns from the broadcasting authorities and what they needed was an independent body to articulate and pass on those concerns.
>
> Out of all these complaints, only a handful have been upheld. All those who complained and had their complaints rejected will feel they wasted their time, just like when they used to complain to the broadcasters themselves. People aren't going to bother writing in any more.

And there is more evidence to support what we see as the weakness of the BSC. According to the BSC's 1992 report it received complaints about different aspects of the first episode of *The Camomile Lawn* (televised in March 1992) adapted from a novel by Mary Wesley which told the story of a group of men and women before, during, and after the Second World War. This was transmitted on Channel 4 between 9 and 11 p.m. and included sexually explicit scenes, bad language, and incitement to child abuse. There were complaints about scenes of simulated copulation in the second episode of the serial. The Council's Complaints Committee, after viewing the first episode, asked the broadcaster for a statement in response to the complaints made against the first two episodes.

In his response, said the BSC, he drew attention to the warning which had preceded its transmission and claimed 'that the language used in the episode and the scenes of female nudity the episode contained were justified by the context and had been appropriately scheduled. The purpose of their inclusion had not been to titillate.'

The Council accepted C4's claim that in the context of a

serial scheduled after the 9 p.m. watershed, the scenes in the first episode of sexual explicitness and those involving the child character were within the bounds of acceptability. It took the same view about the sexually explicit scenes complained of in the second episode.

> On the question of the language which gave offence to some of the complainants, the Council felt that, in general, it too was justified within the context of the plot. Early in the first episode, however, one of the male characters used the word 'fuck' when talking to one of the female characters. The word, whether used as here in its original sense or more metaphorically, retains great power to offend and the Council believes that its use at that point in the serial, when the audience's expectations had still to be formed, went beyond what should have been broadcast relatively soon after the watershed.

So the complaint was upheld – and it was only one 'f' word.

In no time at all the scene changed disastrously. In June BBC 2 transmitted *Do The Right Thing* at 10.30 p.m. when many youngsters, let alone adults, were still viewing. A full stream of obscenities characterized this programme. We decided, for the first time, to make a complaint to the BSC drawing its attention to the constant use (well over 300 times) of the 'f' word and the repetition, more than 30 times, of – what had previously been seen as totally unacceptable by the Council – the word 'mother f—er'.

To say that we were amazed to read that our complaint had been rejected is to put it mildly. I have to admit that its reasons for so doing made us feel that, at best, the BSC lived in Cloud Cuckoo Land! According to its press release the full Council viewed a recording of the film and then considered a statement requested of the broadcaster. In this the BBC claimed that 'its language accurately reflects an aspect of black American culture'; they believed 'that to have edited it would have damaged the integrity of the film'. What about the integrity of the family? I wondered. The report went on to say that 'the Council took the view that the frequent use of offensive language was unacceptable without exceptional justification' but it went blandly on, 'The justification offered was the importance of the subject, its truth to the action portrayed, the scheduling and the warning given. Taking account of these factors, the Council decided not to uphold the complaint.'

I promptly issued a press release to coincide, we hoped, with the publication of the Council's findings. In it we attacked the Broadcasting Standards Council for 'opening the door to whatever kind or amount of obscenity the broadcasters want to transmit', and went on

> The BSC has lamely accepted the BBC's excuse that the language was justified because it 'accurately portrayed an aspect of black culture'. But the question the Council should have asked itself is: was the film suitable for transmission on television bearing in mind the duty laid upon BBC personnel by its Governors 'not to transmit material likely to offend against good taste and decency or give offence to public feeling?'
>
> Furthermore this judgement invalidates the result of the BSC's own research (*A Matter of Manners,* 1991) which found that such language was 'almost universally considered both very strong and offensive' and makes it abundantly clear that the BSC is not operating in the public interest as was envisaged by those, such as ourselves, who fought so hard for its establishment.

'I can assure you that we thought long and hard before deciding to show *Do The Right Thing* in an unedited version,' said John Birt, Deputy Director-General of the BBC in a letter to Bernard Jenkin and other MPs. The film, he told us, was transmitted as part of 'a history of the impact of television on the black race and ethnic minorities'.

How about the impact of television on the rest of us – as individuals and upon the world in which we live? It is not without significance that the programme contained the phrase 'mother f. . . . .' at least thirty times, in spite of the guidance given by the Broadcasting Standards Council that it should never be used, along with almost endless unmentionable obscenities.

'Nothing to offend against good taste and decency': the obligation under which television producers are supposed to function becomes no more than a sick joke and there remains the unanswered question, which does not relate to whether the presentation accurately portrays the behaviour of ethnic minorities. It is this: why, out of all the films available, did this one have to be shown?

In a matter of months we have moved from the transmission of one 'f' word to hundreds in one programme! And yet Lord Rees-Mogg himself, as Chairman of the BSC, writing in the *Daily Mail* only the previous year had said, 'The broadcasters' argument that you could always switch off the set was arrogant. What they are saying is if you don't like it, you can lump it. Broadcasters should not take their decision in a social vacuum.' He went on to point out that in ordinary family life the balance was imposed by what the mother would allow in the home. 'People feel that television is imposing lower standards than they themselves want. They want TV to be careful when children are watching. Adult films at 11 p.m. are not such a problem.'

Nevertheless, it has to be said that Lord Rees-Mogg is making his voice heard in other, but related ways. We were aware that he was a Christian but nothing had really prepared us for his unexpected attack on 'The Permissive Sixties' carried in the *Daily Mail* on the day in 1991 that the Council became law.

How often over the years had we claimed that the so-called 'freedom' of the sixties had been in effect a snare and a delusion? We had often stated our belief that no change for the better would come until the producers of the sixties had worked through the system. It was marvellous to see these convictions being articulated by a person with the position and power of Rees-Mogg. Suddenly they were given respectability and authenticity. He launched an attack on what he called 'children of the sixties' who make programmes in which they impose their permissive values on viewers. He intended, he said, to reverse the trend and put the viewer in charge of what was shown.

The people now making programmes were students in the 1960s when there was a revolutionary change in social conscience and a great breaking down of taboos. That affects what we see on our screens.

We are going through a period in which people taking

the decisions in television are the people who were students at the end of the 1960s, people under 45. The power lies with the producer age group. But the parents of young children are normally in their twenties or thirties.

As for the Broadcasting Standards Council, what is one to say? Perhaps it's better left to the Rt Revd Bill Westwood, Bishop of Peterborough, who was a member of the Council from its inception in 1988 until January 1993. In a letter to a fellow clergyman – and I have been given permission to quote from it – he says that he 'found himself always in a minority' and that he looks upon his 'tenure of that office as one of the failures of my life. In discussion and voting I was regularly defeated by a combination of that sociological and psychological and media-centred thinking which characterizes our generation.'

He went on:

> I believe that the standards of our television have declined and believe that the horrendous material which appears on television programmes and on video is now a major contributory cause of the breakdown of the social fabric of our society. Those responsible for television are more casual in their approach to violence and will go on being so in my judgement, despite the James Bulger tragedy. I believe that the portrayal of sex is for the most part without any context or commitment despite the geometric progression of AIDS throughout the world. I fear that their attachment to the easy and cynical laugh continues, despite the fact that we are in a desperately serious situation as a nation.
>
> All these things continued to grow in my four years on the Council and this most powerful of all influences in a nation, other than the home, continues in its shoddy way. This was probably one of the greatest inventions of the twentieth century and could have done so much more for us.

The Broadcasting Standards Council bears no resemblance to the body we had felt inspired to fight for. It has, most regrettably, become part and parcel of the broadcasting establishment instead of being, as it was first conceived, the independent voice of the viewer and listener.

I find myself increasingly irritated by the realization that, in making a complaint to the BSC, I am not making my own voice heard, but am providing an opportunity for the members of the council to make a judgement on my views. Instead of the Government providing a vehicle for the voice of the viewer it has provided little more than a convenient means for the broadcasters to deflect criticism of their programmes.

Nothing but a thorough reappraisal of the role of the BSC will hold out any hope for its future and in order to keep the ball rolling, I decided to send a copy of my 1993 Convention address to the Prime Minister. Apparently he read it but firmly disagreed with what I had said about the weakness of the Broadcasting Standards Council! He concluded that we wanted it abandoned which was not true. But, in its present form and with its growing acceptance of four-letter language which has always been deemed obscene, it remains, whatever the Prime Minister may say, a great disappointment to those of us who fought so hard for its establishment.

Perhaps it is too early to stand in judgement on the Council and how its work is likely to develop, but one hopes most profoundly that the Chairman's sincerity and deeply held views will permeate it more deeply and that it will review its work objectively. But there can be no doubt that in being so ineffectual the BSC is digging its own grave. If it values its future it needs to take note that Labour is on record as saying that if they win the next election the Council will be terminated. Its role, says Robin Corbett, Labour spokesman on broadcasting, would be passed on to the Broadcasting Complaints Commission. This body was set up to deal with misrepresentation and intrusion of privacy and, one can't help but remember with a rueful smile, was set up as a sop to those who, like ourselves, were campaigning for a Broadcasting Standards Council.

CHAPTER FIFTEEN

SKY'S THE LIMIT

'It must sometimes feel lonely, being you,' said the kind stranger who wrote to encourage us.

Dear Mary Whitehouse

I saw you on TV the other week, about satellite TV and the porn films they are putting on. We got the satellite TV and someone told us to buy a Decoder for 'Filmnet' because they put on better films, so we did. One night my husband put it on and there was hard porn on, it was very bad. We had a row over this and I don't think we will be together long. My husband thinks there is no harm in it, but I do. The Decoders anyone can get and they are putting two films on a week of hard porn one to two o'clock Thursday and Sunday morning, they show and do anything in these films.

I cannot take it in about my husband wanting to see this, I am so strong about it. I don't think I can carry on being with him. But if this is doing us harm what about other people?

I am sorry that I cannot give my address in case my husband finds out – there should be something done. I don't know how they can call it good TV.

(name supplied)

When I presented a paper at the Council of Europe's Parliamentary Assembly's Hearing on Violence at Assisi in September 1982, I referred, first, to the way in which the advent of cable and satellite TV would rapidly change the face of traditional broadcasting. I went on to underline 'the need for far more comprehensive public accountability than has attended broadcasting so far.'

Two years later a meeting, organized by the Council of Europe took place. Reporting on the conference, the *Guardian* carried the headline (23 June 1988) 'One million children kidnapped for sale into sex trade'. A meeting of European justice ministers, then being held in Lisbon, were debating a report that 'a million children fall victim to paedophiles, prostitution racketeers and traffickers in pornography each year', and were calling for 'concerted international action against the sexual exploitation of children'.

The suffering of a million children is beyond comprehension and beyond bearing. These children, we are told, are either bought or kidnapped or made available through false adoption agencies and then sold through middle men to rich clients to 'work' privately or in brothels. And, we're told that 'If the market requires video films featuring toddlers in physically damaging intercourse situations, then these are produced.'

The sex tour industry and the presence of military bases in developing countries had led to 'an enormous increase in child prostitution of boys' the conference was told and it must have drawn little comfort from a report that while European publicity drives against child pornography in 1986 forced its disappearance from shop shelves within a few months, it is feared that it is now increasingly available under the counter.

The conference did, however, pass a number of resolutions and it is important that we are all aware of their nature so that we can pressure the Home Office, our MPs and the Churches, to ensure that the resolutions are translated into reality.

On 9 October 1989 the Home Office assured us of the government's support of the Council of Europe Convention on Transfrontier Television, which it believed demonstrated the government's commitment 'to maintaining acceptable standards of broadcasting and its awareness of the need to protect viewers from pornographic material from abroad'.

The Convention stated:

Member States shall take appropriate measures to ensure that television broadcasts by broadcasters under their jurisdiction do not include programmes which might seriously impair the physical, mental or moral development of minors, in particular those that involve pornography or gratuitous violence. This provision shall extend to other programmes which are likely to impair the physical, mental or moral development of minors, except where it is ensured, by selecting the time of the broadcast or by any technical measure, that minors in the area of transmission will not normally hear or see such broadcasts.

Member States shall also ensure that broadcasts do not contain any incitement to hatred on grounds of race, sex, religion or nationality.

'That doesn't surprise me!' I wrote in my diary on 4 July 1989, the day after the Edinburgh Forum. 'The satellite companies, Sky and BSB, apparently want what they call "a more liberal framework" than that which applies to the BBC and ITV so that they can show films such as Stanley Kubrick's *A Clockwork Orange* and *The Life of Brian*!'

And I poured out my heart, as I so often do, to those long-suffering pages:

So now it looks as though many of us – the young and vulnerable included – far from being saved from the dark and dangerous depths of our own souls are liable to have them stimulated by the same dark passions as characterized the *Clockwork Orange* cult of the sixties. What a thought! Even the Broadcasting Standards Council is not going to be the lifeline it is meant to be if it agrees to the system of 'dual standards' for which the satellite operators are pressing.

According to press reports the following morning, Andrew Neil, Executive Chairman of Sky Television, had told the Forum that he intended to screen uncut films which are generally 'savaged' before they are shown to conform to existing standards. The fact that he added, 'We are not pornographers', left a question mark in my mind. And, in any case, he said, no need to worry because there's always the locking device which would provide all the protection that children need and enable parents to go out for the evening without a care in the world.

Pondering on his comments I asked myself, 'How does one expose the dangers of transmitting a film such as *A Clockwork*

Orange on television? Only by getting them publicized.' I promptly drafted an article, before ringing the features editor of a newspaper which had always been sympathetic to anything I wrote. But not this time. I was told kindly, and I felt regretfully, that as Sky TV had a financial interest in the paper concerned, it would be unable to publish an article critical of its policies. I put down the phone in a state of shock and disbelief: if newspapers and satellite stations are to be as closely linked as this, then a new power of quite frightening censorship is abroad in the land.

So I made some enquiries. 'How effective', I asked, 'is this so-called "locking device" in which Andrew Neil would have us put all our faith?' I set out my findings in a letter to *The Times*. No luck there either. Most unusual. Not even an acknowledgements. Could that, I wondered, be related in any way to the fact that Rupert Murdoch, a director and founder of Sky TV is also owner of News International which publishes *The Times?* I'd been tipped off by someone very close to the heart of the paper that I might not see my letter in print for that very reason.

For many years, National VALA's voice had been ridiculed and silenced by the established broadcasting authorities but the press, for the most part, have been willing to give us a hearing. But, as I wrote in my diary next day, 'all this could well change if the press and satellite television are going to be so closely involved one with another'.

Without waiting any longer I sent my letter to the *Daily Telegraph* which published it as the first one the following day (19 July 1989).

> Sir – In the days since you published your report (5 June) on the Broadcasting Standards Council's forum, we have been making some inquiries regarding the 'locking device' in which Mr Andrew Neil, chief executive of Sky Television, would have us place such confidence.
>
> With this in the hands of parents, Mr Neil would, apparently, be quite happy to transmit films such as *A Clockwork Orange*. This, in spite of the evidence of the part played by this film in some of the most brutal copycat murders carried out not only in the United States but in this country too –

as witness the murder of the elderly tramp David McManus by a 16-year-old schoolboy on his way home after seeing the film at his local cinema.

We are asked to believe that the 'locking device' would give children total protection, but inquiries made on our behalf in Coventry and Croydon, where cable stations have been in operation for three years, reveal that in all that time 'no-one has asked for this facility' in spite of the fact that they have been advertised. At 50p a month that's surely not going to frighten anybody! Apparently, Lord Rees-Mogg's purpose in calling the BSC forum together was to help him resolve the question of whether there should be dual standards for subscription television and 'the rest' – a proposition much favoured by Sky Television and by British Satellite Broadcasting.

One hopes that this information will persuade the Broadcasting Standards Council and its chairman that 'dual standards' was never a responsible, realistic or rational proposition. And that will be a blessing. One lot of standards is almost more than the average parent can cope with.

Yours faithfully, etc.

Several weeks later I heard that this letter had been commented on in Croydon and Coventry and it brought forth the information that since there were no takers of the 'locking device' at 50p they had been offered free. There were still no takers.

Prosecuting counsel in the case of the sixteen-year-old schoolboy told the court, 'The conclusion that the film had some terrible influence on what happened is inescapable', while the psychiatrist who examined the boy said: 'The real explanation is truly macabre and frightening. It seems as though, momentarily, the devil had been planted in the boy's subconscious. In my submission, it is the irresistible conclusion that whatever was planted there followed the violence of *A Clockwork Orange*. It is the only possible explanation for what this boy did.' The boy's defence counsel said there was no evidence whatsoever that he was suffering from any mental disease, he was not drunk, neither had he taken drugs, and asked, 'What possible explanation can there be for this savagery other than the film?' And he went on to claim that 'All responsible people desire to see the mindless violence of this film stamped out.'

But far from being 'stamped out' the British Board of Film Censors had given the film an X Certificate. It became a cult film, and its theme, against a background of masochistic violence, was one which is fundamental to much, now easily available, pornography: woman is there to be raped, she deserves to be raped, and raped she must be. The mascaraed clockwork orange 'droogs' with their anarchic speech, mannerisms and clothes, engaged in chillingly formal acts of rape, robbery and murder, became the 'heroes' upon whom, as Scotland Yard reported at the time, a dozen gangs were modelling their lifestyles.

The most widely publicized tragedy associated with the film was, of course, the shooting in the United States of Governor George Wallace by Arthur Bremer. He had written in his diary that he 'saw *Clockwork Orange* and thought about getting Wallace all through the picture'. When asked whether he had anything to say before he was sentenced he answered, quite simply – but how poignantly – 'I only wish someone had saved me from myself.'

Just to make sure that Andrew Neil was in no doubt about our feelings, I wrote to him and sent a copy of the letter in the *Daily Telegraph* to each member of Sky's board of directors including Mr Rupert Murdoch who had, of course, been closely involved in the channel from its inception.

I was intrigued to receive a reply from Jonathan Miller, another famous television entrepreneur and felt what he had to say was important enough to put on the record, which I do with his permission. He wrote as a member of the Board of Sky TV.

21 July 1989

Dear Mrs Whitehouse

Rupert Murdoch has received your letter of 7 July and wishes you to know that he is always interested in your views on programme standards. He has asked me to reply to the points you raised.

You should know, firstly, that we shall not transmit any

film on Sky Movies unless it has been certificated with a rating of 18 or below by the British Board of Film Classification.

At this time, *The Clockwork Orange* is not available for broadcast, nor does it have a certificate from the BBFC for transmission on subscription television.

I am sharing your concerns about this film with all the relevant personnel at Sky.

I would add that in the almost six months we have been on the air we have received some 4,500 enquiries (2,800 telephone calls and 1,700 letters) from Sky Television viewers and members of the public.

We have received no complaints whatsoever about the portrayal of sex, violence or the use of bad language. I feel this is an outstanding record.

Yours sincerely, etc.

At the time of writing *A Clockwork Orange* has not been shown on Sky TV or on any other television channel in this country. I was both intrigued and encouraged to hear what Rupert Murdoch had to say when he was interviewed by Mary Goldring on Channel 4: he said that he believed that a 'major revival of high moral and religious values' was taking place in Britain and that if newspaper – and television – editors 'do not have high moral values they should have'. Whether or not this means that he intends to use his own influence on decisions affecting, shall we say, page three of the *Sun* remains to be seen. But what a prospect his apparent change of heart opens up! Incidentally, I heard that Mr Murdoch had been both touched and impressed by the nationwide evangelical campaign, led by Dr Billy Graham, which moved so many hearts in the early autumn of 1989. However, other people, it seemed, stagnated in the soft 'trendy' values of the so-called 'permissive sixties'.

I stayed up on 5 November 1989 to watch the BBC1 programme *Heart of the Matter* which looked at the situation created by the presence of cable and satellite television. My own belief that there is little that can be done to control satellite television realistically in spite of agreements among members of the European Community was reinforced and it would have been easy to feel depressed at the end of it. The measure of the task ahead for government and viewers alike is incalculable, and that came across strongly.

I was interested to hear Joan Bakewell, who presented the programme, say that formal agreements cannot, in the end, be enforced because of the nature of satellite television in particular and that the only defence against the soft porn programmes already being transmitted from Holland and France is the character of the individual viewer – whether or not they are prepared to accept such material in their home. She spoke of the need to move towards 'a culture which is good and caring' and for us, collectively and individually, 'to reject that which is cruel, brutal and exploitive'.

It's the old and eternal truth: everything, in whatever circumstances, depends upon the outcome of the battle between good and evil, a battle which is both personal and collective, but which now must move into a dimension never previously experienced. What a challenge.

We are asked from time to time how many members we have and the answer to that inevitably varies from year to year. As National VALA is not a charity, we do not have to present annual membership figures. Our concern is with whether the tide of new members keeps steady, which it does at around 175,000 per year composed of individuals and groups. Certainly the financial support for our work has been remarkable over the years. The basic annual subscription which has risen only to £2 has been much supplemented by gifts and legacies so that the finance for our various activities has always materialized. As time went on it became apparent that opinion, conviction, even experience, would not be enough to counteract the attacks of those who wanted for whatever reason – financial, political, ideological – to destroy our case.

Ridicule, both of persons and ideas, was perhaps their strongest weapon. Yet their own arguments and claims were wide open to similar treatment. The charge that we wanted to act as censors was heard almost daily yet the boot was, as they say, 'on the other foot'.

We realized that to look for authentic evidence of the impact of, for example, TV violence upon human behaviour within Britain was something of a lost cause, not because it did not exist but because of the actual censorship of such material within many parts of the media.

To obtain our ammunition, therefore, we had to search further afield both in person and by gathering the results of research done elsewhere and sent to us by well-wishers in many countries and this I have quoted widely wherever appropriate in speeches, on television and in writing.

CHAPTER SIXTEEN

JUST A PASSING FANCY?

Alexander Solzhenitsyn: 'Once I hoped that experience of life could be handed on from nation to nation, and from one person to another . . . But now I am beginning to have doubts. Perhaps everyone is fated to live through every experience himself in order to understand . . . Our Russian experience is vitally important for the West, because by some chance of history we have trodden the path the West is taking seventy or eighty years before the West. And now it is with a rather strange sensation that we look at what is happening to you, when many social phenomena are repeating what happened in Russia before its collapse. Our experience of life is of vital importance to the West, but I am not convinced that you are capable of assimilating it without having gone through it right to the end yourselves.'

Michael Charlton: 'Give me an example of what you mean by the Russian experience being repeated in the West.'

Solzhenitsyn: 'One could quote here many examples: for example, a certain retreat by the older generation, yielding their intellectual leadership to the younger generation. It is against the natural order of things for those who are youngest, with the least experience in life, to have the greatest influence in directing the life of society. One can say to them that this is what forms the spirit of the age, this current of public opinion, when people in authority, well-known professors, scientists, are reluctant to enter into an argument even when they hold a different opinion. It is considered embarrassing to put forward one's counter-arguments lest one becomes involved. And so there is a certain abdication of responsibility, which is typical here where there is complete freedom.'

Charlton: 'You are, in some respects, an impassioned critic'.

Solzhenitsyn: 'Firstly, I am not a critic of the West. I repeat that for nearly all our lives we worshipped it – note the word 'worshipped'. I am not a critic of the West, I am a critic of the weakness of the West. I am a critic of a fact which we can't comprehend; how one can lose one's spiritual strength, one's will-power and possessing freedom not value it, nor be willing to make sacrifices for it ... Human nature is full of riddles and contradictions. One of these riddles is: how is it that people who have been crushed by the sheer weight of slavery and cast to the bottom of the pit can nevertheless find strength in themselves to rise up and free themselves – first in spirit and then in body – while those who soar unhampered over the peaks of freedom suddenly lose the taste for freedom, lose the will to defend it and, hopelessly confused and lost, almost begin to crave slavery? Or again – why is it that societies which have been benumbed for half a century by lies they have been forced to swallow, find within themselves a certain lucidity of heart and soul which enables them to see things in their true perspective and to perceive the real meaning of events; whereas societies with access to every kind of information suddenly plunge into lethargy, into a kind of mass blindness, a kind of voluntary self-deception? A moral stance, even in politics, always safeguards our spirit; sometimes, as we can see, it even protects our very existence. A moral stance can suddenly turn out to be more far-sighted than any calculated pragmatism.'

Panorama, BBC 1, 1 March 1976

In 1934 J. D. Unwin published a massive socio-anthropological study called *Sex and Culture*, in which he investigated some 80 primitive and 16 sophisticated societies. His purpose was, without any preconceptions, to consider the effect on a cul-

ture of the sexual attitudes which prevailed in it. His conclusion was that strong cultures were those in which self-
restraint, monogamy and fidelity prevailed. When these attitudes broke down in favour of permissiveness, the culture
swiftly declined and became subject to other cultures. There
were no exceptions.

'I don't think I am being paranoid when I say that the
media in Britain have steadfastly neglected to look objectively
at the consequences of the sexual revolution. Implicitly and
explicitly the media purvey the notion that anything goes,
ignoring the massive evidence that such a course is ultimately disastrous.

There is a refusal to accept the evidence of hugh
increases in sexually transmitted diseases, broken marriages,
disturbed children, and most of all the sheer joylessness of
so many sexual relationships. And when a Mary Whitehouse
has the courage to stand up and protest at prevailing attitudes she is vilified and attacked on all sides. It is not too
hard to identify some of our contemporary 'powers of this
dark world'.

> Peter Kimber M.A., M.Ed.,
> Assistant Director of the Scottish Examination Board
> speaking at the National Prayer Breakfast
> in the presence of Lord Mackay the Lord
> Chancellor, 13 May 1991

'Solidarity fights for control of the media' ran the headline
in *The Times* on 30 August 1989, the morning after a visit to
our home of Father Balicki, a Polish priest and professor of
moral philosophy with particular concern for the media and
its influence in one of the main Polish universities. He was a
supporter of Solidarity and anxious to hear at first hand how
we had conducted our campaign, the kind of problems we
had faced and the success we had achieved.

The Times article spoke of how the Communist Party in
Poland, as in every Warsaw Pact country, controlled television
and most of the press. And it was fascinating, particularly in
the light of what our visitor had had to say the previous day,
to read of how, while a Solidarity government was prepared to

hand over the interior, defence and even the economic portfolios to Communists it was not prepared to bargain over the control of the media. We found ourselves with much common ground. Father Balicki was particularly concerned about the tactics used by the Communist government on both radio and television and he emphasized particularly their techniques of 'undermining character and their encouragement of drinking, immorality, pornography and obscenity'.

We felt both honoured and privileged to think that we could make any positive contribution to the great battle being waged by Solidarity and we were able to give him much in the way of printed material which would give him the background, history and ongoing activities of National VALA. But it was almost uncanny to listen to this cultured and knowledgeable man tell us of how the media is acknowledged, by friend and foe alike, to be at the very centre of the struggle for freedom and for quality of life.

Among the material we were able to give him was a copy, suddenly very topical, of an extract from the book *The Naked Communist* by W. Cleon Skousen, the manuscript of which was placed in the United States Congressional Record for 10 January 1963. Mr Skousen served for several years with the American Federal Bureau of Investigation and it was through his work there that he was able to draw up a 'list of 45 objectives, aimed at political, economic, industrial and moral disruption in free, democratic societies' put together by the Communists.

Among those objectives were:

21. Gain control of key positions in radio, television and motion pictures.

22. Continue discrediting [American] culture by degrading all forms of artistic expression . . . eliminate all good sculpture from parks and public buildings and substitute shapeless, awkward and meaningless forms.

24. Eliminate all laws governing obscenity by calling them 'censorship' and a violation of free speech and free press.

25. Break down cultural standards of morality by promoting pornography and obscenity in books, magazines, motion pictures, radio and television.

26. Present homosexuality, degeneracy and promiscuity as 'normal, natural and healthy'.

27. Infiltrate the Churches and replace revealed religion with 'social' religion. Discredit the Bible and emphasize the need for intellectual maturity which does not need a 'religious crutch'.

28. Eliminate prayer or any phase of religious expression from schools.

I was amazed when I first saw that document years after its publication. I realized just how far these aims had already been achieved in Britain and without any awareness of the vast majority of people, including me, of the profound significance of what was happening. I couldn't help but think how far the object of presenting, for example, homosexuality as 'normal, natural and healthy' has gone as I watched *Them and Us* at 7.30 p.m. – in the middle of 'family viewing time'. We were treated to Sir Ian McKellen discussing homosexuality in the Isle of Man with residents who were critical of it, all of whom were, and looked, thoroughly aggressive and unpleasant – no advertisement whatever for Christian love and understanding. All the watching children would be drawn towards Sir Ian, and be 'put off' by the anti-homosexuals. Clever stuff.

The battle against any attempt to control pornography has seeped deep into our culture and the truth is that, by and large, many of our academics and so called 'liberals' have been, to put it mildly, less than supportive of our work. What effect the changes which have been wrought so spectacularly in the USSR will have upon those who are, and have been for so long, committed to the destruction of Christian ideals and values in the West remains to be seen. The battle, because more open, may well be won in the former openly Communist world than in those countries where the poison has permeated so deeply.

Maybe some of my readers will respond to this by thinking that, now, following the break-up of the USSR and the growing impact of democracy within former Communist states, this is irrelevant. But nearly a century of indoctrination and infiltration of Western, basically Christian, countries does not melt away with the breaking down of political boundaries. The truth is that so profound has been the effect of such left-wing ideology that it has come to be part and parcel of so-called 'liberal' philosophy. The battle to reverse that trend should involve us all.

In September 1992 there was daily news from Germany of the uprising of neo-Nazi youth and I turned again to the address given by Count Nikolai Tolstoy to the 1980 Convention of National VALA:

> History shows the pattern of progress – eventually it was real blood in the Roman circuses that the crowds were after. Audiences no longer appreciated gladiatorial skill, etc. – if there was no blood they howled for a new act . . . That's what we shall see here.
>
> At present most of the pornographers agree that what is right for adults is not right for children. I suspect that we shall see that age limit slipping lower and lower. Amongst the pornography supporters I detect a strident note that they object to any who in their own homes still resist all this . . . the day may not be far off when you cannot even escape in your own homes. This is an area where my historical interests have often directed me . . .
>
> The whole of civilized society is based on subtle relationships of trust, faith and honour between people . . . a central theme of all Shakespeare's plays is the essential upholding of honour and trust between people . . . when this breaks down there is appalling bloodshed, chaos and destruction.
>
> Germany's Weimar Republic [1919–33] was just the sort of society which most of us are trying to prevent arriving here. A distinguished historian of that period says of the pre-Nazi German Republic: 'Morality came to be divorced from sexual matters and in Berlin all manner of sexual licence and aberrations could be indulged without shame or restraint. Virginity lost its esteem and contraceptive practices gained official recognition. Nudism, homosexuality, sadism, masochism flaunted themselves with immoderation that shocked visitors from Latin countries. The repulsive licence of republican Germany was a preparation for the callous immorality indoctrinated by the Nazi creed. The ascendance of cruelty had begun.
>
> The Brownshirt movement [over a million strong when

Hitler came to power] was led by the chief of staff Ernst Rohm, a practising homosexual. Nearly all Brownshirt leaders were part of a ring of homosexuals . . . this was drawn to Hitler's attention, but, as he said, the Nazi movement was not a training ground for high school girls.

Hitler himself would not have disapproved of the tendencies we see in England today. I quote from someone who knew him for many years before breaking with him and escaping from him before the war broke out . . . 'Hitler had a room with obscene nudes on the wall concealing nothing. Such pictures have no artistic intention or appeal. He revels in this style of painting . . . and keeps by his bed pornographic magazines to read in privacy.'

It's an odd coincidence that a high official of the Soviet political police who defected to the West learned from officers of the Kremlin guard that Stalin, too, delighted in pornography which he kept in secret by his bed.

In Nazi Germany the epitome of all pornography was Julius Streicher's *Der Stürmer* newspaper which Hitler described as Germany's respectable form of pornography. Under the guise of attacking Jews and Roman Catholics there were graphic descriptions and illustrations of hideous sexual crimes supposedly committed by Jews and nuns. Some of Hitler's staff complained about it but Hitler himself always protected Streicher and his newspaper.

Most pornography, of course, is hostile to women, presents women in degrading positions and much of it of course goes in for actual cruelty.

It's not without significance that much of this pornography deals in Nazi symbolism – jackbooted men with swastika armbands whipping women – all this not very far beneath the surface.

If we are to preserve ourselves from such a society – and I don't think it's alarmist when you look at the shortlived Weimar Republic and how logically the Nazis extended the violence and cruelty permeated in the thought of that society and used it to their own ends.

Much the same happened in the destruction of the old Russian society. These trains of thought are of course part of the spirit of the times – they're not consciously worked out. There are documents, some genuine, which show that the KGB was implicated in spreading pornography in an attempt to dissolve the links of family life and personal loyalties ... Today the KGB fully recognizes the danger of the family unit, of religion and other non-state, non-totalitarian standards and ethics.

One of the horrifying aspects of the Gulag camps (which at their peak in 1945 probably had some 20 million inhabitants working on forced labour) was the fact that the moment people were deported to these camps the men were instantly separated from their families. I quote from Russian orders captured by Germans in 1941 issued by Deputy Commissar Shirov on 4 June 1941 about deportation of Balts from their occupied lands: 'In view of the fact that a large number of deportees must be arrested and distributed in special camps ... it is essential that the operation of removal of the deportee's family and its head should be carried out simultaneously without notifying them of the separation confronting them.'

So even in the camps, far from any civilized life and guarded by a million NKVD guards, the Soviet state still felt threatened in its authority by the mere existence of husbands, wives and children together. I think it's on behalf of families as much as anything else that I hope we will go out from this gathering and continue our struggle.

As I reread this in the spring of 1993 I was struck by how much of what Count Tolstoy said is history and yet it still has great significance for us.

The Russians have made a fresh start, albeit in many places a very stormy one, but we surely would be foolish indeed if we just smiled a blessing and turned our backs on the history of the last three-quarters of a century. It has been the attack of materialism upon the quality of character and upon faith, which has permeated the thinking and affected the actions of the West, an attack that has soaked deep into the essence of how we live and think. The fight against Communism was clear cut, the challenge to rescue our so-called Christian democracy faces us all.

CHAPTER SEVENTEEN

A
PUBLIC SCANDAL

Extract from a letter to me from a man who must remain anonymous:

> For years I have 'enjoyed' these filthy magazines. They had almost ruined my marriage and I truly wonder if they did not contribute to almost killing my wife. This filth is like a drug. The more you get the more you want. The more you want the more you hate yourself for wanting – and then you get again and hate yourself for getting. One moment it seems a desirable private dream, then later it is empty – and so is life, and you are always so awfully alone in your own private Hell.
>
> Since the war this class of publication has become easier to obtain, even to the point of being almost impossible to avoid in most ordinary newsagents, in the last few years being strategically placed so as to create 'impulse buying' as it is termed in the retail trade. Then along comes the same theme on television. It started in very subtle and cunning ways, gradually feeling its way from one step to another. I particularly felt this when I was in a mood of some resistance to this curse. Then I used to feel trapped and unable to get away from it wherever I have turned ... I mention this to endorse the terrible seductive forces, television in particular, which confront me and others in my position.

From his wife:

> Last year I was in hospital with a coronary thrombosis, due to emotional disturbances over a long period. I am in the distressing position of having witnessed in action the so-

called 'arts studies' [pornography]. It is far worse than just 'looking' at pictures. No wife is going to be able to satisfy her husband sexually, once he has indulged in these books or other forms of depravity . . .

I must say that the present attitude of my husband, plus the fact that he is now prepared to give any help of which he is capable in combating the present permissive trend, has wiped out many long years of terrible bitterness and future of complete meaninglessness.

I have now nothing but the highest regard for his moral strength and courage in that he is prepared to take the line he is now taking at cost only to himself.

Letter from a stranger:

My memories, some of them, date back before I ever started school. As I got older, things didn't improve. The father of a friend of mine would only allow her to go places if I would allow him to handle me, so I would so she could go. My friend's father kept nude magazines under his bed. The man next door to him also used to abuse me. He had nude pictures on his walls; he also allowed his young son to have these on his bedroom walls.

As a child I was taught to never say no to adults, this was disrespect for your elders. I too accepted this behaviour as being normal. I mean what could you do? For a long time I had a bad attitude towards men and sex. I put all men into one group including my husband. And to me sex was a man's game not intended for females. I couldn't even stand for my husband to touch me, because all of the others touched me.

I have had some really horrid nightmares over the years concerning sex and men – dreams of being raped by many men, dreams of men treating me so mean and making fun of me, dreams of little girls being messed with and not being able to help the poor little child. I've had nightmare after nightmare. A lot of times, I woke crying after having such horrid dreams.

It's really sad, the price my husband and I have paid because of the sexual abuse I suffered as a child. I have been a victim, but my husband is also a victim of another sort. Praise God for His healing power to heal such scars and wounds caused from pornography and men. No one could reach my scars and wounds except Christ, and He is healing me.

Parliamentary, police and civil efforts to deal with pornography here in Britain over the years have until now failed. The heart of the problem has lain in the ineffectiveness of the 1959 Obscene Publications Act – which can be laid at the door of the present Lord Jenkins who saw it on to the statute book and resisted efforts then and afterwards to make it more effective. Lord Denning, when Master of the Rolls, had this to say about it in 1972: 'Unfortunately, this legislation against pornography seems to have misfired. Experience has shown that much material – which at first sight would appear to be pornographic in the extreme – has escaped the reach of the law.' He went on to argue that: 'The law has misfired because of the wording of the Statute and the way in which courts have applied it.'

Eight years later in the appeal court, Lord Denning repeated this assessment and commented ruefully that pedlars of pornography were 'cocking a snook at the law'. The Williams Committee Report on Obscenity and Film Censorship 1979 concluded that the law on these matters is, in short, 'a mess'. Home Secretary William Whitelaw declared that 'The obscenity laws are in ruins.'

Because the police in Britain were not, until the autumn of 1989, under any instruction to take note of the presence of pornography at scenes of sex crimes, we have had to turn to the USA for hard facts. From there has come incontrovertible evidence that the trade in illegal drugs and pornography is backed by organized crime.

A message to National VALA from a nationwide law enforcement conference in Denver, Colorado, in 1985 told us that 'Many of those involved in organized crime in the United States deal in drugs and in obscene material. However, organized crime makes more money dealing in drugs than dealing in obscene material. Make no mistake, if more enforcement efforts were directed towards curbing drugs then that would result in an increase in the illicit marketing of pornography.' The message went on to warn us that 'If British authorities increase enforcement against drug trafficking then we feel sure you can expect an increase in the sale and distribution of obscene materials in your country.' And there can be no doubt that that is happening.

It was the growing conviction that 'it is now or never' which lay behind our launching in 1991 of the COP (Campaign to Outlaw Pornography) petition. We realized, because Customs officers told us, that because Britain was going into Europe it would be even more difficult than it is now to control obscene material coming into Britain from the Continent. 'Even when seized the chances of a conviction are just about nil,' a disillusioned officer explained. And there has already been news of companies being set up to import and market the most extreme of continental pornography, Dutch in particular.

The need for the law to be made effective is greater than ever. No matter how much public concern exists and how sympathetic individual MPs and ministers are, all our efforts collapse at the wording of the 1959 Obscene Publications Act.

Kenneth Baker, then Home Secretary, was the guest speaker at our 1991 Convention and we were honoured to have him and grateful for his friendship and support. But his final statement on the matter of the obscenity law left us faced with the same old problems. I quote from his speech:

> I do not suggest that our present legislation is immaculate and beyond improvement. The 1959 Obscene Publications Act is widely recognized to be difficult to understand and apply: the 'deprave and corrupt test' is problematic enough but its defects are compounded by the need to look at the work as a whole and the uncertainties of the public good defence. However, as so often in government, the problem is not one of diagnosis but of prescription. Any proposed new legislation must meet stiff criteria. First, it must be clear in its meaning and reasonably predictable in its effects so that publishers and prosecutors know in advance where the line is to be drawn. Second, it would have to adopt a test which is neither too slack nor too oppressive but which reflects broad public sentiment. Finally, it must be fair in its application. We are rightly proud in this country of our prospering cultural life. This draws its strength from inno-

vation, with writers and artists prepared to try out new techniques and, in certain cases, to push back the boundaries of what was previously considered acceptable.

Shortly afterwards I wrote to the Prime Minister, John Major, asking him if he would 'include a commitment to the tightening up of the present ineffective obscenity law' in his 1992 election manifesto, and adding, 'about the depth of the public interest and concern over this matter there can be no doubt'. I went on to say that I felt sure he would

> ... be aware of the kind of emotive controversy which has surrounded this issue for many years ever since Lord Jenkins, as Labour Home Secretary, was largely responsible for its controversial and unhelpful wording.
>
> Child abuse cases, which have figured so prominently in the press in recent weeks, have served to bring the matter to the forefront of public interest and concern, and we, here, have been very conscious of this. You will not need me to persuade you that the suffering associated with pornography is very great. The recent case of the 10-month-old baby whose genitals were very badly bruised and damaged by a paedophile hooked on pornography haunts my mind and I am sure must have similarly affected many other people's minds.

In replying to my letter Mr Major assured us that:

> The government entirely shares your concern about pornography and its possible effects and we are in favour of strengthening and clarifying the law in this area so that the boundaries of what the law regards as acceptable are well defined and objectionable material is effectively dealt with ... There can be little doubt that pornography has an insidious and dehumanizing effect on attitudes to women and family relationships. Regardless of whether or not it encourages violent crime, pornography degrades all who come into contact with it. That is why we have taken such tough action to control it.

He was referring to his party's support for legislation to control indecent displays, sex shops, video recordings and child pornography but was not, I fear, committing himself and his party to amending the Obscene Publications Act. I remembered – struggled not to be cynical – with what speed the government had moved to deal with the then topical issue of dangerous dogs when objections were overruled and legislation was introduced in the House of Commons almost in a matter of days! Surely, if it was possible to move at such a speed against a physical danger it ought to be a priority for the government to move at speed to control pornography?

Clearly we needed to know where the Labour party stood in this matter. I had written to Neil Kinnock in March 1991 asking him to clarify his position in relation to the Obscene Publications Act. Weeks passed and I received no reply from him. It was only after a further letter had been sent to him that one of his staff replied saying that Mr Roy Hattersley was the party's spokesman in that field and that he would be replying to me. However, that was as far as it went – although my travels around the country have left me in no doubt that Labour supporters are as concerned about the prevalence of pornography and the abuse of children as are the great majority of those who vote for other parties.

The BBC sent a television team to talk to me during the election campaign – they were interested in my 'implied suggestion that if anyone wanted action in this field they should vote Tory!' They also did an interview with the Labour MP Diane Abbott, and I see that I wrote in my diary next morning that, 'I was very pleasantly surprised by the attitude of the TV crew that came – one I feel sure was a Christian and stayed behind afterwards for a chat. Another told me he was very sympathetic to our work because he has children. Amazing the difference in the way we get treated by the BBC these days!'

It was around the same time that Superintendent Michael Hames, head of New Scotland Yard's Obscene Publications Squad said that:

> Paedophiles who collect child pornography must be made to undergo treatment to break their obsession with youngsters as sexual objects.... We need to break into the circle much earlier than when dealing with offences of distribution

and possession of obscene material – child pornography is
made largely by abusers for themselves and for other abusers.
It is part of a circle of abuse and is used to seduce youngsters,
to justify behaviour and add an instrument of blackmail to
ensure the child's silence after.

Superintendent Hames told the meeting that his department
keeps a paedophile index listing of more than 4000 names.

It was as I was reading a report on the BBC 2 programme *Q –
The Winged Serpent*, which I mentioned earlier, that my mind
went back to the concern that we, along with others, had
expressed about the failure of the Director of Public Prosecutions to take action over the sale in this country of the
Marquis de Sade's book *Juliette* in the autumn of 1991. 'Insufficient evidence' was the reason he had given to us, various
MPs and other concerned people for his decision. Perhaps
what he meant was 'insufficient evidence' to make an almost
totally ineffective law effective! I concluded that if there was
insufficient evidence of corruption, lasciviousness and cruelty
beyond description in this tome, then there never could be
sufficient to persuade him, or his successor, to move on any
other publication.

As Moyra Bremner, writing in *The Times* in August 1991
said,

> The black-leather, naughty-fun image that surrounds de Sade
> is utterly misleading. The 2500 victims of both sexes in *Juliette*
> are not consenting, most are under 16 and many under
> eight. This catalogue of atrocities belongs to the torture
> chamber not the bedroom: rapes split children open, preg-
> nant women are disembowelled, babies cut to shreds,
> children flayed alive, eyes gouged out, boys castrated, parents
> forced to eat their children.

Ms Bremner's article was very important, not least because,
as she herself says, she has always been against censorship. But
Juliette was different. Having made it clear that she was not
suggesting that the book could turn normal men into rapists,
she went on,

[It is] only that for some individuals, reading his work both heightens sexual tension and pushes back the frontiers of social taboos, converting potential into actual rapists, and rapists into torturers or killers.

De Sade both describes acts liable to excite such people and justifies every fantasy cherished by sex offenders and the violent *Juliette*, for example, enjoys torturing but she also seeks pain and degradation, miraculously recovering overnight from 200 lashes with a metal-tipped whip. Sex offenders often claim their victims really want their attacks and are not harmed by them.

Two experts on the treatment of sex offenders, Ray Wyre of the Gracewell Clinic in Birmingham and Dr Eileen Vizard, a pioneer in the treatment of child abusers, say that sex offenders typically refuse to accept that what they do is wrong and seize on any signs that suggest society secretly endorses their crimes. Both experts believe the appearance of this book in high street bookshops seems to give its atrocities a stamp of approval. This is my greatest objection to the publication. ... At stake is not freedom of speech, but whether we should set the freedom of one publisher above the safety of women, children, the old and the vulnerable: it is whether we are a civilized society.

What more can one say? Except that until we get effective obscenity law on the statute book, a publication such as this will still be available.

Opening the adjournment debate on 2 July 1992 Liz Lynne, MP for Rochdale, said:

The aim of tonight's debate is to draw the Minister's attention to problems in the way in which the Obscene Publications Act 1959 operates.

I am a passionate believer in freedom of speech, which is one of the great freedoms on which our society is built. Any limitations on the right to a free press and the right to publish need to be kept to a minimum. But I also believe that freedoms are balanced by responsibility.

When I was asked to add my name to the list of supporters of early-day motion 312 about *Juliette*, my initial reaction was to say no; I do not believe in censorship. However, as soon as I had been read excerpts from that violent and horrific book, I was so disgusted and felt so physically sick that I agreed to add my name to the early-day motion. When I read further extracts, I was pleased that I had made that decision and decided to go further and ask for this Adjournment debate.

It is not just about this one book. *Juliette* is an example of some of the horrendously violent material that is available in booksellers. In June 1991, Arrow published in paperback the first British edition of *Juliette* by the Marquis de Sade, who gives his name to sadism. This is not a book of literary merit; it is too ill-translated. Nor is it about sadism as most of us think of it. The main victims are children. Its characters revel in the gross abuse, multiple rape, sodomy and extreme torture and murder of more than 2100 children and young teenagers and more than 450 women. And, throughout, the murders and tortures are glorified, admired and rewarded.

The Obscene Publications Act 1959 attempted to provide a new balance between freedom to publish and responsibility to others. The responsibility element was expressed in the now notorious phrase that material could be found obscene if it had a 'tendency to deprave and corrupt'.

This test has proved a nightmare for juries. There have been perverse decisions about similar material in different parts of the country. The Director of Public Prosecutions has decided not to act against some horrific publications. In some instances the police have been uncertain about what will be found obscene. In the case of *Juliette* and books of this ilk, I do not see how there can be any doubt.

I had thought of quoting from the book this evening. I consider myself to have a reasonably strong stomach, but I am afraid that *Juliette* is too horrible for me to do so. Furthermore, I would not wish to give the impression that there are one or two isolated incidents that are particularly bad. It is the whole book that is the problem. Throughout all his books Sade positively advocates attacks on the vulnerable and finds excuses for child abuse, and thereby justifies it.

The public has been led to believe that our obscenity and pornography laws are strong. In fact, they are a mess. For example, the law on obscene photographs of children is effective, but, as the case of *Juliette* shows, the law on books is useless. It seems incredible that a publisher would decide to release such a book and that booksellers would sell it. However, some chains, such as W. H. Smith and John Menzies, have refused to stock it, which is very welcome. Sadly, however, there are people willing to buy such books and publishers can make money from them.

Earlier today I met Superintendent Michael Hames who is in charge of the Obscene Publications Squad at Scotland Yard to discuss his work with him. He was quite forthright about the problems that the police have with the Obscene Publications Act. Because of a series of court cases, they can no longer prosecute all the material that they consider to be obscene. It seems as if the rug has been pulled from beneath their feet because written material such as *Juliette* has escaped the current law even though the images that it creates are so powerful. Psychologists working with sex offenders believe that such material can directly influence the actions of those carrying out child abuse and other sex offences.

Dame Peggy Fenner, MP for Medway, said:

The book was first drawn to my attention by a prison chaplain who wrote to me pleading that it should not be provided in the prison library. Whereupon I wrote to the Home Office asking whether that was the sort of material that criminals and sex offenders should have in prison for recreational reading. I received a wet reply from the Home Office Minister telling me that, as the book was available in bookshops, it was available in prison libraries. Will the Minister please read the book for himself, even if he feels that it is likely to deprave, as I am sure he will? It is disgraceful, not only that it should be in bookshops but that we should give it to prisoners as recreational reading.

Ms Lynne went on:

I agree with the Hon. Lady. It is appalling that the book is available in prisons. It is available in prisons because it is available in the bookshops. If we took it off the bookshelves, it would not be available in the prisons.

Can anyone believe that it is a coincidence that the Moors murderers made notes from de Sade justifying rape and murder? That case still haunts the area that I represent.

Some of us probably associate the obscenity law with prudery and material that simply gives offence. I emphasize that that is not the issue on which I sought this debate. There is ample evidence that grossly violent pornography can do real life harm to individuals and society.

The last time there was a review was in 1978 when the Williams Committee looked at the matter. Its report now seems strangely out of date. So much has happened in the area in the past fourteen years. All the evidence suggests that pornographic material has become much harder and more violent in its content since that time. Perhaps the only lasting impact of the Williams Report was its suggestion that the written word should not be prosecuted because of its importance to literature. I wonder whether members of the Williams Committee would take the same view now if they were to read *Juliette*. I doubt it very much.

Mrs Ann Winterton, MP for Congleton, spoke of how

The *Juliette* case demonstrates the total inadequacy of the current law on obscenity. *Juliette* is not a book; it is a vile manual, and a thick one at that, that encourages the sexual abuse, murder, and torture of children and other vulnerable people. It is not literature; it is the glorification of extreme violence.

I was pleased to learn that the government agree that the law on obscenity has deficiencies, and that they are willing to support attempts at reform. However, although this sounds so promising, it rapidly runs into the sand, by mistakenly making this suggestion: 'Recent attempts to reform the law ... have failed to attract sufficient parliamentary support. This is an area for Private Member initiative.'

And it was just such an initiative that Dr Robert Spink, MP for Castle Point, undertook on 27 October 1992 when he declared to an attentive House of Commons that he raised

a subject of considerable concern to Members on all sides

of this House and to millions of people throughout this country. The unprecedented national concern is vividly illustrated by a petition, signed by over 350,000 people, which I will be formally presenting to this House today on behalf of the National Viewers and Listeners Association.

The current obscenity laws are not working properly. The Secretary of State called them unsatisfactory, the Minister said they are inadequate . . .

The law in the UK on obscenity and pornography is a patchwork quilt of different provisions. We have different statutes dealing with, for example, broadcasting, videos, films, the theatre, sex shops and child pornography. This patchwork quilt of provisions is overlain with a blanket called the Obscene Publications Act 1959 which started life as a ten-minute rule bill moved by the then Roy Jenkins.

That blanket is designed as a 'catch all' defining the content of material which can be held to be obscene. The police use the Obscene Publications Act 1959 to control the most severe kinds of material, whether it be videos, child pornography or films.

For some of these media other statutes are already in place, but for other kinds of material, the Obscene Publications Act 1959 is the only statute which can be used. For example, it is the only restriction on the sale of magazines and books.

It is clear therefore that the Obscene Publications Act 1959 is the keystone in the legislative arch of our obscenity and pornography law. The problem is that not only is the arch itself shaky and incomplete, but this keystone is fundamentally loose. The source of that weakness lies essentially with the discredited 'tendency to deprave and corrupt' test . . . This test is fast becoming impossible to prove and the authorities are reluctant to prosecute cases involving even the most extreme material like de Sade's *Juliette*. The government readily acknowledge the problem. It is not therefore tenable for the government to take no action. It is the job of a caring government, however difficult this may be, to protect society and to set sound standards. This is not the job of a Private Member.

Hon. Members may recall the evil and vicious murder of Rachel Nickell on Wimbledon Common. I see that the

Hon. Member for Tooting is here today in his seat and I thank him for his support. The psychologists employed by the police believe that the man who carried out that brutal killing was addicted to reading pornography. You know, therefore, why the government must act.

Valerie Howarth, of the now sadly impoverished Childline, which receives thousands of calls, tells us: 'Many distressed children say they are shown pornography and asked to perform similar acts.' Tim Harding, Director of NSPCC, says: 'Pornography is used to entice other youngsters into child sex abuse.'

This is irrefutable evidence.

Superintendent Hames, Head of New Scotland Yard's Obscene Publications Squad, called for tougher laws to enable him to fight what he calls: 'a rising tide of child pornography'. He went on to say: 'The vast majority of murderers, serial rapists and child molesters indulge in pornography.' I want their oxygen supply of violent pornography cut.

If more evidence is needed we can look at Oklahoma City which clamped down on pornography in 1984. Rape has since fallen by over 20 per cent while at the same time, in the rest of the State where pornography remained, rape increased by over 20 per cent.

We must fight to protect society from evil monsters who purvey pornography for profit. We must denounce those sick people who claim that the mutilation, torture and murder of children and women, for sexual gratification, can somehow be acceptable as art or as literature. That's not freedom of expression, that's simply rubbish.

Scotland Yard calls for action because the law is unworkable. It is these very police who are saying, 'Please, please, give us a law that works – we want to tackle this problem, we must stop this evil.'

My Bill would require the government formally to review the operation of all the legislation in this area and bring forward proposals for the government themselves to change the law.

Mine is a paving Bill, very fashionable these days. It encourages the government to suggest alternative routes for reform, perhaps in a Criminal Justice Bill, with a free vote of this House. I am sure all parties would co-operate and would scrutinize such legislation.

Perhaps it's more than time for all of us to assess the research that launched the sexual revolution, which provided society, so we are told by US News, with 'the cornerstone of almost everything known about human sexuality' and which gave rise to the notion (now mercifully being questioned) that 10 per cent of the nation is homosexual, which forms the foundation of much modern sex education.

The research in question is none other than that carried out by the famed, notorious Dr Alfred C. Kinsey, described as 'one of the 100 most important Americans of the 20th Century', according to *Life* magazine's 1990 special autumn issue. However, in their new book *Kinsey, Sex and Fraud* (Lochinvar, 1990), authors Judith Reisman and Edward Eichel and editors Gordon Muir and John Court document the Kinsey team's research chicanery so devastatingly that a reviewer for the leading British medical journal the *Lancet*, put it quite simply: '[They] demolish the foundation of the two [Kinsey] reports' (*Sexual Behaviour in the Human Male*, 1948; *Sexual Behaviour in the Human Female*, 1953).

Is the claim in the Reisman-Eichel book that Kinsey's research is the 'most egregious example of science fraud in this century' merely another abstruse fact to be noted by a few academics and then forgotten? It may turn out that way but it shouldn't, for a number of good reasons that are also well documented.

Kinsey's research, although forty-plus years old, has given rise to a philosophy that is the foundation of modern sex education. It also presented a picture of what was supposedly being done sexually in American society. Since this is what people were believed to be doing, it was considered to be normal. Ground-breaking experiments, not well reported at the time, also laid a scientific base for a new view of human sexual behaviour which was claimed would prevail once 'repressive and damaging Judeo-Christian codes' were recognized as mere prejudices and taboos of a superstitious past.

The media presented Kinsey as a skilled researcher dispelling age-old myth with scientific truth. He is still seen like that by many academics and by those who control sex education and who are trying to engineer Kinsey's vision of sex in society. As the writers of *Kinsey, Sex and Fraud* point out, it requires a suspension of disbelief to accept the 'science' that is claimed to underpin this vision. It is important to understand that the results of this wacky science are taught as truth in classrooms across the nation and it is necessary also to know that Kinsey became an atheist during his college years and was reportedly 'indignant' about what, he claimed, Judeo-Christian traditions had done to society.

Kinsey claimed that any form of sexual behaviour found in animals was normal in humans. Monogamy and taboos against child-child sex and adult-child sex were, on the other hand, abnormal because they were the product of 'cultural restraints'. Kinsey and his team provided experimental data that young children had orgasmic potential from infancy. This was the scientific basis for presenting early sexual activity as the ideal (particularly if the children were helped by adults).

The notion that children are 'sexual' – not just affectionate – from a very early age, and should learn to use this capacity appropriately with other children and adults, comes from the 'science' of masturbating hundreds of young boys and babies (some as young as two months) by trained paedophiles attempting to elicit 'orgasms'. Yet this is presented as scientific in Kinsey's Male Report, as proof of normal childhood sexual capacity. These experiments have gone unchallenged by the media and by academic sexology for over forty years, a fact almost as bizarre as the experiments themselves. Until now.

Professor John Court faced the picket line when he arrived on 23 March to address the 1991 National VALA Convention at the RAF Club in London, but Dr Court, British born and living for several years in Australia and America, is well used to controversy.

He first hit the headlines in Britain several years ago when he gave evidence at a number of major obscenity trials, testifying to the damage that pornographic and obscene material can do to people's psychological health and well-being. 'Back in the 1970s it was', he said, 'an uphill battle to put across the view that pornography might be harmful. It went completely against the fashionable views of the day. But now, thanks partly to the commitment and determination of people who continue to publish and reveal the truth about what was going on, things are changing.'

He spoke of how the battle has moved a very long way on in recent years. 'There is now a big movement at many levels and there is a large body of psychological opinion which recognizes that obscene material is harmful. That is a great shift from where things were in the days when I was a lone voice.' He said that he was greatly encouraged that in Britain the law has recently changed so that obscenity legislation now applies to broadcasting but went on,

> We should not get complacent and think that because things are beginning to swing in the right way then everything is all right. For instance, there has been an upsurge of concern about child pornography and about the abuse of children. But there will be a reaction against that. People will get sick of the subject, and there will also be renewed pressure in a different direction from paedophiles who in America are already starting to campaign to be regarded as a legitimate 'minority group' with rights that have to be respected. They like to see themselves as visionaries with a new and important message which will liberate society from its old taboos, and are keen to press the message that traditional values no longer apply because the old family structures have broken down.

Himself a family man with children and grandchildren, he warned against losing hope in the family as the fundamental unit of the nation:

> The latest expression is to talk about the 'mosaic family', meaning a couple with a relationship not based on marriage, and their various children and other friends. We need to be careful about looking at alternative family patterns of this kind. For instance, we hear a lot about child abuse but what is not emphasized enough is that natural fathers rarely abuse their children. The vast majority of cases involve a mother's boyfriend who is not married to her and is not the father of her child.

Dr Court said he would like to see the Churches taking a firmer stand on some of these issues and giving clear leadership and direction to ordinary people who may be confused and disorientated. He owes a lot to his own faith, and has written a book, *Rainbows Through the Rain*, to explain how to reach God even when things seem difficult. 'I certainly know all about dryness in spiritual life, about wondering whether there is any point to things at all,' he said. 'I think that as a therapist it is actually useful to have gone through that, in order to be able to be of real help to others.'

Dr Court views the future with optimism. 'We have won certain battles,' he said. 'But the most important thing is still for ordinary people to affirm what they know to be right, and live by it, and for Christians to work together to show leadership.'

CHAPTER EIGHTEEN

OUR GREATEST ASSET

Children are subjected to an ugly cultural climate which accepts, as facts of life to be tolerated, bad manners, violence in speech and deed, casual sex and the ethics of do-as-you-please. The minds of the young have been opened to moral brutality to an extent inconceivable a few decades ago, and children are affected not only directly but by the erosion of the values of adults generally.

Ronald Butt, writing in *The Times*, 15 February 1991

25 October 1991

Dear Mrs Whitehouse,

Despite our never having met or previously corresponded, I am nevertheless writing to offer you my sincere apologies. Allow me to explain.

I was a student at the time when you came to public notice and began your campaign against the screening of unsuitable material on TV. And did I, and my compatriots, criticize you! We were furious at what we regarded as your arrogance, and I was particularly loud and long in my oft-expressed opinion that you were (and you should pardon the expression) bitter, repressed and possessed of a nosy and interfering nature, and that I was damned if I was going to have you start telling me what I should or should not watch. Each time you 'lost' such a battle over one programme or another, I saw it as a victory; when you won, I saw moral repressiveness winning over the freedom of the individual.

Twenty years on, I look back at my brash vehemence

and twist in shame at my folly and immaturity. A parent now, and possessed of a more objective nature, I am well capable of seeing what such 'freedom' has done, in helping to make Britain a sick, 'nudge-nudge' society, and I recognize that I, and many thousands like me, stood by, unable to see what was happening. You, of course, were right all the time. So, please accept my apology.

With my now better understanding of human nature, it is my bet that you will have received a great many letters of this sort over the last few years. Yet I feel that we have a very long way to go to experience a full scale reaction whereby the views of like-minded people to yourself become the norm.

I would, therefore, like to write a play for either television or radio, on this theme. Its working title is *I Used to Laugh at Mary Whitehouse,* and it actually ends with a letter to you, expressing something like the view in this letter. I would like to know if you would have any objection to my including such a reference, and if you could spare me just a couple of lines to indicate your feelings on this, I would be most grateful.

Yours sincerely, etc.

It seems to me that however short we, in the Western world, have fallen from the perfection Christ was and taught, however much of His teachings may have been twisted or ignored, it remains that it has been within the Christian culture that man has reached the highest level of personal, social and political freedom. We trivialize the argument about what is and what is not acceptable in public and private attitudes and behaviour if we reduce the issue to one of personal taste.

In denying the young this awareness we deny them all things. It is a manifestation of hate not love, to talk about such 'freedom' to the young. The truth is that our children today are the victims of a cruelty which is uniquely modern, a travesty of the love which, historically, one generation has had for the next. Not only are their personalities, their individualities, the very essence of their being, at risk in the culture of the age in which they have been born, but so is the family which sustains them.

My own deepest fear is that the young growing up in a

culture soaked in coarseness, crudity and cruelty, may react against sex, and therefore, against life and the God who gave it; that we shall, between us, raise a generation which either grasps at sex as a physical lust or treats it simply as a passing fancy, no more. On the other hand, rejecting the crudity of sex, fearful of its flaunted harshness, the young may fail to discover its wonder and beauty, or experience that strength and newness which can spill over into creativity on every level. The consequences of such a turning away from life are incalculable – in human relationships, culture, spirituality, indeed in every aspect of our existence.

I often ask myself, Whatever happened to anger? Plenty of it about, you may say. But where is the anger that a man worth calling a man should feel at the misuse and gross exploitation of women, at the way in which even the hearts and minds – and now the bodies – of children are considered fair game and have become unprotected territory?

A dreadful, almost all-pervasive silence has vindicated the evil, which has denied our humanity and endorsed the primitive savagery let loose between the covers of 'dirty' magazines. I still cannot live with the knowledge of the dead babes in the moors, or feel anything but contempt for the men – clerics among them – who will defend as 'enlightened' precisely the kind of obscenity which, so pitifully, cost those children their lives. Neither do I care if millions have to go without their quota of pornography if that is the limitation we have to set upon ourselves to ensure it does not happen again. And while it is true that children are rarely murdered by those obsessed with pornography, it is equally true that their minds are constantly raped by the kind of material which meets their eyes on every side. Is not the greatest threat to us all that we shall become desensitized, that we shall no longer be moved by suffering, no longer capable of recognizing the obscene when we see it, so far removed from the magic of childhood ourselves that we no longer preserve it for our children?

But children *are* the future. Unless we can ensure their freedom to discover and experience the beauty, the pain, the mystery, the wonder and the joy of life at a pace dictated by their own natural development and not by sexual manipulators, whose profits are tied to the rate at which the child can be pressurized into premature sexual awareness, then we shall raise an emotionally and spiritually stunted generation, a generation which will not find it easy to respect women, for they will find it impossible to believe that their fathers did.

We know, when we have our feet on the ground and our heads safely out of Cloud Cuckoo Land, as history teaches, that society, like a tree, will sprout fresh healthy growth only from roots that are deep, strong and constantly nurtured. Yet so simple a truth is, perhaps because of its simplicity, too suspect in the eyes of the 'progressives' to be given credence and children grow up in an intellectually and emotionally stunted environment. It is they who are most at risk in our anarchic culture. Children are now 'free' as never before, we are told. But are they?

It was Sir John Wheeler MP who, as chairman of the Commons Select Committee on Home Affairs, spoke out uncompromisingly in favour of a move to lower the age of homosexual consent to eighteen or even sixteen. Has he any experience of working with teenagers? I have, and in such a capacity one quickly discovers that there exists a wide disparity – as much as four or five years – in the ages at which teenagers mature. Consequently, while some mature youngsters may be able to measure up to and, hopefully, reject approaches from predatory homosexual adults, others less mature may find themselves involved with talk and behaviour that violates their privacy and person and denies their right to mature at their own pace. Behind the bland persuasive talk of those who equate with freedom such a lowering of the age of consent, there lies a streak of cruelty and exploitation which should have no part in a truly free, let alone Christian, society.

BBC 2's *Public Eye* (29 May 1992) transmitted a programme on this very issue which made absolute nonsense of the Corporation's obligation 'not to take sides on matters of public interest'. If any programme ever took sides this one most certainly did! Totally biased in the smoothest and most persuasive way in favour of the lowering of the age of consent, it also claimed to have the support of the Prime Minister. But that was not true.

Earlier this year I wrote to Mr Major expressing concern about a press report to the effect that he was considering lowering the age of homosexual consent. In his personal reply to me (9 March) he stated that he has 'no plans to alter the current age of consent affecting homosexuals' and trusted that his letter offered me 'the reassurance' I was seeking. It did.

Public opinion long ago condemned and outlawed the exploitation of child labour by nineteenth-century industrialists. Yet today our society ruthlessly exploits the minds and emotions of young people for financial and political capital. Children are fodder, not for industry, but for ideas. They are no longer sent up chimneys, but they are pressurized into alien patterns of behaviour to line the pockets of unscrupulous publishers, and to further the cause of revolution by stealth.

A nation's youth is its greatest asset. We are poor guardians if we do not ensure its inalienable right to childhood, mystery, dreams, tenderness and love; if we do not realize that by ceasing to provide authority we may also cease to care; if we do not conscientiously maintain the spiritual foundations without which the young cannot build anew; if we do not teach that there is a third way, neither reactionary nor libertarian, which still waits to be explored.

Dear Mary

I have read in the papers that you are against the play *The Romans in Britain* currently running at the National Theatre. I am fifteen years old and I must say that I support you in your campaign to have these people prosecuted. From what I have read and heard this play sounds obscene and filthy and if this sort of 'smut' is all the National Theatre can do with our money then I suggest that they close down. We, the teenagers of today, are labelled troublemakers and hooligans but if that is the sort of example we are being set by our more intelligent elders who are more 'experienced' than us then all I can say is 'God help us!'

I have written to the National Theatre to express my disgust but I doubt if my letter would change their minds so I am also writing to you in the hope that this, after you have read it, can be passed on to some higher authority. I have spoken to many people before writing this letter and young and old we all express the same feeling so it is not one person's cry for reform.

Please, please, please take heed of this letter. I am willing to help you in any way and don't let the press and that upset you. As my father would say, 'you're doing a grand job, lass!' Keep it up.

Yours faithfully,

Alison (aged 15)

10 February 1989

Dear Mrs Whitehouse,

I know from my own experience that children need to be told what is right and wrong – they do not instinctively know and cannot differentiate between reality and fantasy. What disturbed me most about the pornography I saw as a child was the fear that what I saw was normal adult behaviour and that I would be expected to do the same when I became an adult. It was after one picture in particular I saw, which I vividly remember now, that I suddenly had a massive conviction that porn was all wrong, and I told the person concerned that I would have no more to do with it ever again. The person concerned was someone I was close to and trusted, and I remember shaking violently at the thought of having thrown away the security I had in this person. Looking back now, I am sure that the conviction came from the Holy Spirit. I had no one else to tell me porn was wrong. I could not tell anyone else in the family about it for fear of worse consequences. Having no one else to turn to, I turned to God. I wanted to show you how God can use evil to bring us to Him. It was through the pornography that in my fear I turned to God and I praise God that he brought out good of something so evil.

A young man

23 January 1989

Dear Mrs Whitehouse,

I am an 18-year-old A level student and from the age of five I can say that the effects of pornographic material disturbed and totally distressed me with no one to explain or reassure me, I grew up with an extremely distressed and warped view of life. Only recently have I really come to terms with the aftermath of such experiences and the harrowing memories.

I would like to say how much I support you – if you are ever apt to feel discouraged by the weak people who oppose you: remember that if the children had a voice, they would raise it in support of you: and if the children benefit and are protected (though they cannot thank you) it is surely more than worthwhile.

These two letters touch the heart of the origins and motivation of our work. The campaign was born and grew in strength as evidence multiplied of the impact upon the heart and mind of the child of the grossness, the insensitivity and the cruelty which characterizes the 'permissive' society. And indeed upon the rest of us. The price in human suffering has been and remains incalculable. While it is true that there are signs, not least among the young, that such a concept is increasingly seen as a snare and a delusion, its effects have sunk deeply and destructively into our everyday lives.

One thing, above all, I have learnt is this: whether or not individually and collectively we are able and willing to make an effective and positive contribution to the great moral debates of our time depends upon in whose strength we do it. I have learnt that God will take us not only into unknown ways but also into unimaginable ones, if only we will let him.

The story of the Apostle Peter walking on the water is never far from my consciousness, and it holds an all-pervading challenge to me. If we move only in those circumstances and with those people of whom we have at least some knowledge and experience, then we are simply humanist – however sincere our intention. I have learnt, too, that we need constantly to live beyond our depth and outside our own circle of friends. Especially we must not be limited by our natural gifts. I sometimes think that these gifts can be a hindrance rather than a help. The more of them we have, the less we feel the need to throw ourselves upon the mercy and sustaining power of God. It is when we are sure of ourselves that we stand most in danger of failure – at least, in God's terms.

The early days of the campaign are as vivid to me now as ever they were – the sleepless nights which followed some response I had made to an enquiring journalist, the horror I had of seeing my name in the newspapers, even more, the fear and anxiety that surrounded the business of 'being talked about', especially as many of the newspapers and television producers set no limits on the misrepresentation and calumny in which they indulged. Mind you, I came to see that this had its positive side, since packed meetings have been a characteristic of our years of campaigning. I'm sure that at least some (if not many!) people came to see what this cranky woman looked like, 'Bun on top of the head, an' all!' The fact that I did not and that what I had to say was very different from what was expected reinforced my theme about the power of the media to mislead.

I had no training or experience in public speaking and the state of my nerves before beginning to speak was such that my legs often lost their feeling and my mind its power of conscious thought. But I came to realize that it is the Holy Spirit, and not some gift of oratory, which makes our words touch people's hearts. There is nothing so flat as the speech which has been delivered over and over again. And it is that prayer, at the moment of emptiness before one stands up to speak, which makes the words flow with freshness and conviction. And what do I say? Much as follows though it usually comes out different each time!

Could anyone, anywhere (psychopaths excepted), agree with the proposition that there should be no limits imposed on the public presentation of sex and violence and in the use of language? This would mean accepting the public display of the violation of children and the use of television to advocate violent elimination of coloured people, perhaps along the lines of the Nazi atrocities against the Jews. It would mean freedom to batter the sensitivities of young and old with an undiluted stream of the foulest obscenities.

The whole current debate on censorship takes place in a climate of unreality. No group has practised censorship more rigidly than those who bellow, in and out of season, for the abolition of all controls. The same group has not hesitated to suppress the voices of those who hold opposing views. That's why the sixties, as society is just beginning to recognize, was such an illiberal decade. Monopoly, authoritarianism, exploitation, those bogeys of the 'progressive' left, formed the bedrock of its own strategy. No views could be seen, heard or given publicity unless they advocated permissive humanism. The rest must be censored out by ridicule, denigration or exclusion. The age-old mechanism by which new ideas were filtered through the sieve of experience, or refined through conflict with respected values, was sabotaged. As a consequence, the avant-garde flooded our culture and society with its dirty water, churning up foundations, overturning standards, confusing thought and leaving in its wake an all too obvious trail of insecurity and misery. Any serious discussion of censorship in the nineties must take these facts into account.

One of the most frequently heard arguments against censorship is that it would emasculate and inhibit genuine art. But modern advocates of obscenity do not seem to realize that by claiming exemption from the law for every kind of creative activity, however sick or subversive, they are obliterating the distinction between art and trash. And in so doing are depriving themselves of the ground upon which, for work of real quality, they might claim exception.

It's no good being pro- or anti-censorship in some kind of ideological or intellectual vacuum. 'No censorship' became a parrot cry, the ultimate in with-it slogans, the password to approval in all kinds of political, literary and theological groupings.

It is no secret that pornography is a growing and highly lucrative industry, and it is truly extraordinary – if it didn't stink – how many of those who shout loudest against commercial exploitation wherever they detect it are quite prepared to encourage a market which is dependent on human exploitation of the crudest kind. Hypocrisy, the shame of the Victorians we are told, is the stock in trade of those who grossly capitalize on the degradation of human dignity.

Other powerful and subtle pressures towards total abolition of control come from politically motivated interests. The radical left are convinced that sexual permissiveness and moral relaxation are primary conditions to the establishment of the alternative society. But those who think that the increasing acceptance of blasphemies and obscenities is simply part of an evolving contemporary society are being dangerously naïve.

Pornography and obscenity are seen not simply as a matter of personal taste but as accepted ideological weapons. The question now arises: Do we have the right to expect government and law, while protecting the free flow of ideas, to establish sufficient control to ensure that society remains coherent and capable of resisting the pressures of that statistically minute group who are committed to its destruction? I believe, profoundly, that we do. Censorship, effectively but sparingly used, is a liberal concept since it would protect the lifestyle of the vast majority.

The civil libertarians object to censorship on the grounds that no one has the right to interfere in the private affairs of others. 'Let a man go to hell in his own way,' they say. But, whom do they take with them, and what rights do the victims have?

It is unrealistic to imagine that laws which allow the distribution of porn for adults can, at the same time, ensure that children are not corrupted. The porn merchants themselves accept that a – by no means insignificant – percentage of their products inevitably falls into the hands of children, since there are no conceivable means by which a publication can be controlled once it is in circulation. A society which exploits its young, for whatever purpose, has in it the seeds of its own destruction. If the censorship laws of the country are not straightforward enough to protect the young from some of the more obscene and subversive publications now so freely distributed, then the government itself may be challenged in terms of the UNICEF Declaration of the Rights of the Child which states that 'The Child shall enjoy special protection, and shall be given opportunities and facilities, by law and by other means, to enable him to develop physically, mentally, morally, spiritually and socially in a healthy and normal manner and in conditions of freedom and dignity. In the enactment of laws for this purpose the best interests of the child shall be paramount.'

And that, it seems to me, says it all.

POSTSCRIPT

So often the accusation of being 'negative' is thrown at those who fight against the moral and cultural anarchy of our times. When it comes my way I take comfort from the story of Nehemiah and the vision he had of a new Jerusalem. (The foundations of the city had been destroyed seventy years before and had to be relaid before the city itself could be rebuilt.)

The first thing Nehemiah and his friends did was to rebuild the wall around the city. And so it is, metaphorically speaking, in our own time. Nothing will be gained and much, indeed everything, could be lost, if we fail to take the true measure of the calculated and continued threat to the Judeo-Christian foundation of Western democracy. The Queen is Defender of the Faith, our law is based upon the Ten Commandments, and Parliament begins each day with prayers.

At this time of crisis there is much we can learn from Nehemiah (Ezekiel 33:1–6). He spared himself nothing. He and his friends faced, and refused to run away from, every kind of threat, and public and private ridicule from those who were opposed to the rebuilding of the city. He set no limits to his mental, physical and spiritual commitment. He used his brains. Above all, he had a vision, and he had great perception of the way in which the devil would do his best to destroy him. He was quite uninhibited by any false modesty, which can so easily cloak an unwillingness to expose oneself to the full implication of what total commitment means.

Nehemiah went to see the King and asked permission to rebuild the city. The King gave it to him. Nehemiah set his watchers around the wall with their trumpets at the ready so that everyone would be alerted at the first sign of danger. The builders worked from the first light of dawn until the stars came out. The opposition never let up for a moment; but, wonder of wonders, the wall was completed in fifty-two days. At that point, I have to confess, my sense of identification with Nehemiah and his stalwart warriors disappears!

It would be foolish for me to give anyone the idea that getting involved in this fight, which inevitably touches the essence of what people believe and fear and care about, is a bed of roses. Far from it; and I would have backed out of it many years ago if I hadn't known the Source of the replenishing of my strength and of the vision of what we were called upon to do. One lesson I have learnt is that the task is far and away too large to cope with in one's own strength.

Out of all the things that have happened, all the places I have visited and all the people I have met, one experience stands out above all others. It occurred at a time of great physical and mental stress, when no day seemed to go by without some crisis to be resolved. These strains were associated not only with the work but also with family affairs, not least because my husband's brother and his wife were killed in a mid-air collision over France leaving three teenage children. I had been into the office of the Press Association in Fleet Street, and as I came out I missed my footing on the steps and went flying across the pavement. Several people came to my aid and I wasn't seriously hurt, only badly shaken. I stood for some minutes against the wall to recover my breath. And as I walked on I simply felt that I had come to the end of my tether, that I could not possibly go on.

It was at that point that the Lord came to me. He said with unforgettable love, but with great clarity and challenge, 'Mary, you feel as you do because you carry the burden on your own shoulders instead of giving it to Me. The burden is Mine, not yours.' That releasing and joyful experience remains for me as vivid today as when it happened; and while I would not, and could not, claim that since then I have never felt strained or tired – that would be a nonsense – it taught me two things: first, that the burden is the Lord's, that the forces with which we have to reckon will destroy us unless we constantly draw on His strength, acknowledging always that our minds and bodies are inadequate for the fight; second, that when we put ourselves into His hands, and set no limit on what we will do and give in terms of time, energy and resources, then He leads us,

He gives us experiences far beyond anything we could have imagined, and 'goes before' to protect, prepare and achieve.

I think many people ask themselves the question, 'How on earth did we ever get into this mess?' and then go on to wonder how we can get out of it. I know I did; and discovering the answer has taken me and those who work with me deep into the ramifications of political, personal and financial interests both here in Britain and in many countries across the world.

But may I say, with all understanding and gentleness, that if we are to make a constructive contribution to this debate then any kind of a 'passing by on the other side' will be a kind of betrayal.

Many times people have asked me: 'Who will take over the work of National VALA when you can no longer lead it?' I have always had to answer, 'I do not know.' Not because I have been unwilling to know, far from it; not because there is a shortage of people who could most effectively take over. There are two reasons: I have always had a deep sense that 'the work is the Lord's' and that He will make His purpose clear in His own time; and I have increasingly realized that with the passing of the years the nature of the work changes and continues to change, as it is bound to do if it is genuinely 'free' and not tied to human ambition or preconditions.

But time does pass, and I come to understand that the privilege *and* the burden need to be carried by more and more people. I would go so far as to say 'by everyone who cares'. That, I imagine, means just about all of us!

I'd always said that I would not even consider giving up the work until we have effective obscenity law on the statute book. Without that, it seemed to me that so much of our work would remain unfulfilled. It was, after all, the ineffectiveness of the 1959/64 obscenity laws that had propped up so many of the defendants in obscenity cases. However, broadcasting is no longer exempt from that act and that is a step in the right direction. It is by no means the end of the battle: only an effective law will provide the means of controlling the obscenity and pornography which despoil our culture. Safely on the statute book also lie the Indecent Displays Act, the Video Recordings Act and the Child Protection Act.

But I write in the spring of 1993 just after I have informed our Executive Meeting that at our 1994 Annual Convention I intend to retire as President though not, of course, from National VALA. I never thought the day would come, so why?

First of all, it has to be said that age and health have played a key role: Ernest is now eighty-one and I am eighty-three and it really has been nothing short of a miracle that we have both been able to work, often a twelve-hour day or more, week in and week out, without setting limits on what we did or how far we travelled. Suddenly things have caught up with us and, in particular as far as I am concerned, the pain and discomfort caused by the fracture of my spine has been much exacerbated by me being smitten by what the doctors – three in one day – described as 'a very vicious virus' which undermined my strength, affected my eyes and left me with a very inadequate memory – all temporary, I trust!

Could it be, I asked myself and then Ernest, that the Lord is trying to tell us something? Are we meant, in the years we have left, to spend more time together, discover more fully the beauties of the wonderful Constable country in which we live and spend more time with the family? It would not mean, we tell one another, that we would cut ourselves off from the work of National VALA or that the organization itself would be in any way diminished. Far from it! I can foresee more, not less, people taking responsibility – as is already happening with more spokesmen and women becoming experienced in the art of public speaking and instant comment. And here, in particular, I want to mention John Beyer, General Secretary of National VALA. He has been, as they say – and certainly I do – 'worth his weight in gold'. His clear mind, gift of immediate recall, no matter how long the time involved, his loyalty and total integrity lie at the core of our success and will remain so I trust in the years that lie ahead. But he, of course, has not been the only one. Members of our executive committee, of our branches, countless individuals have over the years been bravely and imaginatively committed to the work. And that has been wonderful. Without them all, none of the miracles of the last thirty years would, or could, have happened. Bless them.

And me? I am both impressed and grateful for the Lord's timing. I had no idea when I began this book before the accident to my spine, now six years ago, that it would have to be put on ice for so long, but this has allowed much more material to be included! Neither did I have the faintest idea that its publication would coincide so closely with the announcement of my retirement as President at our 1994 Convention.

Quite remarkable, really, and I feel the move is positive rather than negative. There are now countless people in this country and abroad to whom the challenge to get involved is an increasing reality. I hope and trust that *Quite Contrary* with its very serious as well as its light connotations will make some contribution to the ongoing fight for external values to which Dr George Carey, Archbishop of Canterbury, referred in his address to Community leaders in Harrogate in 1992.

INDEX

Hope Price
Angels £12.99

Dazzling golden haloes, harps, swords and flowing white robes – these are the traditional images that spring to mind when people think of angels. But do they still exist today or are they merely the stuff of fantasy, myth and legend?

In *Angels*, Hope Price has gathered together compelling evidence from people of all ages and experience who are convinced beyond any doubt that they have benefited from the extraordinary intervention of angels in their lives. As many hundreds of rational people can testify, angels can and do appear miraculously in mundane modern settings on British motorways and in anonymous urban streets and homes. In every instance they are described as carrying out practical missions of mercy and comfort that in some way echo those portrayed in the scriptures of the Old and New Testament.

These personal accounts offer astonishingly consistent images of robust, physically strong beings, shimmering with lights, who, after rendering assistance, usually disappear from sight very abruptly. Angels have been seen to rescue children and adults from disaster, to give early warning of impending tragedy and to offer protection in times of fear, danger and bereavement. Invariably, they leave behind a lasting sense of divine peace, tranquillity and harmony.

With a foreword by David Suchet.

Emma Foster — ? dressing rooks
New Inter — proms in Aug

All Pan Books are available at your local bookshop or newsagent, or can be ordered direct from the publisher. Indicate the number of copies required and fill in the form below.

Send to: Pan C. S. Dept
            Macmillan Distribution Ltd
            Houndmills Basingstoke RG21 2XS

or phone: 0256 29242, quoting title, author and Credit Card number.

Please enclose a remittance* to the value of the cover price plus £1.00 for the first book plus 50p per copy for each additional book ordered.

*Payment may be made in sterling by UK personal cheque, postal order, sterling draft or international money order, made payable to Pan Books Ltd.

Alternatively by Barclaycard/Access/Amex/Diners

Card No.   ☐☐☐☐☐☐☐☐☐☐☐☐☐☐☐☐☐☐

Expiry Date ☐☐☐☐☐☐☐☐☐☐☐☐☐☐☐☐☐☐

                    Signature_____

Applicable only in the UK and BFPO addresses.

While every effort is made to keep prices low, it is sometimes necessary to increase prices at short notice. Pan Books reserve the right to show on covers and charge new retail prices which may differ from those advertised in the text or elsewhere.

NAME AND ADDRESS IN BLOCK LETTERS PLEASE

....

Name ....

Address ....

....

....

....

                                                                                    6/92